Teacher's Resource Book

UPPER INTERMEDIATE
BUSINESS ENGLISH

Bill Mascull

Longman

FINANCIAL TIMES
World business newspaper.

Introduction

1 Course aims

Market Leader is an extensive new Business English course designed to bring the real world of international business into the language teaching classroom. It has been developed in association with the *Financial Times*, one of the world's leading sources of professional information, to ensure the maximum range and authenticity of business content.

The course is intended for use either by students preparing for a career in business or by those already working who want to improve their English communication skills.

Market Leader combines some of the most stimulating recent ideas from the world of business with a strong task-based approach. Role plays and case studies are regular features of each unit. Throughout the course students are encouraged to use their own experience and opinions in order to maximise involvement and learning.

An essential requirement of Business English materials is that they cater for the wide range of needs which students have, including different areas of interest and specialisation, different skills needs and varying amounts of time available to study. Market Leader offers teachers and course planners a unique range of flexible materials to help meet these needs. There are suggestions in this book on how to use the unit material extensively or intensively, and how the material in the Practice File integrates with the Course Book. There are optional extra components including a Business Grammar, Videos and a series of special subject books to develop vocabulary and reading skills. This book contains extensive extra photocopiable material in the Text bank and the Resource bank.

2 The main course components

Course Book

This provides the main part of the teaching material. It is divided into 14 topic-based units, plus two revision units. The topics have been chosen following research among teachers to establish the areas of widest possible interest to the majority of their students. The Course Book provides input in reading, speaking and listening, with guidance for writing tasks too. Every unit contains vocabulary development activities and a rapid review of essential grammar. There is a regular focus on key business functions, and each unit ends with a motivating case study to allow students to practise language they have worked on during the unit. For more details on the Course Book units, see *Overview of a typical unit* below.

Practice File

This gives extra practice in the areas of grammar and vocabulary, together with a complete syllabus in business writing. In each unit students work with text models and useful language, then do a writing task to consolidate the learning. Additionally the Practice File provides regular self-study pronunciation work (with an audio CD and exercises), and a valuable survival language section for students when travelling.

Audio materials

All the listening activities from the Course Book (interviews with business practitioners and input for other activities such as role plays and case studies) and the Practice File (pronunciation exercises) are available on cassettes and audio CDs, depending on users' preference.

Teacher's Resource Book

This book provides teachers with an overview of the whole course together with detailed teaching notes, background briefings on business content, the Text bank (28 optional extra reading texts) and the Resource bank (photocopiable worksheets practising communication skills).

Test File

Five copiable tests are available to teachers and course planners to monitor students' progress through the course. There is an entry test, three progress tests and an exit test which reviews the work done throughout the course.

3 Overview of a Course Book unit

A typical unit consists of the following sections.

Starting up

Students have the opportunity to think about the unit topic and to exchange ideas and opinions with each other and with the teacher. There is a variety of stimulating activities such as answering quiz questions, reflecting on difficult decisions, prioritising options and completing charts. Throughout, students are encouraged to draw upon their life and business experience.

Vocabulary

Essential business vocabulary is presented and practised through a wide variety of creative and engaging exercises. Students learn new words, phrases and collocations, and are given tasks which help to activate the vocabulary they already know or have just learnt.

There is further vocabulary practice in the Practice File.

Discussion

There are a number of discussion activities in the book. Their main purpose is to build up students' confidence in expressing their views in English and to improve their fluency.

Reading

Students read interesting and relevant authentic texts from the *Financial Times* and other business sources. They develop their reading skills and acquire essential business vocabulary. The texts provide a context for language work and discussion later in the unit.

Listening

The authentic listening texts are based on interviews with business people and experts in their field. Students develop their listening skills such as prediction, listening for specific information and note-taking.

Language review

These sections develop students' awareness of the common problem areas at intermediate level. They focus on accuracy and knowledge of key areas of grammar. If students already know the grammar point, this section works as a quick check for them and the teacher. If they need more explanation they are referred to the Grammar reference at the back of the Course Book.

There is further grammar practice in the Practice File and in the *Business Grammar and Usage* book (see *Extending the course* below).

Skills

This section helps learners to develop their communication skills in the key business areas of presentations, meetings, negotiations, telephoning and social English. Each section contains a useful language box which provides students with the support and phrases they need to carry out the business tasks in the role play activities.

Case studies

Each unit ends with a case study linked to the unit's business topic. The case studies are based on realistic business problems or situations and are designed to motivate and actively engage students. They use the language and communication skills which they have acquired while working through the unit. Typically students will be involved in discussing business problems and recommending solutions through active group work.

All of the case studies have been developed and tested with students in class and are designed to be easy to present and use. No special knowledge or extra materials are required. For teaching tips on making the best use of the case studies, see *Case studies that work* below.

Each case study ends with a realistic writing task. These tasks reflect the real world of business correspondence and will also help those students preparing for Business English exams. Models of writing text types are given in the Writing file at the end of the Course Book.

4 Using the course

Accessibility for teachers

Less experienced teachers can sometimes find teaching Business English daunting. They may be anxious about their lack of knowledge of the business world and of the topics covered in the course. *Market Leader* sets out to provide the maximum support for teachers. The *Business brief* section at the beginning of each unit in the Teacher's Resource Book gives an overview of the business topic, covering key terms and suggesting a list of titles for further reading and information.

Authenticity of content

One of the principles of the course is that students should deal with as much authentic content as their language level allows. Authentic reading and listening texts are motivating for students and bring the real world of business into the classroom, increasing students' knowledge of business practice and concepts. Due to its international coverage the *Financial Times* has been a rich source of text and business information for the course.

The case studies present realistic business situations and problems and the communication activities based on them – group discussions, simulations and role plays – serve to enhance the authenticity of the course.

Flexibility of use

Demands of Business English courses vary greatly, and materials accordingly need to be adaptable. *Market Leader* has been designed to give teachers and course planners maximum flexibility. The course can be used either extensively or intensively. At the beginning of each unit in the Teacher's Resource Book are suggestions for a fast route through the unit if time is short. This intensive route focusses mainly on speaking and listening skills. If the teacher wants to extend this concentration on particular skills, optional components are available in the course (see *Extending the course* below).

5 Case studies that work

The following teaching tips will help when using case studies.

1 Involve all the students at every stage of the class. Encourage everyone to participate.

2 Draw on the students' knowledge of business and the world.

3 Be very careful how you present the case study at the beginning. Make sure your instructions are clear and that the task is understood. (See individual units in the Teacher's Resource Book for detailed suggestions on introducing the case study.)

4 Ensure that all students have understood the case and the key vocabulary.

5 Encourage the students to use the language and communication skills they have acquired in the rest of the unit. A short review of the key language will help.

6 Focus on communication and fluency during the case study activities. Language errors can be dealt with at the end. Make a record of important errors and give students feedback at the end in a sympathetic and constructive way. Note good language use, too, and comment on it favourably.

7 If the activity is developing slowly or you have a group of students who are a little reticent, you could intervene by asking questions or making helpful suggestions.

8 Allow students to reach their own conclusions. Many students expect there to be a correct answer. The teacher can give their own opinion but should stress that there usually is no single 'right' answer.

9 Encourage creative and imaginative solutions to the problems expressed.

10 Encourage students to use people management skills such as working in teams, leading teams, delegating and interacting effectively with each other.

11 Allocate sufficient time for the major tasks such as negotiating. At the same time do not allow activities to drag on too long. You want the students to have enough time to perform the task and yet the lesson needs to have pace.

12 Students should identify the key issues of the case and discuss all the options before reaching a decision.

13 Encourage students to actively listen to each other. This is essential for both language practice and effective teamwork!

6 Extending the course

Some students will require more input or practice in certain areas, either in terms of subject matter or skills, than is provided in the Course Book. In order to meet these needs, *Market Leader* provides a wide range of optional extra materials and components to choose from.

Teacher's Resource Book

The Text bank provides two extra reading texts per unit, together with comprehension and vocabulary exercises.

The Resource bank provides copiable worksheet-based communication activities, linked to the skills introduced in the Course Book units.

Business grammar

For students needing more work on their grammar, this book provides reference and practice in all the most important areas of Business English usage. It is organised into structural and functional sections.

Video

Two *Market Leader* videos are available at the intermediate and upper intermediate levels – a drama and a documentary.

Alliance is an exciting story about an international airline alliance and the pivotal role played in it by a rapidly-expanding catering service firm. The video illustrates key business functions such as meetings, socialising and negotiating and extends work that students will have done in these areas.

Business leader briefings is based on interviews with leaders and thinkers from international businesses. It is organised into six topical units. Students have the opportunity to revise key vocabulary and take part in discussions stimulated by what they hear from the interviewees.

Each video is accompanied by a set of photocopiable worksheets and a transcript. The videos are also available separately.

Special subject series

Many students will need to learn the language of more specialised areas of Business English. To provide them with authentic and engaging material, *Market Leader* includes a range of special subject books which focus on reading skills and vocabulary development.

The first books in the series are *Banking and Finance*, *Business Law* and *International Management*. Each book includes two tests and a glossary of specialised language.

Longman Business English Dictionary

This is the most up-to-date source of reference in Business English today. Compiled from a wide range of text sources, it allows students and teachers rapid access to clear, straightforward definitions of the latest international business terminology.

Market Leader website: www.market-leader.net

This website offers teachers a wide range of extra resources to support and extend their use of the *Market Leader* series. Extra texts of topical interest will be added regularly, together with worksheets to exploit them. Links to other relevant websites are posted here, and the website provides a forum for teachers to give feedback on the course to the authors and publishers.

Contents

Resource Bank

Communication

	Classwork – Course Book	Further work
Lesson 1 *Each lesson (excluding case studies) is about 45–60 minutes. This does not include administration and time spent going through homework.*	**Starting up** What makes a good communicator? Written and spoken forms of communication. **Vocabulary: Good communicators** Ss look at vocabulary related to good and bad communicators. **Listening: Improving communications** Ss listen to an expert on communications within and between companies.	**Practice File** Vocabulary (page 4)
Lesson 2	**Reading: Communication problems in organisations** Ss read an article, complete a chart and answer questions about communication in organisations. **Language review: Idioms** Ss do language awareness and practice activities on some common idioms.	**Text bank** (pages 136–139) **Practice File** Language review (page 5) **ML Grammar and Usage**
Lesson 3	**Skills: Problem-solving on the phone** Ss listen to a phone conversation between a customer and a supplier, and one between a manager and her PA, and practise skills involved in problem-solving on the phone.	**Resource bank** (page 196) **Practice File** Survival Business English (page 63)
Lesson 4 *Each case study is about 1½ to 2 hours.*	**Case study: Creating a sense of identity** An international engineering group has communication problems between different parts of the organisation.	**Practice File** Writing (page 6)

For a fast route through the unit focussing mainly on speaking skills, just use the underlined sections.

For 1 to 1 situations, most parts of the unit lend themselves, with minimal adaptation, to use with individual students. Where this is not the case, alternative procedures are given.

Business brief

Within companies, communication falls into two main areas. There is the communication of information and technical knowledge needed to do the job at hand. Here, paper-based communication is being replaced by the company **intranet**, with internal websites only accessible by employees. Some very large companies are appointing **knowledge officers** to exploit the information in a company to the full and communicate it effectively to those who need it. (But in this age of increasingly accessible information, there will no doubt always be the **information hoarders**, employees and managers who find power and pleasure in keeping information for themselves, even if it would be useful to their colleagues.)

There is also what might be called 'celebration-exhortation'. The internal **company magazine** is the classic **communication channel** here. It may be produced **in-house** by a 'communications department' or **out-of-house** by journalists who specialise in this area. It may try to demonstrate how the company is putting its **mission statement** into action: the management may try to change employee behaviour by exhortation and by praising the performance of particular departments and individuals.

Externally, **advertising** has been the most visible form of communication with customers. Usually this is designed to increase product sales, but there is also **institutional advertising**, designed to improve **perceptions** of the company as a whole. Companies naturally like to be seen as human and environmentally aware. But the communication between companies and their customers is increasingly becoming two-way, with **customer service centres** designed to gather information, not just complaints, from customers about all aspects of use of a company's products. Ideally, this information feeds back into product modification and new product design. (See Unit 10 for more on **customer relationship management**.)

Equally, a company must communicate with its investors, and **investor relations** are becoming an important specialised area of **public relations**. Investors want to know how their money is being used and what their prospects are.

And then there is the wider public audience to attend to. **Press conferences** may be called to announce important events, such as product launches. **Press releases** may be issued to communicate more routine information. There is also the specialised area of **crisis management** and **damage control**: see Unit 11.

Whatever a company does, it has an **image**. It might as well try to influence (some would say 'manipulate') the moulding of this image. This is one reason why the **communications industry**, in all its forms, is a multibillion-dollar business.

Read on

Paul Argenti: *Corporate Communication*, McGraw-Hill, 1998

Scott Cutlip: *Effective Public Relations*, Prentice Hall, 1999

Steven L. Guengerich (ed.) et al.: *Building the Corporate Intranet*, Wiley, 1996

Richard B. Higgins: *Best Practices in Global Investor Relations*, Quorum, 2000

Cees van Riel, Wally Olins: *Principles of Corporate Communication*, Prentice Hall, 1995

Lesson notes

Lesson notes

Warmer

- Divide the board into areas and write one or two words in each area, like this:

drums pigeon post	painting ... ...
newspapers radio	language sign language ... ...

- Get the Ss, in pairs, to list all the forms of communication they can think of by adding to each group. Elicit their responses and complete the table on the board, perhaps to produce something like this:

drums pigeon post smoke signals semaphore Morse code telephone	painting sculpture music
newspapers radio television Internet interactive television	language sign language body language dance

- Invite comments and encourage discussion. (The Ss may come up with other responses, or organise them in other ways, but it doesn't matter.)

Overview

- Tell the Ss that they will be looking at communication, especially in the context of organisations.
- Ask the Ss to look at the Overview section on page 6. Tell them a little about the things on the list, using the table on page 8 of this book as a guide. Tell them which points you will be covering in the current lesson and in later lessons.

Quotation

- Write the quotation on the board.
- Tell the Ss that it is a quotation from a philosopher.
- Ask the Ss to discuss, in pairs, whether they agree with the quotation. (Some might mention music or painting as communicating emotions that cannot be expressed in words.)

- In whole-group discussion afterwards, ask pairs for their opinions, and then ask the group why some areas, like philosophy and law, can be very difficult to understand.

Starting up

These questions introduce the theme of communication, and provide an opportunity for some speaking practice.

 A

- Divide the class into groups of three or four.
- Ask the Ss to choose the three most important criteria in the context of
  a) native speakers   **b)** non-native speakers of a language
  (The emphasis on grammatical accuracy will probably be different for **a)** and **b)**.)
- Discuss answers.

 B

- Discuss in small groups or with the whole class. Rather than doing this in the abstract, take some well-known figures from television, politics, etc. and ask Ss what makes them good communicators (or not). Be tactful when discussing political figures. Ss might mention body language, speaking style, ease that people have in identifying with them, etc. You could discuss what makes for charisma, the way that some people have a powerful attractive quality as communicators and leaders that makes people admire them and want to follow them.

C

- Again, divide the class into threes or fours.
- Ask Ss to discuss how much they use each form of communication, and with whom.
- Elicit feedback.
- If you are doing this lesson at the beginning of a course, and these issues have already been covered in needs analysis, don't spend too much time on them here. Have the needs analysis results available and use this activity to elicit further information.
- If you are doing this lesson at the beginning of a course and you have not done a needs analysis, this exercise forms a good basis for one. Agree with the Ss which communication forms are most important for them/or need most practice. Note down what they say and refer to these notes regularly while you are planning and doing the rest of the course, so as to modify activities, emphasis of the course, etc.

---

1 to 1

This forms a good basis for a needs analysis, if you haven't already done one. It may give you ideas for role play of specific activities to complement those in the Course Book, based on your student's particular work situation.

Vocabulary: Good communicators

Ss look at vocabulary typically used to describe good and bad communicators.

Ⓐ–Ⓑ

- Work on pronunciation of the words, without going into meanings at this stage. Get individual Ss to repeat the difficult ones after you, paying particular attention to stress: arTICulate, etc.

- Put the Ss in threes and get them to put words into groups: the good and the bad, and then into the more specific groups in Exercise B. If available, get each three to consult a good general dictionary, such as the *Longman Dictionary of Contemporary English*.

A
Good communicators: articulate, coherent, eloquent, fluent, focussed, lucid, persuasive, responsive, sensitive, succinct
Bad communicators: hesitant, inhibited, rambling, tongue-tied

B
1 focussed, succinct   – concise
2 hesitant, inhibited, tongue-tied – unable to speak
3 rambling   – conf
4 fluent, eloquent, sensitive – exp well
5 articulate, coherent, lucid – easy/underst
6 persuasive, responsive   – influen ly pl

Ⓒ

- Go round class quickly to elicit opposites.

---

opposites: inarticulate, incoherent, unfocussed, uninhibited

- Point out that the opposite of many, but not all, adjectives are formed using *in-* or *un-*. (See Revision Unit B, 12A, Course Book page 127, for more on opposites.)

Ⓓ

- In pairs or class discussion, get examples of good communicators. Prompt the Ss by mentioning different occupations: politicians, actors, news presenters, advertisers, etc.

Listening: Improving communications

Penny Logier is Retail Director at the London-based communications agency MediaComTMB. She talks about

- communication between companies and their customers
- breakdowns in communication
- whether it is possible be a poor communicator but a good manager

Ⓐ 🎧 1.1

- Get the Ss to listen once or twice to the recording, depending on their level. Stop at points where Ss can answer questions 1–4.

---

1 New technology and the idea that communications, education and training is important.
2 E-mail means companies can talk to clients more easily. This will go on improving as people become more sophisticated at sending e-mail attachments. (By 'structures', Penny is referring to attachments like text documents, spreadsheets and so on.)
3 An intranet is a confidential computer network where information is only accessible to people in specific organisations (unlike the Internet, where information is accessible to anyone). VW employees can gain access to any work that her consultancy is doing for them in order to suggest changes, etc.
4 She mentions a number of instances where her consultancy has nearly lost clients because of communication breakdown.

- Encourage discussion of any points arising, for example, the importance of communications training and the frustrations of voice mail.

Ⓑ 🎧 1.1

Play the last section two or three times, stopping at the end of each sentence so the Ss can fill in blanks.

---

1 understand
2 strategy
3 development
4 aims
5 Verbal
6 one-to-one
7 confidence
8 rapport
9 relationship

- Ask the Ss if they agree that communicating with employees in this way is one of the most important roles of managers.

Reading: Communication problems

This article is about the importance of informal communication between employees, and how this is possible in organisations of less than 200 people, but becomes more difficult in larger organisations. However, even in smaller ones, people need the right conditions for this informal communication to take place.

A

- Get the Ss to discuss pre-questions in pairs. Discuss the findings with the whole group and ask the Ss about their personal experiences of the effect the size of an organisation has on communication. (Pre-work Ss can talk about large vs small educational institutions.)

B

- Rather than treating the whole article in the same way, vary the treatment of each paragraph, perhaps in the way outlined here. Read the first paragraph with the whole group, explaining and / or practising pronunciation of difficult words and expressions where necessary, e.g. in paragraph 1: *hierarchical* (line 5), *chaos* (line 6), *quid pro quo* (line 15). You may want to avoid explaining expressions like *quid pro quo* which are covered in Exercise C, or you could explain them anyway and see if the Ss have picked up on your explanation.

- Get the Ss to read the second paragraph silently and individually, or to read and discuss in pairs. Circulate and monitor for difficulties, e.g. *cohesive* (line 20), *reciprocal alliances* (line 21), *panacea* (line 24: it means 'over-simplistic solution'), *casual* (line 28), *inhibits* (line 30).

- Get the Ss to complete the diagram in pairs after reading the first two paragraphs.

Communication

```
                    Communication
                         |
          ----------------------------------
          |                                |
  Small organisations            Larger organisations
  Less than 200                  More than 200
                                         |
                                 Need either a
                                 hierarchical structure or a
                                 line management system.
          |                              |
  Already have a free            Costs of above
  flow of information            1 Information can only flow
                                   along certain channels
                                   because only certain
                                   people contact each other
                                   regularly.
                                 2 Lack of personalised
                                   contacts means less
                                   personal commitment.
                                 3 Favours will only be done
                                   where there is a clear quid
                                   pro quo (= where there is
                                   a clear and immediate
                                   benefit to doing so).
                                 4 Large organisations are
                                   less flexible.

                                 One solution
                                 Divide larger organisations
                                 into smaller units.

                                 In addition
                                 Avoid maintaining too
                                 formal a structure by
                                 allowing staff to:
                                 1 build reciprocal alliances
                                 2 interact in a casual way.
```

- Read the final paragraphs with the whole group, explaining and / or practising pronunciation of difficult words and expressions where necessary, e.g. *dispense with something* (line 48), *idle time away* (line 52), *inadvertently* (line 53), *snippets of information* (line 57). If there is not enough time, get the Ss to read it as homework.

C

- Get the Ss, in pairs, to answer the questions. Check and discuss them with the whole group.

> 1 a) the decision not to have a coffee room
>   b) the architects who designed the new building
> 2 a) destroyed without realising it
>   b) small groups of people who know each other well
>   c) *empowered* usually means 'given the authority to do something without having to ask permission from managers each time', but here it means something more like 'drove forward': *It was the intimate social networks that drove forward the organisation and made it successful.*
> 3 a) (You can make a joke about distractor c) if your Ss are familiar with the informal British English meaning of *quid!*)
> 4 a)
> 5 designed and built with a particular use in mind

D

- Get the Ss to prepare by writing notes of key ideas for a few minutes and then to give individual mini-presentations.

E

- Discuss with whole group.

> Examples might include conversations in the lift, in work place canteens, during drinks after work. The Ss will no doubt think of others in relation to their own workplace / place of study.

 F

- Get the Ss to prepare in pairs or threes for a few minutes, and then to give reports about their own workplace or place of study. Deal with this tactfully, for example where you are dealing with people from different workplaces.

Language review: Idioms

In this section, the Ss look at different idioms. (Ss usually love them.)

A

- With books closed, explain what an idiom is (an expression with a meaning that can be difficult to guess from the meanings of its separate words) and ask the Ss if they have any favourite idioms in English.

- Discuss the Language review box with the whole class.

- Get the Ss to complete the exercise in pairs and then discuss the answers with the whole class.

```
1 c   2 h   3 d   4 a   5 b   6 e   7 f   8 g
```

B

◎ Go through the exercise with the whole group.

```
1  shop
2  tip
3  gift (Gift of the gab is gift of gab in AmE.)
4  loss
5  cuff
6  language
7  head
8  tail
```

Skills: Problem-solving on the phone

In this section, the Ss discuss some customer–supplier problems that can occur on the phone, and listen to conversations about different problems.

A

◎ Get the Ss, in pairs, to brainstorm possible customer–supplier problems, then to report to and discuss with the whole group.

```
Delivery: late delivery, delivery to the wrong place, delivery
of the wrong goods, damaged goods
Payment: late payment, payment sent to the wrong place,
bouncing cheques, non-payment
Quality control: goods not to agreed specifications,
defective goods, breakdowns
```

B 🎧 1.2

◎ Play the recording 1.2 once and get the Ss to summarise the problem and the solution offered.

```
There's a labour problem at the supplier's (Martin) plant,
and they can't deliver the air conditioning equipment
ordered by the customer's (Elena) firm on time. Martin
suggests that Elena's firm might be able to get similar
equipment from a German supplier.
```

C 🎧 1.2

◎ Get the Ss to predict the answers before they listen to the conversation again.

◎ Play the recording for Ss to check their predictions.

```
a) customer
b) supplier
c) supplier
d) customer
e) customer
f) supplier
g) customer
h) supplier
```

D 🎧 1.3

◎ Play recording 1.3 once or twice and get the Ss to summarise the situation.

```
The manager's (Patricia) flight has been delayed and she
can't get back on time to chair an important meeting. Her
PA (personal assistant) suggests that participants deal
with the less important points first, by which time Patricia
might be back. The PA suggests the meeting could be
chaired by Rachel. Patricia agrees to the idea, and says she
will think of other possibilities in case Rachel can't do it.
```

E 🎧 1.3

◎ Replay relevant parts of the recording in order to point out key phrases. Discuss how well the situation was dealt with. (The Ss response may depend on their perception of the role of the PA. In some cultures, it might not be appropriate for a PA to make suggestions like this.)

Lesson notes

(F)

In this exercise, the Ss look at useful language for dealing with problems, and apply this language to role play two situations.

◎ Go through the expressions and practise intonation, getting individual Ss to read the expressions. Get them to complete the unfinished expressions with possible endings, e.g. *I do apologise for the late delivery of the goods you ordered.*

◎ Get the Ss to role play the situation in simultaneous pairs sitting back-to-back, using expressions from the Useful language box. Circulate and monitor. When the students have finished, praise strong points and mention one or two things that Ss should pay particular attention to. Then get 'public' performances from one or two individual pairs in front of the whole group.

◎ Use the same procedure, this time getting other pairs to give the 'public' performances. (Alternatively, if you don't have enough time, and class numbers allow, get some pairs to prepare Situation 1 and other pairs to prepare Situation 2 at the same time.)

◎ There are more situations like these to role play in the Resource bank, on page 204 of this book.

Case study

Creating a sense of identity

In this case study, the Ss look at the communication problems in an international engineering group with offices all over the world, and suggest solutions.

Stage 1

◎ Get the Ss to read silently the Background section, the letter from Aldo Renato to the editor of the company magazine, and the e-mail from the new Communications Director to KMB's Chief Executive.

◎ Circulate and answer any queries. Discuss common queries with the whole group.

◎ Quickly put the headings in the left-hand column of the table below on the board and elicit information from the group so as to complete the column on the right.

◎ Make sure the Ss understand the situation by getting individual Ss to expand orally on different parts of the table, using complete sentences.

Company	KMB
Activity	Construction and engineering
Based in	Munich, Germany
Structure	Manufacturing subsidiaries and associated companies all over the world
Key points of Aldo Renato's letter to the editor of the company magazine	◎ Feels isolated and uninformed ◎ At recent sales conference, other members of staff felt the same ◎ Wants more information about new developments, e.g. the strategy behind a recent takeover ◎ Should share knowledge of best practice between the subsidiaries ◎ New Communications Director should improve communications so that all staff are informed of the group's strategy
Key points of Communications Director's e-mail to KMB's Chief Executive	◎ Renato's complaint quite common ◎ Overseas staff do not have enough information about developments within the group, acquisitions, etc. ◎ Need to improve communication system so as to strengthen sense of common purpose

Stage 2: Brainstorming

In the task the Ss are members of a working group which will discuss suggestions for improving the communications system. They will also come up with their own ideas for solving the problems that have been outlined. Before the meeting, Ss brainstorm ideas for the agenda.

- In threes or fours, get the Ss to brainstorm possible ideas.
- Write the ideas in the form of agenda items on the board.
- If more than three ideas are suggested, 'shortlist' the ones that are to be put on the meeting agenda by getting the whole group to vote for each suggestion with a quick show of hands. Add the three most popular suggestions to the agenda.

Other possible ideas, if the Ss fail to come up with enough of their own:
- a system of **mentoring**, where more senior managers would advise junior ones about their careers and at the same time explain and discuss the company's strategy.
- a system of **reverse mentoring**, where junior employees would 'educate' senior managers in technology developments such as Internet applications.
- more frequent in-house **training courses**. The courses would inform managers about new developments in business and engineering, but their main purpose would be to bring people together from different subsidiaries.
- more **management by walking around**, where senior managers would be encouraged to visit overseas subsidiaries more often and talk to managers and employees.

1 to 1

Go through the Background section and get your student to complete the table with key points. Get the student to come up with some ideas for the agenda and then discuss advantages and disadvantages of both in a 1 to 1 meeting. Get the student to cost each activity.

Stage 3: Meeting

- This meeting can be run more or less formally, depending on Ss' level, time available, etc. If this is the first time a meeting has been role played on the course, appoint a self-confident student as chair for each meeting.
- If the class is large, run parallel meetings with four or five participants each.
- Make sure the chair knows what the final agenda is: show it on the board, and underline that participants should discuss the cost implications of each suggestion.
- Suggest timings for each item depending on overall time available, and get the chair to follow the timings.
- Circulate and monitor discussions, noting down language strengths and difficulties.

- Discuss language strengths and difficulties in front of the whole group, pointing out 'models' to follow that may have been uttered during the role play, and mistakes to avoid, pointing out the correct form, and getting individual Ss to use it in context.
- When the meeting is over, ask participants to list quickly the suggestions that were approved, showing relative costs like this:

Suggestion	Cost
Regular e-mail newsletter	$
Employee of the month scheme	$$$
... etc.	

The Ss should 'guesstimate' the relative costs; the more $ symbols there are, the more expensive the suggestion would be to implement. The number of $ symbols is not meant to show an actual, real cost.

Stage 4: Writing

- The Ss write up the decisions of their meeting in memo form. This should
  - inform the heads of all KMB's subsidiaries that the meeting took place
  - outline the plan of action agreed
  - ask for their cooperation in implementing the suggestions.

 Writing file page 141

1 to 1

This forms a good basis for a needs analysis, if you haven't already done one. It may give you ideas for role play of specific activities to complement those in the Course Book, based on your student's particular work situation.

UNIT 2 International marketing

At a glance

At a glance

	Classwork – Course Book	Further work
Lesson 1 *Each lesson (excluding case studies) is about 45–60 minutes. This does not include administration and time spent going through homework.*	**Starting up** The advantages and problems of marketing globally; Coke advertising slogans around the world. **Vocabulary: Marketing collocations** Economic vocabulary in an international context and the vocabulary of international marketing.	**Practice File** Vocabulary (page 8)
Lesson 2	**Reading: International marketing mix** Ss read an article about marketing brands internationally, fill in a chart about different brands, discuss some of the issues in the article, do comprehension tasks and work on some of the vocabulary. **Language review: noun compounds and noun phrases** Ss work on the structure of noun compounds and noun phrases.	**Text bank** (pages 140–143) **Practice File** Language review (page 9) **ML Grammar and Usage**
Lesson 3	**Skills: Brainstorming** Ss look at the principles of brainstorming, listen to a brainstorming session, and work on expressions used in sessions like this. They then put these ideas into action in their own brainstorming sessions.	**Resource bank** (page 197) **Practice File** Survival Business English (page 65)
Lesson 4 *Each case study is about 1¹/₂ to 2 hours.*	**Case study: Zumo – Creating a global brand** A multinational based in Spain looks at ways of developing one of its products into a global brand.	**Practice File** Writing (page 10)

For a fast route through the unit focussing mainly on speaking skills, just use the underlined sections.

For 1 to 1 situations, most parts of the unit lend themselves, with minimal adaptation, to use with individual students. Where this is not the case, alternative procedures are given.

16

Business brief

'The world's youth prefer Coke to tea, trainers to sandals,' wrote one marketing specialist recently. This implies that tastes everywhere are becoming similar and **homogeneous**. But as the article in the main Course Book illustrates, the watchword should still be **Think global, act local**. Acting local means having local market knowledge: there are still wide **variations** in taste, customs, behaviour and expectations between consumers in different markets, even markets that from the outside look very similar, such as those in Europe. It means, for example, recognising attachments to local brands, how business is done in each place and so on.

Of course, these are issues that a company with a **global presence** has to address. But even companies that seem as if they have been global for ever had to start from a home base. For example, it took Marlboro 30 years and McDonald's 20 years to become truly global organisations.

How to enter overseas markets in the first place? Philip Kotler enumerates the various methods.

- **Indirect export**. Exporters use an **intermediary**, such as an **export agent**, to deal with buyers in the overseas market.

- **Direct export**. Companies handle their own exports, for example by setting up **overseas sales offices**.

- **Licensing**. Companies sell the rights to use a **manufacturing process**, **trademark** or **patent** for a **fee** or **royalty**. In services such as hotels, the company may negotiate a **management contract** with a local business to run the hotels on its behalf.

- **Joint ventures**. Two companies, for example an overseas firm and a local one, may work together to develop a particular market.

- **Direct investment**. The company buys a local firm, or sets up its own **manufacturing subsidiaries**.

Of course, these different arrangements require different levels of commitment, investment and risk. Kotler talks about the **internationalisation process**, where firms move (hopefully) through these stages:

- no regular export activities;

- export via independent representatives / agents;

- establishment of overseas sales subsidiaries;

- establishment of production facilities abroad.

This process will help them to progress towards global thinking and local action as they expand internationally. At different stages, companies will have different levels of understanding of the markets where they are trying to develop. Each step in the process requires different levels and types of support.

Read on

Philip Cateora, John Graham: *International Marketing*, McGraw-Hill, 1998

Harold Chee, Rod Harris: *Global Marketing Strategy*, Financial Times Prentice Hall, 1998

Financial Times: *Mastering Marketing*, Pearson Education, 1999, ch. 10: 'International Marketing'

Philip Kotler: *Marketing Management*, Prentice Hall, 1999 edition, ch. 12: 'Designing Global Market Offerings'

Warmer

- Ask Ss to consider the place of the international products on the left in the table below in relation to the products on the right in their country / countries. (Write them quickly on the board.) For example:
  - Who drinks Coke or Pepsi? Is it all generations? What do people drink with meals?
  - Who goes to fast-food hamburger restaurants? Do families go there for snacks and family meals?
  - Who wears trainers? Is it only younger people? Do business people wear them to work and then change into shoes when they get there? etc.

Coca-Cola and Pepsi Cola	Tea, coffee and local soft drinks
Fast-food hamburgers	Traditional food of the country
Trainers	Shoes or sandals
Jeans	Trousers
Western rock music	Popular music of the country

- Whole class discussion about the place and use of these products.

Overview

- Tell the Ss that they will be looking at international marketing.
- Ask the Ss to look at the Overview section on page 14. Tell them a little about the things on the list, using the table on page 16 of this book as a guide. Tell them which points you will be covering in the current lesson and which in later lessons.

Quotation

- Ask the Ss what they understand by the quotation on page 14. (It goes against the usual principle of marketing, which is that marketers should understand customers' needs and provide products and services that satisfy them.)

Starting up

This section introduces the theme of international marketing and provides an opportunity for some speaking practice. Get the Ss to discuss in pairs or small groups with one member of each group taking notes. Then ask the notetaker in each group to report their findings to the whole class.

The warmer will have given them some ideas. Others include:
- Cars: Ford, GM, Toyota
- Clothes: Gap, Benetton
- Food: Nestlé, Danone
- Cleaning products: Unilever, Procter & Gamble

1. Advantages include being able to buy raw materials in large quantities at lower prices, and being able to spread administrative and other costs over a larger number of products sold.
2. Problems include not understanding local tastes and habits, and not understanding the structure of local distribution networks.
3. For methods of entering overseas markets see Business brief on page 17.

- In addition to discussing the slogans that impressed them, you could ask the Ss to translate into English the slogans that Coke uses in their country / countries.

- If you have time, you could get the Ss to sketch out advertising hoardings, showing the products and the slogans. Get each pair / group to work on a different type of product.

Vocabulary: Marketing collocations

These exercises develop some of the vocabulary needed to talk about a country's economy.

- Get Ss to work individually or in pairs. Then go round the whole class and elicit answers.

1. monetary regulations (Point out that *currency regulations* would also be possible here.)
2. government bureaucracy
3. political stability
4. buying habits
5. economic situation
6. Income distribution

- Talk about a particular country, using these and related expressions. Don't ask the Ss to 'make up sentences' with the expressions, but have a natural discussion. *In [name of country], the economic situation is good, with low inflation and low unemployment. The country is politically stable …,* etc. Get the Ss to use correct related forms, e.g. *politically stable* and *political stability*.

(B)

- Get the Ss to discuss the questions in pairs or small groups, and then report to the whole class.

> 1 For business, benefits include stable environment for planning, investment, etc.
> 2 Talk about inflation, growth, general prosperity, etc.
> 3 Treat this one with caution. Some Ss might argue that unequal distribution allows some people to accumulate wealth that can then be used for new investment. Others may say that on principles of fairness, wealth should be more equally distributed.

(C)

- Get the Ss to do the exercise in pairs or small groups.
- Then check answers with whole group. Here, it's particularly important to discuss with the Ss *why* the odd one out is the odd one out. For example in question 1 a), b) and c) all are used to talk about markets that are increasing in size, but d) is not.

> | 1 d | 2 b | 3 c | 4 b | 5 c | 6 d |
> |-----|-----|-----|-----|-----|-----|
> | 7 d | 8 c | 9 d | 10 d | | |

Reading: International marketing mix

This article, from the *Financial Times*, looks at how global companies try to cater for consumer tastes in different parts of the world.

(A) – (B)

- Get the Ss to discuss in pairs or small groups and then bring findings together in the whole class.

> A
> Cars: The Ss might mention adapting car interiors for different national tastes: for people, on the one hand, who prefer functional-looking dashboards, instruments, etc., or, on the other hand, for those who like a lot of 'wood' veneer (even if it's plastic). Advertising for the same car might emphasise performance in one market and comfort in another.
> Fast food: Do the international chains try to cater for local tastes with additional items only available in particular countries?
> Soft drinks: Do drinks companies try to satisfy varying tastes in fizziness and sweetness? (They do, in fact, as the article will point out.) Does advertising emphasise fun and youth, or does it show specific situations of use, like family meals?
> B
> The disadvantage is higher costs, hopefully offset by the advantage of higher sales in each market. Companies have to find a balance.

(C) – (D)

- Get the Ss to read the first three paragraphs (lines 1–51) of the article silently.
- Then work on pronunciation of difficult words like *integration* (line 2), *differentiating* (line 17), *exorbitantly* (line 23), *pioneer* (line 25).
- Ask one student to summarise the article so far in a couple of sentences.
- Get the Ss, in pairs, to complete the first three rows of the table.

Company	Product	Marketing approach
Nissan	cars	reduced number of chassis designs
Kellogg	breakfast cereal	ignored research and introduced cereal in France; changed consumption patterns
Coca-Cola	cola	changes flavour to suit local tastes

- Quickly write on the board the pre-question: 'What is the difference between customisation and standardisation?'
- Get the Ss to read the next two paragraphs (lines 52–92). Circulate and monitor. Ask the Ss for words that are causing difficulty and explain them. You may want to avoid explaining expressions that are covered in Exercise F below, or you could explain them anyway and see if the Ss pick up on your explanation.
- Get individual pairs to answer the pre-question in their own words.
- Paragraphs 6 and 7 (lines 71–113) and Exercise D can be skipped if time is short. Otherwise, tell Ss to read the questions in Exercise D.
- Get the Ss to read paragraphs 6 and 7 (lines 71–113). Circulate and monitor. Ask the Ss for words and phrases that are causing difficulty and explain them. Some, e.g. *mining markets for information* (= gathering information from different markets) and *melding* (= combining) *product ideas* might need explaining to the whole class.
- Get the Ss to answer the questions in Exercise D.
- Get the Ss to read the last two paragraphs (lines 114–162) and complete the rest of the table in pairs. You may need to work on *tailored*, *positioning* and *premium price* (= a higher price paid for a luxury, upmarket product).

Rolex	watches	same approach everywhere – for high achievers, upmarket distribution outlets, premium price
Unilever	Lifebuoy soap	different ingredients in India and East Africa, but same positioning – inexpensive, everyday, antibacterial

Lesson notes

- Even if you have explained these words earlier, this exercise will provide a useful recap. Get the Ss to do it in pairs and then check with whole class.

| 1 a | 2 a | 3 a | 4 a | 5 a |

Language review: Noun compounds and noun phrases

This section looks at a feature which can cause difficulty, particularly to those from certain language backgrounds, such as Latin-based ones.

- Go through points 1, 2 and 3 with whole class, commenting where necessary.

- Get the Ss to work on these expressions in pairs. If you are short of time, get some pairs to do items 1–5 and others 6–10.

1 country-specific differentiating features
2 changing consumption patterns
3 new product development strategies
4 global research laboratories
5 software development establishments
6 formal market research methods
7 product development schedules
8 marketing mix decisions
9 upmarket distribution outlet
10 premium price

- Get the Ss to work in pairs. Point out that not all the columns have to contain an item. Ss could use the expressions from Exercise A. Here are some examples:

Adverb	Adjective / -ing participle	Noun / Gerund	Head noun
markedly	different		ways
	changing	consumption	patterns
	new	product	strategies
		development	
	global	research	centres

- Check with whole class.

- Get the Ss to work in pairs. Then go round the whole group quickly to get answers.

1 really impressive sales figures
2 new public relations department
3 highly ambitious market research programme
4 expanding overseas operations
5 rapidly improving balance sheet
6 extremely volatile exchange rate
7 highly confidential marketing report
8 incredibly successful trade fair

- Ask individual Ss to use appropriate intonation, pretending that they are company managers talking to an audience and putting the expressions into short contexts, e.g.

  Ladies and gentlemen, last year we had some really impressive sales figures. As you can see from the chart, ...

Skills: Brainstorming

The idea here is to introduce the Ss to the idea of brainstorming, if they are not already familiar with it.

(A)

- Get the Ss to go through the points in pairs or small groups. Circulate and monitor.
- Round up the findings with the whole class. There are no right or wrong answers, but some of the issues below may emerge.

1 Yes, but sometimes it is good to be vague about the purpose of the meeting, so that participants don't look immediately at the specific situation. This will keep the discussion more open-ended and throw up ideas that otherwise might not have occurred.
2 Theoretically, no. The idea is to get everyone involved as equals. But people in some cultures would always expect the most senior person to speak first, whatever the type of meeting.
3 Probably a good idea.
4 This should be one of the main features of brainstorming, but sessions where this actually happens must be rare.
5 In theory, yes, but extremely bizarre suggestions would probably be seen as such.
6 Easier said than done, but it's probably more acceptable to interrupt in brainstorming than other types of session.
7 Theoretically, the speculation should be as wide-ranging as possible, but most participants would probably set limits as to what is relevant.
8 Probably a good idea. Details can come later in developing particular ideas.

(B) 🎧 2.1

- Play recording 2.1 once and get the Ss to say what the purpose of the meeting is – to develop promotional ideas for the Business Solutions website.

- Play recording 2.1 once or twice more and get the Ss, in pairs, to note the different types of promotional activities mentioned. Then check with whole class.

> advertising on television and radio; on-line promotion; direct mailing; press advertising in traditional newspapers, business magazines and journals

(C) 🎧 2.2

- Play recording 2.2 once or twice and get the Ss, in their pairs, to note the answers to the questions. Then check with the whole class.

> 1 send a mailing to the names of the contact base, containing a brochure and / or a CD Rom; an event, for example on a river boat; billboard advertising
>
> 2 next meeting in three weeks; information on the budget and the cost of the different promotional activities

(D)

- Get the Ss, in pairs, to categorise the expressions. At the same time you could ask them to say whether they are tentative / neutral (T/N in table below) or strong (S). Then check with the whole class.

Stating objectives	
The purpose of the meeting this morning is ...	T/N
Encouraging contributions	
Anything goes ...	S
Fire away!	S
Would it be worth sponsoring some kind of event?	T/N
What about that?	T/N
Expressing enthusiasm	
That's great!	S
Excellent!	S
We should definitely do some of that.	S
Absolutely!	S
Making suggestions	
I think we could send out glossy brochures ...	T/N
I think we'd reach a wide audience ...	T/N
What about press advertising?	T/N
Would it be worth sponsoring some kind of event?	T/N
It would be great to do a presentation. ...	S
Agreeing	
Yes, that's a good idea.	S
Excellent!	S
We should definitely do some of that.	S
Absolutely!	S
That might be one way ...	T/N

(E)

- The idea here is to put into action some of the principles of brainstorming.

- Organise the class into groups of three or four for maximum participation.

- If there is more than one group, get different groups to do different situations in parallel. Appoint someone in each group who will note down the ideas produced, ready to report them to the whole class at the end of the activity.

- Make sure students are clear about the background to their situation.

- Start the activity. Circulate and monitor.

- When students have finished, get the notetaker in each group to say what ideas they came up with.

- Praise strong points from your monitoring of the brainstorming sessions and mention language points that the Ss should pay particular attention to. Get individual Ss to go back to the context where the mistake occurred and say the new, improved version.

> **1 to 1**
> - Encourage the student to come up with ideas for each situation as quickly as possible. Do not interrupt. Afterwards praise and correct language as in the final bullet point above.

Lesson notes

Case study

Zumo – creating a global brand

A multinational company based in Spain wants to develop one of its existing products, currently sold only in Europe, for the global market.

Stage 1

- Get the Ss to read the first two sections.
- Circulate and answer any queries. Discuss common queries with whole group.
- Quickly put the points in the left-hand column of the table below on the board and elicit information from the group so as to complete the column on the right.
- Make sure the Ss understand the situation by getting individual Ss to expand orally on a part of the table, using complete sentences.

Background: Zumospa

Company	Zumospa
Activity	food and drinks
Based in	Valencia, Spain
History	developed nationally, then globally, with acquisitions worldwide
Methods	innovative advertising and marketing; careful selection of products; marketing round the world through regional offices
Products	many food and drink products, household names

Background: Zumo

Sales	€30 million, 20% of Zumospa's total sales
Profit	€4.5 million
Position in Zumospa's product portfolio	cash cow
Ambitions	to make Zumo a global brand
Global competitors	Coca-Cola, Pepsi-Cola and Heinz

Stage 2

- Write the points in the following two tables on the board and follow the same procedure as above.

Zumo's key features

Ingredients	caffeine, vitamins, glucose, plus secret ingredient 'herbora' (rare African plant root)
Properties	body absorbs Zumo faster than water or other soft drinks; unique formula – tasty and thirst-quenching

Zumo as a global brand: initial strategy

Positioning	global; play down Spanish associations
Markets for initial launch	South America, Mexico, southern US, Japan, where Zumospa already has regional offices
Advertising campaign	standard throughout all markets, with local language and content adaptation
Advertising media	TV and radio; some adaptation of media (different media in different places)

Stage 3: Task

- Divide the class into small groups of three or four. Explain the purpose of the brainstorming session and remind them that they shouldn't spend too long on each point.
- Circulate and monitor, noting strong and less strong language areas.
- Praise the strong points and talk about areas for improvement, getting relevant students to reformulate what they said with the corrections you suggested.
- Make sure that Ss understand the situation by getting individual Ss to expand orally on different parts of the table, using complete sentences.

Stage 4: Writing

- Get the Ss to write a memo concentrating on two or three key points from the brainstorming session, saying what their particular group came up with in those areas, and whether they, as Marketing Manager for Zumospa, agree with the ideas produced.

 Writing file page 140

---

1 to 1

Get your student to glean the information to complete the tables and then have a 1 to 1 brainstorming session, where you both come up with ideas. Move on quickly from point to point.

Building relationships

At a glance

	Classwork – Course Book	Further work
Lesson 1 *Each lesson (excluding case studies) is about 45–60 minutes. This does not include administration and time spent going through homework.*	**Starting up** Ss discuss different business relationships, listen to an interview and do a quiz about their ability to build relationships. **Vocabulary: Describing relations** The vocabulary of relationships, including typical word combinations with *relations*. **Listening: Ways of entering markets** Things to be aware of when doing business in Latin America and China.	**Practice File** Vocabulary (page 12)
Lesson 2	**Reading: Relationship marketing** The importance of retaining existing customers.	**Text bank** (pages 144–147)
Lesson 3	**Language review: Multi-word verbs** Ss look at multi-word (phrasal) verbs and practise them in the context. **Skills: Networking** Ss study networking language in a series of networking situations, and practise the language in role plays.	**ML Grammar and Usage** **Practice File** Language review (page 13) **Resource bank** (page 197)
Lesson 4 *Each case study is about 1½ to 2 hours.*	**Case study: Getting to know you** Ss analyse an Asian car manufacturer, and suggest ways of strengthening customer loyalty to deal with increasing competition.	**Practice File** Writing (page 14)

For a fast route through the unit focussing mainly on speaking skills, just use the underlined sections.

For 1 to 1 situations, most parts of the unit lend themselves, with minimal adaptation, to use with individual students. Where this is not the case, alternative procedures are given.

Business brief

Both employers and employees have expectations about what is reasonable behaviour in a work context. There is a certain level of **trust** between people, and even if the newspapers are full of stories of breakdowns in this trust, we think of them as exceptions to **established norms** in **social relationships**.

Business-to-business relationships

Some say that first impressions count. Others think that someone's character can only be judged after a lot of contact in business contexts and socially. This is why deciding on a **supplier** or **distributor** takes varying lengths of time in different cultures. To emphasise the importance of relationships like these, companies may refer to each other as **partners**.

A new trend is for companies to set up **e-marketplaces** on the Internet where they work together on **procurement** (purchasing) of materials and parts. Suppliers can make bids in competition with each other.

When firms work together on a particular project, they may enter into a **strategic alliance**. This may take the form of a **joint venture** between two or three companies, or a **consortium** between several organisations. An alliance may be the prelude to a **merger** between companies. Journalists often use the language of betrothal and marriage in situations like this.

Companies may overcome legal and other barriers in order to merge, but, as in marriage, there is no guarantee that the relationship will work. The cultures of the two companies may be so incompatible that the promised increase in profitability and **shareholder value** does not materialise.

Relationship networks

Stakeholder theory holds that society is made up of a web of relationships, and that each member of this arrangement has its **stake** of interest and of responsibilities. In a company, the interested parties are its owners (shareholders), managers, employees, suppliers, distributors and customers who may or may not be end-users of its products or services. A large company's activities have an effect on the places where it operates (think especially of **company towns** dominated by one company) and on society as a whole. Some companies publish an independent **social audit** that goes beyond the traditional **annual report** and attempts to give a bigger picture of the company's place in society, the benefits it brings, the effects of its activities on people and the environment (see Unit 1, Communication). Some say that social audits give a false sense of **social responsibility**. Optimists reply that pressure from stakeholders such as shareholders and customers can bring positive changes in the way companies work, and benefits to society as a whole. Companies are increasingly sensitive to accusations of causing pollution, tolerating **racism** or using **sweatshop labour**. In a company, the interested parties are its owners (shareholders), managers, employees, suppliers, distributors, and of course its customers, who may or may not be the actual end-user, of its products or services.

Read on

E. Robert Dwyer, John Tanner: *Building Business-to-Business Relationships*, Irwin, 1998

Francis Fukuyama: *Trust: The Social Virtues and the Creation of Prosperity*, Free Press, 1996

Robert Hargrove: *Mastering the Art of Creative Collaboration*, McGraw-Hill, 1998

Gary Heil: *One Size Fits One: Building Relationships One Customer and One Employee at a Time*, Van Nostrand Reinhold, 1996

James E. Post et al.: *Business and Society: Corporate Strategy, Public Policy, Ethics,* McGraw-Hill, 1995

Lesson notes

Warmer

◎ With the whole class, build up on the board a 'mind-map' of a typical individual and their relationships. Draw a circle in the centre of the board showing the individual, with 'spokes' going out to other circles representing family, colleagues, boss, friends, clubs the individual belongs to, etc.

◎ Then get the Ss to draw individual mind-maps for themselves, talking about each type of relationship, how important it is and so on. You could get more confident Ss to come and do this in front of the whole class.

◎ Invite comments and encourage discussion of each map.

Overview

◎ Tell the Ss that they will be looking at Building relationships, especially in organisations.

◎ Ask the Ss to look at the Overview section at the beginning of the unit. Tell them a little about the things on the list, using the table on page 24 of this book as a guide. Tell them which points you will be covering in the current lesson and which in later lessons.

Quotation

Ask the Ss to look at the quotation and say if they agree with it. (Explain *shark* and who Woody Allen is if they don't know.)

Starting up

This section develops some of the ideas from the Warmer activity, and focusses the Ss on the subject of the unit. There is also a brief listening extract.

Ⓐ

◎ Get the Ss to discuss the questions in pairs. Each individual student should draw a mind-map like the one in the Warmer activity, this time concentrating on company and professional relationships, and the benefits they bring.

◎ Get one or two individual Ss to draw their map on the board and explain it to the whole class, not forgetting to talk about the benefits of each relationship.

Ⓑ

◎ In the listening activity in Exercise C, the Ss will listen to Ward Lincoln, the Business Relations Manager of an international training organisation talking about how companies can build good business relationships.

◎ Before listening to the recording, tell the Ss specifically that Ward Lincoln is going to talk about the key factors companies must consider when communicating with their clients. With the whole group, get the Ss to say what they think the key features of this communication might be and write them on the board. Some examples are:

    – they should get to know each other well

    – they should talk to each other regularly.

Ⓒ 🎧 3.1

◎ Play recording 3.1 once or twice and get the Ss to say:

    – which of the points they came up with were mentioned, and in what order, marking this on the list prepared on the board in Exercise B

    – the points they didn't anticipate, adding them to the list.

◎ Play the recording again, confirm the key points about communication, and work on remaining unfamiliar vocabulary, e.g. *restless*.

Ⓓ

◎ Get the Ss to do the quiz individually, then check their answers on page 152.

◎ Get two or three Ss to say what their 'profile' is and whether they agree with it.

Vocabulary: Describing relations

This section deals with the vocabulary of relationships, looking at some typical word combinations, and prepares the Ss to talk about relationships in the later activities in the unit.

Ⓐ

◎ Ask the Ss to work in pairs, getting them to say whether the words they know are positive or negative. With the whole class, put these verbs into a table on the board.

◎ Then, with the whole class, explain the verbs they don't know, using full sentences, like this:

    – If something *jeopardises* a relationship, it puts it in danger.

    – If people *resume* a relationship, they start it again after a period when it had stopped.

◎ After each of your definitions, ask the Ss if the expression is positive or negative and put it on the table on the board.

Positive meaning	Negative meaning
build up relations	*break off* relations
cement	cloud
develop	cut off
encourage	disrupt
establish	impair
improve	jeopardise
maintain	sever
promote	sour
restore	spoil
resume	
strengthen	

(B)

- Get the Ss in pairs to put the adjectives that they know on to the scale.
- Explain the adjectives they don't know, again using full-sentence definitions, such as
  - A *strained* relationship is difficult, one where people do not fully like or trust each other.
- Get the Ss to complete the chart.

Very bad	Very good
stormy strained cool	*amicable friendly close excellent*

(There might be some discussion about the order, especially with the 'Very good' words.)

(C)

- Explain any unfamiliar words, e.g. *imposition*, to the whole class.
- If the Ss are unfamiliar with this type of matching exercise, point out that they can look for clues like full stops at the end of the numbered elements, indicating that the following element will be a new sentence. Here, there are no full stops, but in 4, for example, the plural *excellent relations* shows that the continuation must have a plural verb, so a) or b) must be the continuation, but only a) makes sense.
- Get the Ss in pairs to match the two parts of the expressions quickly.
- Round up the results with the whole class.

1 e	2 d	3 b	4 a	5 e

- In getting the Ss to make up sentences, it's good to give them specific contexts. You could prompt them to talk about relations between:
  - their country and another country
  - their company and its customers
  - their department and the rest of the company they work for
  - two well-known celebrities or politicians.
- Give the Ss time to think about their sentences and write them down. Don't 'put them on the spot' in front of the whole class.
- Once the Ss have had time to think about their sentences, do a whole-class round-up, writing the best sentences on the board.

Listening: Ways of entering markets

Ss listen to Miguel Adao, who talks about doing business and building relationships in Latin America, and Tong Yan, who talks about China, and compare the two business cultures.

(A) 🎧 3.2

- Use the points as the basis for a brief whole-class discussion about what they think they will hear. (*Intermediary* and *loyal* may need explaining.)
- Of course, if there are students from a Hispanic or Chinese background, they will have views on this.
- Get Ss to tick the appropriate column(s) for each point.
- Play recording 3.2 once or twice.
- Get Ss to say whether their predictions were correct or not.

	Latin America	China
1 It is important to find an intermediary.		✓
2 These people tend to work with friends and relatives.		✓
3 You may need to shake hands and even hug.	✓	
4 Long lunches or dinner meetings may be important.	✓	
5 These people trust those who are loyal to them and show respect.		✓
6 The best way to build a business relationship is through networking.	✓	

(B)

- Get individual Ss to summarise the similarities and differences between the two cultures, using the points in Exercise A as a guide.
- Get the Ss to say if they think some of the things are true even if they were not mentioned. For example:
  - Do they think long business lunches are common in China?
  - Is loyalty and respect important in Latin America?

(C) 🎧 3.3

- Play recording 3.3 and get the Ss to summarise what Tong Yan says about how business decisions are made in China.
- Ask the Ss if what he says about China is true of other cultures, including their own.

Reading: Relationship marketing

Ss read about the importance of retaining customers, something that for a long time was overlooked.

 A

◎ Do not look at the article yet. Get the Ss to guess answers to Questions 1 and 2 with a show of hands.

◎ Get the Ss to read the first two paragraphs. Explain any difficult vocabulary.

◎ Get Ss to summarise paragraph 1 and another S to summarise paragraph 2.

◎ Ask the Ss to answer questions 1 and 2.

1 a	2 c

B

◎ Ask the Ss to look at the questions as preparation for reading the rest of the article.

◎ Get Ss to read the last four paragraphs. Explain any further vocabulary.

◎ Ask for answers to the questions.

> **1** A 5% decrease in the number of defecting customers led to profit increases of between 25% and 85%. Domino's Pizzas estimates that a regular customer is worth more than $5,000 over ten years.
>
> **2** Established customers 1) tend to buy more, 2) are predictable and 3) usually cost less to service than new customers. 4) Furthermore, they tend to be less price sensitive, and 5) may provide free word-of-mouth advertising and referrals. 6) Retaining customers also makes it difficult for competitors to enter a market or increase their share of a market.
> The article also mentions, as its main theme, that keeping customers leads to increased profitability.
>
> **3** Advocate   Supporter   Client   Customer   Prospect

 C

◎ Get the Ss to work in pairs on these words. Print out the line numbers when they occur. Ss should look at these words in a sentence context but without looking at the whole article and try to guess their meaning from among the alternatives.

◎ Ask the Ss for their answers, and discuss briefly how they chose them.

humdrum	(line 11)	b)
defecting	(line 30)	a)
nurturing	(line 43)	b)
correlation	(line 51)	a)
customer retention	(line 51)	b)

 D

◎ Ask the Ss to match the words to make possible combinations.

◎ Then get the Ss to go through the article again to look for the word combinations as they actually occur in the articles. (Other possible combinations include *financial opportunities* and *price implications*.)

1 c	2 a	3 b	4 e	5 d

E

◎ Ask the whole class to give their ideas about this.

> If the Ss need prompting, you could mention:
> ◎ special offers offered by many types of organisations and retailers
> ◎ loyalty cards with supermarkets
> ◎ frequent flier programmes with airlines
> ◎ 'free' minutes with mobile phone companies.

Language review: Multi-word verbs

Ss look at verbs made up of more than one word, otherwise known as phrasal verbs, and study them being used in context.

A 🎧 3.4

◎ Tell the Ss to look through the sections of the conversation. Answer any queries about meaning.

◎ Get the Ss, in pairs, to put the conversation in the correct order.

◎ Play recording 3.4 once or twice so that Ss can check their answers.

f	c	b	d	g	j	h	e	a	i

◎ Ask the Ss to read the conversation in simultaneous pairs. Circulate and monitor, especially for realistic intonation.

◎ Ask one or two pairs to perform the conversation in front of the whole class.

B

◎ Get the Ss, in pairs, to underline the multi-word verbs in the conversation and then match them to their meanings.

1	get on (really well)	**6**	sounded out
2	count on	**7**	let (us) down
3	build up	**8**	set up
4	hold on to	**9**	draw up
5	put (it) off	**10**	call (it) off

◎ Check the answers with the whole class.

⊚ Point out the separable multi-word verbs, for example *build up something* and *build something up*. Point out that when using *it* as the object, the verbs must be separated; for example, you can say *build it up* but not *build up it*.

(c)

⊚ Ask the Ss, in pairs, to rephrase the comments.

> 1 We'll have to *call* the meeting *off* tomorrow. / We'll have to *call off* the meeting tomorrow.
>
> 2 Let's *put off* the presentation until next week. / Let's *put* the presentation *off* until next week.
>
> 3 We know our suppliers will never *let us down*. / We can *count on* our suppliers to meet their deadlines.
>
> 4 We have now *set up* a first class distribution network in Europe.
>
> 5 Could you please *draw up* a contract as soon as possible. / Could you please *draw* a contract *up* as soon as possible.
>
> 6 Could you *set up* a meeting with them for next week. / Could you *set* a meeting *up* with them for next week.
>
> 7 We've *held on* to the same market share that we had last year.
>
> 8 The new sales manager *gets on* very well with his team.

⊚ Check the answers with the whole class.

⊚ Again, point out the separable multi-word verbs, as in 1, 2, 5 and 6. (4 is theoretically separable, but *up* after *network* would be a long way from *set*, and would sound rather odd.)

⊚ If there is time, your Ss could discuss the questions below in pairs. Write them on the board, and invite different pairs to talk about different points. The idea is to use as many multi-word verbs as possible (not just ones from this section) when answering the questions.

⊚ Try to have a phrasal verb dictionary to hand, for example the *Longman Phrasal Verbs Dictionary*.

> 1 How can businesses build up market share?
>
> 2 How can companies hold on to their most valued employees?
>
> 3 What preparation should be made before setting up a meeting with an important potential customer?

⊚ Circulate, monitor and assist if necessary. Note how each pair is using multi-word verbs.

⊚ With the whole class, go over the multi-word verbs you have heard, correcting problems where necessary.

Possible answer for question 1

Of course, before companies can *build up* market share, they have to *get into* the market in the first place. They have to *find out about* how the market works, how distribution is *set up* and so on. When they have *put together* enough information, they can *set out* to attack the market, perhaps *starting off* in just a small area to begin with. They may try to *set themselves apart from* competitors by offering a product with special features, or they may compete on price.

Skills: Networking

Ss look at networking language in a series of networking situations, and use it themselves to role play two situations.

(A) 🎧 3.5

⊚ Tell the Ss that they are going to listen to a series of conversations in the context of people networking.

⊚ Ask them to look through the statements as preparation for listening, saying they will have to decide which statements are true and which false.

⊚ Play recording 3.5 and stop at the end of each situation to give time for the Ss to make their choice.

⊚ Ask the Ss for their answers.

> 1 a) false b) true   2 a) false, b) false
> 3 a) true, b) false   4 a) false, b) true

(B) 🎧 3.6

⊚ Ask the Ss to look at the questions.

⊚ Play recording 3.6 once or twice and ask for the answers.

> 1 Valentin Perez (A) wants advice on franchising contracts. A friend has given him the name of the person that he calls, saying that they might be able to help. B (whose name we do not learn) is unable to help, but gives Valentin Perez the name of someone who might be able to: Stephanie Grant.
>
> 2 The call is successful in the sense that Valentin Perez gets Stephanie Grant's name.

Lesson notes

© 🎧 3.6

◎ Before playing the recording again, ask the Ss to look at items 1–6, and to think briefly about what the missing words might be.

◎ Play recording 3.6 again, and have the Ss fill in the blanks.

---

1 I <u>hope</u> you don't <u>mind</u> me <u>phoning</u>. Silvana said it would probably be OK.

2 Is it a <u>convenient</u> time to ring or could I call you <u>back</u> at a better time?

3 Silvana <u>mentioned</u> that you might be able to <u>advise</u> me on franchising contracts.

4 Mmm, I don't know. I could maybe give you a little help, but I know someone <u>who's</u> <u>an</u> <u>expert</u> in that area.

5 You haven't got her phone number <u>by</u> <u>any</u> <u>chance</u>?

6 Can I <u>mention</u> <u>your</u> <u>name</u> when I call her?

Ⓓ

◎ Before role playing the situations, tell the Ss to look at the Useful language box.

◎ Get the Ss, in pairs, to practise saying the expressions using friendly intonation.

◎ Ss take turns to say one of the expressions from the Useful language box, and to make an appropriate reply. For example:

A Haven't we met somewhere before?

B Yes, it was at the group sales conference in Portugal last year.

A Oh yes. Very good conference, wasn't it!

B We both went to that presentation on networking skills.

A That's right! It was one of the most interesting at the conference!

◎ You can demonstrate with one student to give the Ss the general idea. Then get the Ss to practise in pairs.

◎ Praise and correct as usual, concentrating on friendly intonation.

◎ Keep the class in pairs. If you are short of time, some pairs can role play situation 1 and others situation 2.

◎ For situation 1, encourage the owner to think of a name for their notional colleague, and the contact to think of a typical Russian name, such as Ivan(a) Pavlov(a).

◎ For situation 2, the Ss can invent names for themselves or use their own names.

◎ Make sure that the Ss understand the situation they are going to role play before they start.

◎ Start the activity. Circulate and monitor.

◎ Praise good points and correct weaker ones, again concentrating on intonation.

◎ Ask for one or two public performances of each situation.

Case study

Getting to know you

Kimsoong, a Korean car manufacturer, wants to strengthen customer loyalty as a way of dealing with increasing competition.

Stage 1

◎ Instruct the Ss to read the section on the company's background in pairs.

◎ Circulate and answer any queries. Discuss common queries with the whole group.

◎ Quickly put the points in the left-hand column of the table below on the board and elicit information from the group so as to complete the column on the right.

◎ Make sure the Ss understand the situation by getting individual Ss each to expand orally on a part of the table, using complete sentences.

Background

Company	Kimsoong
Activity	Car manufacturer
Based in	Korea, European HQ near Paris
Structure	◎ Retail franchises in most European countries; also tyre- and exhaust-fitting services

Special features of the company	◎ Reliability at low prices
	◎ Basic models include many features that are usually options
	◎ Environmentally aware
	◎ Social conscience
	  – makes donations to environmental groups
	  – Eco-car under development

◎ Ask the Ss to read the sections on problems and their possible solutions and elicit the points below.

◎ As before, invite individual Ss to summarise the situation using complete sentences.

Actions	Hoped-for benefit
◉ Look after existing customers well. Develop better understanding of customers through accurate customer profile. ◉ Customer loyalty programme (cost shared 50/50 with franchises). ◉ To encourage staff to be more active in building up good customer relations.	◉ To build up long-term customer relationships – customers may buy 3 or 4 cars over 10-year period thereby increasing profits.

1 to 1

Use these three points for the task as the basis for a discussion about existing customers and a possible loyalty programme.

Stage 2

◉ Before doing the task itself, Ss should study, in pairs, the Kimsoong customer profile for a couple of minutes.

◉ Go round the class quickly and ask individual Ss to make statements about different points, for example:

  – Nearly half the buyers of Kimsoong cars are under 30.

  – Less than 1 in 6 of buyers buy another Kimsoong.

Stage 3: Task

◉ Get the Ss to work in pairs or threes on their ideas for the customer loyalty programme.

◉ Invite representatives of the groups to present their ideas to the whole class. The representatives can write key points on the board and explain them briefly.

◉ Have the whole class discuss the various ideas and choose the best ones, perhaps by voting on them. You can run this discussion yourself or ask a student to chair the meeting. (The student should be briefed beforehand on the time available.)

Stage 4: Writing

Ss write to an existing customer of a company in order to make an offer that will increase customer loyalty.

◉ Go round the class and ask individual Ss which company they might write about and what the special offer might be.

◉ Ask for possible openings to the letter, for example:

  – Dear Mr Eastwood, You are one of our most valued customers. That's why we're making you this special offer. ...

◉ The Ss could write letters in pairs collaboratively in class. Circulate, monitor and assist. Alternatively, set the activity as homework.

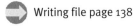 Writing file page 138

Lesson notes

Success

At a glance

	Classwork – Course Book	Further work
Lesson 1 *Each lesson (excluding case studies) is about 45–60 minutes. This does not include administration and time spent going through homework.*	**Starting up** Ss look at language for describing successful people and organisations and talk about success symbols in their own culture. **Listening: Successful people and companies** A business woman talks about the ingredients for personal success, and for the success of companies. **Discussion: Epic failures** Ss read about two classic product failures and discuss them.	
Lesson 2	**Reading: Mobile phones** Ss read about Nokia, the mobile phone manufacturer, answer questions and complete a profile. **Language review: Present and past tenses** The tenses are compared and contrasted. Ss look at how they are used in the Nokia article and then use them to write about another company's history.	**Text bank** (pages 148–151) **Practice File** Language review (page 17) **ML Grammar and Usage**
Lesson 3	**Vocabulary: Prefixes** Ss look at how the prefixes *over-* and *out-* are used with particular verbs. **Skills: Negotiating** The language of signalling, checking understanding and summarising is examined. Ss analyse how it occurs in a negotiating situation and use it themselves to role play a situation.	**Practice File** Vocabulary (page 16) **Resource bank** (page 198)
Lesson 4 *Each case study is about 1½ to 2 hours.*	**Case study: Camden Football Club** Ss take part in the negotiations between a football club and a big media company.	**Practice File** Writing (page 18)

For a fast route through the unit focussing mainly on speaking skills, just use the underlined sections.

For 1 to 1 situations, most parts of the unit lend themselves, with minimal adaptation, to use with individual students. Where this is not the case, alternative procedures are given.

Business brief

People are fascinated by success. Business commentators try to understand the **success factors** that make for successful individuals, products and companies, and for economically successful countries.

People Different types of organisation require different types of leaders. Think of start-ups with their dynamic entrepreneurs, mature companies with their solid but hopefully inspirational CEOs, companies in difficulty with their turnaround specialists. Each also requires managers and employees with different **personality make-ups**. Think of the combination of personality types needed in banks compared to those in advertising agencies.

Products Successful products are notoriously hard to predict. There are subtle combinations of social, cultural and technological circumstances that mean that something will succeed at one time but not another. People talk rightly about a product 'whose time has come'. The technology to meet a particular need may exist for a long time before the product on which it is based **takes off**. In the beginning, cost may be a factor, but after a time, a **critical mass** of users develops, costs come down, and no one 'can understand how they could have done without one'.

Companies Success factors here include **energy, vision** and **efficiency**, but many of the companies that were thought to possess these attributes 30 or even five years ago are not those we would think of as having these qualities today. **Management fashions** are a big factor: **gurus** and management books have a lot to answer for. Once something becomes a **mantra**, everyone starts doing it, but objective measures of the relative efficiency of each type of company are hard to find.

Countries Economic success stories such as Japan, Germany and Sweden became models that everyone wanted to imitate. In the 1970s, government experts and academics went to these places by the plane-load looking for the magic ingredients. In the 1980s and early 1990s, they went to the emerging economies of the Asian tigers. Now the US economy is again held up as a model for all to follow. At various times, commitment to **self-improvement**, **entrepreneurial flair**, efficient **access to capital**, vibrant **institutions** and a good **education system** are held to be important factors for success, but the countries mentioned above possess these to very varying degrees. The exact formula for success at a particular time is hard to pin down.

In any case, how do you successfully imitate companies and countries? Companies have a particular **culture** that is the result of their history, short or long. If managers and their consultants change them radically, for example by downsizing them, they may be ripping out the very things that make them tick. On the other hand, change may be really necessary, and companies with cultures and structures that were successful under earlier conditions are very hard to change in a genuine way, even if they go through the motions of adopting the latest management fashion. Unless convinced otherwise by a **charismatic leader**, there will always be a number of **refuseniks**: managers and employees who refuse to change because they can't understand how the things that made the company successful in the past are no longer valuable, and can even be a cause of failure. One reason for developing new products in **start-ups** is that they can develop a culture and a recipe for success from scratch.

With countries, how do you imitate social structures and habits that have evolved over centuries elsewhere, often with an entirely different starting point? The old joke about not wanting to start from here if you're going there is applicable. In any case, by the time the model has been identified as one worth imitating, the world economy has moved on, and your chosen model may no longer be the one to follow.

The ability to **adapt** is key. Here, the US is world leader in adapting old organisations to new technological conditions – Ford and IBM, for example, have had amazing **turnarounds** from earlier difficulties. But radical **innovation** is equally important. The US is also good at generating entirely new companies that quickly become world leaders – witness Microsoft and Intel. The US economy is as dominant as ever.

Read on

Here is a very limited selection of books about managers, companies and countries respectively.

Michael Gershman: *Getting It Right the Second Time: Remarketing Strategies to Turn Failure into Success*, Management Books, 2000

Richard Koch: *The Successful Boss's First 100 Days*, Financial Times/Prentice Hall, 1998

Lesson notes

Warmer

- Ask the Ss to name the most successful business person / people in their own country / countries. (In a multi-country group, this is a good chance for Ss to learn about each other's business heroes.)

Overview

- Tell the Ss that they will be looking at success and failure, in business people and in organisations.
- Ask the Ss to look at the Overview section at the beginning of the unit. Tell them a little about the things on the list, using the table on page 32 of this book as a guide. Tell them which points you will be covering in the current lesson and which in later lessons.

Quotation

- Get the Ss to explain the joke in the quotation.
- Ask them if they think it's true. Do they think, for example, that some people are successful by luck, perhaps by being in the right place at the right time?
- Invite some quick comments, but don't anticipate the content of the rest of the unit too much.

Starting up

In this section, the Ss look at the vocabulary for describing successful people and organisations and talk about success symbols in their own culture.

Ⓐ

- Get the Ss to discuss the words in pairs. Tell the Ss that they can add vocabulary that came up during the warmer session to their lists if they want to. Circulate, monitor and assist, for example by explaining *ruthlessness*, *stamina* and *nepotism*, helping with pronunciation, and suggesting words where necessary to describe particular character traits.
- Ask individual pairs to give their five most important characteristics and ask them why they have chosen them.
- Invite comments and encourage discussion. The Ss may say, for example, that the characteristics depend on the type of person. The characteristics of a successful novelist overlap with, but are not identical to, those for a successful chief executive. (Drive and discipline might be common to both.)

Ⓑ

- Ask the Ss, in pairs, to talk about individuals in relation to the five words they chose in Exercise A, and report their findings to the whole class. Say that they can relate the characteristics to the people that they mentioned in the Warmer activity if they want to.

Ⓒ

- Get the Ss to work on the success symbols in pairs. Ask them also to name the particular cars, jewellery, holiday destinations, leisure activities, etc. that successful people choose at the moment. (This will not apply to all the points here, of course, e.g. respect.) Invite comments and encourage discussion with the whole group. Where there are different nationalities in the class, treat the status symbols of each culture tactfully, of course.

Ⓓ

- Get the Ss to work again in pairs, this time changing partners. Ask them to study the statements and decide which they agree with and why. For example, they may think that a company could be in the news continually, but often for the wrong reasons. Or they might think that all publicity is good publicity. Invite pairs to present their opinions to the whole group.
- If you have time, get pairs to think of a successful company that they admire, and ask which statements in the exercise apply to this company. (In the case of successful recent start-ups, it may be that not many of the points apply.) Round up the discussion with the whole group.

Listening: Successful people and companies

Ss listen to a business woman talking about the ingredients for personal success, and those for the success of companies.

Ⓐ 🎧 4.1

- Play recording 4.1 and ask the Ss to listen for the general gist.
- Then play the recording again, stopping after each key point so that the Ss have time to make notes.
- Play the recording a third time, again stopping after each key point so that the Ss have time to check their answers and fill in any gaps.

Successful business people

- know their job very thoroughly
- are good at managing people under them
- have a clear idea of the direction of their business
- can make a profit
- are good team players
- are good at managing relationships, making people feel comfortable in the organisation
- are ambitious and wanting to succeed
- need a good collection of people around them, e.g. in finance, marketing, etc.
- manage their work/life balance: they manage their own life as well as their business life.

◎ Go through the answers with the Ss, if necessary playing parts of the recording again if they didn't get something. (If a student asks about it, point out the unusualness of *capable in making a profit*, saying that the normal form would be *capable of making a profit*. Say that in natural speech, these variations are normal. The speaker was probably thinking of *capability in something*.)

◎ Ask the Ss if they agree with all these points. Can they think of counter-examples, for example, successful business people who are not very good managers or successful people who have no leisure activities?

(B) 🎧 4.2

◎ Follow the same procedure again for recording 4.2.

Successful companies

◎ often have well-known brand names
◎ are good places to work
◎ have been in existence for some time
◎ have a strong management team
◎ are financially successful
◎ learn from the mistakes of unsuccessful companies
◎ have sometimes been in existence for only a short time
◎ were sometimes unsuccessful ones that have been taken over and turned round.

◎ Go through the answers with Ss, if necessary playing parts of the recording again if they didn't get particular points.

◎ Ask the Ss if they agree with all these points. Can they think of counter-examples, for example successful organisations that are not good places to work, ones without well-known brand names? (Many companies selling to other companies rather than to consumers have names and brands that are relatively unknown outside their industries.)

(C)

◎ Ss can do this writing task individually or in pairs. Recap quickly some of the ideas about success that they have seen so far in the unit and get the whole class to brainstorm others.

◎ If your Ss are writing about a business person, they could choose the person they mentioned in the Warmer activity above. Suggested text length 200–300 words.

Discussion: Epic failures

Ss read about two classic product failures, the Ford Edsel and New Coke, and discuss them.

(A)

◎ Ask the Ss to work in pairs, A and B. Student A reads about New Coke and Student B about the Ford Edsel. Each takes notes about their article, ready to summarise it to their partner.

◎ Circulate, monitor and assist, noting strong points and those that need correction.

◎ Get pairs to explain their articles to each other as a simultaneous class activity, using their notes and without referring to the original articles.

◎ Ask one or two Ss to explain their article to the whole class.

◎ Praise strong language points and work on the weaker ones as usual.

(B)

◎ Write the following structures on the board, presenting them in a table as here:

Coca-Cola	could might should should not	have ...

◎ Ask the Ss, in pairs, to practise talking about what Coca-Cola and Ford could have or should have done.

◎ Circulate, monitor and assist. Note strong and weak points as usual, focussing particularly on the structures in the table above.

◎ Praise strong points and correct weaker ones.

◎ Get individual Ss to repeat particular sentences using the structures above to the whole class.

◎ Have a whole-class discussion about the lessons to be learnt from the two product failures.

Reading: Mobile phones

Ss talk about the benefits and disadvantages of having a mobile phone, read about Nokia, the mobile phone manufacturer, and complete a company profile.

◎ Ask the Ss to discuss the questions in pairs.

◎ Get pairs to report to the whole class.

◎ Tell the Ss to read the first four paragraphs of the article in pairs, and answer the first three questions. Circulate, monitor and assist.

◎ Ask whole class for their answers to the first three questions. Get the Ss to explain what they understand by *focus* (line 53) (= concentrating on the things you do best) and *value-added* (line 53–4) (= delivering the highest profits as well as the best customer benefits).

1	Country of origin	Finland
2	Chief Executive	Jorma Ollila
3	Chief Executive's main objectives	◎ telecom-orientated ◎ global ◎ focus ◎ value-added

- Get the Ss to read all but the last paragraph in pairs and answer questions 4–8. Circulate, monitor and assist, explaining difficult words and expressions like *outstrip* (line 81–82), *offset* (line 101), *fulsome in their praise* (line 125–126). (GDP is gross domestic product, the total value of all the goods and services produced in a country in a particular period.)
- Ask the whole class for their answers to the questions.
- With the whole class, get individual students to reformulate the reasons for success in their own words, using complete sentences. For example, *Nokia has been successful partly, perhaps, because of luck*; for example, *it decided to concentrate on the GSM segment which became the world standard*. (GSM stands for 'Global System for Mobile communication'.)

4	Industry position	◎ world's biggest mobile phone maker
5	Market share	◎ 30 per cent and growing
6	Market capitalisation (= total value of its shares on the stockmarket)	◎ €142 billion
7	Main competitors	◎ Motorola, Ericsson
8	Reasons for success	◎ luck ◎ decision to concentrate on GSM segment ◎ decision to get out of chemicals, tyres, etc. ◎ strong brand (some thought it was Japanese) ◎ fashionable, reliable, user-friendly handsets ◎ short product cycles ◎ launches new products just when older ones are becoming unprofitable ◎ increases volumes (quantities sold) to offset falling prices ◎ unbureaucratic despite growth culture of innovation ◎ best logistics (= organisation) ◎ incredibly efficient

- Invite students to say what they think potential threats might be, before asking them to read the last paragraph in pairs and to complete the table.

9	Potential threats	◎ new rivals, including US Internet giants ◎ new technologies ◎ market has high expectations

- Check with the Ss whether they had foreseen the threats actually mentioned.

Ⓓ

- Ask the Ss to work in pairs on the company they think is the most successful in their country / countries. They can both choose the same company and work on it together, or different companies and explain to each other why they have chosen them.
- Ask the Ss to work specifically on the reasons for the success of their chosen companies, as for Question 8 above in relation to Nokia.
- Circulate, monitor and assist.
- With the whole class, get each pair to talk about their chosen company / companies.

Language review: Present and past tenses

The tenses are compared and contrasted. Ss look at how they are used in the Nokia article and then use them to write about another company's history.

Ⓐ

- Get the Ss to work, in pairs, on the questions. Circulate, monitor and assist.
- Get individual Ss to make statements about their own company or educational institution using the different tenses.
- Discuss the rules with the whole class and get the Ss to complete the statements.

1	present simple
2	past simple
3	present continuous
4	present perfect

1 *took over, wrote down, saw*
   Past simple, because these are completed actions which took place at a particular time in the past.
2 *has outstripped, has allied, has produced*
   Present perfect, because these are present results of past actions.
3 *are snapping* or *living up to*
   The present continuous is used because this is a current situation.
4 *has happened* and *has happened* –
   Present perfect, because these are present results of past actions.
   has and *is* – present simple, because these situations are generally true.
   has played – present perfect, because this is a present result of past actions.
   realised – past simple, because this took place at a particular time.
   would move – conditional, depending on *realised that*.
   to concentrate – infinitive (decision to do something).
   was – past simple, because this decision took place at a particular time.
   has become – present perfect relating to the present result of a past action.

(B)

- Go through notes with the whole class, explaining the task and any unfamiliar words (e.g. *revive, turning a company around, surge*).
- Get individual Ss to come up to the board in turn and write the first sentence of each section, so that they see present simple, past simple and present perfect in context.
- Ask the Ss to use these sentences as the basis for writing the complete article, individually or in pairs in class, or as homework.

> **The company and its markets**
> Chupa Chups, based in Barcelona, is the world's 25th biggest sweetmaker, with an overall market share of 0.9%. Its share of the global lollipop market is 34%. It has manufacturing sites in five countries and its products are familiar to children all over the world.
>
> **How the company started**
> In 1954 Enric Bernat tried to revive the sweet manufacturer Granja Asturias, and he succeeded in turning the company around. In 1985 he bought all its shares and dropped the entire product range (except lollipops) to concentrate on the new Chups lollipop.
>
> **What it is doing now**
> The company is now building its adult customer base. It is attracting older customers with new flavours.
>
> **Recent events**
> Chupa Chups has recently launched its highly coloured 'tongue-painter' lollipops. It has also diversified into sugar-free mints with the Smint range, and the resulting sales surge has been spectacular. The company's revenues have grown enormously, and last year it sold 4 billion lollipops.

Vocabulary: Prefixes

Ss look at how the prefixes *over-* and *out-* are used with particular verbs.

(A)

- Go through the possible prefix–verb combinations. Explain where necessary, giving explanations like the ones in brackets in the box below.

> overbid (= to offer to pay too much for something in relation to its value);
> overbook;
> overcharge;
> overrun;
> oversubscribe (If a company issues shares on the stock market and they are oversubscribed, the demand for shares is more than the number of shares available.);
> overtake
> outbid (= to bid more than others);
> outmanoeuvre;
> outnumber;
> outrun;
> outstrip;
> outvote.

Lesson notes

(B)

- Ask the Ss which take both prefixes (*bid, run*).

(C)

- Get the Ss to complete the exercise in pairs. Circulate, monitor and assist.
- Invite answers from the whole class.

> 1 overtook
> 2 outstripped
> 3 outbid (Point out that the past tense and past participle of *outbid* are also *outbid*: it follows the same pattern as *bid*.)
> 4 outvote
> 5 outmanoeuvred
> 6 outnumber
> 7 overbooked
> 8 overran
> 9 overcharged
> 10 oversubscribed

(D)

- Ask the whole class about the meanings of *over-* and *out-*, but don't spend too much time on this.

> *Over-* is used, among other things, to say that something is higher than something else.
> *Out-* is used, among other things, to say that something is not inside something, and to talk about leaving or movement away from a place, and to say that something goes beyond a particular level or number.

(E)

- Ask the Ss to answer questions in pairs, referring again to the Nokia article if necessary.
- Ask the whole class for answers.

> 1 c   2 b   3 b

- If Ss are interested, for homework, ask them to look in a good dictionary, for example the *Longman Dictionary of Contemporary English*, at the definitions of *over-* and *out-*. In the following entries, they will also see the many verbs that begin with these prefixes.

Skills: Negotiating

The language of signalling, checking understanding and summarising is covered. Ss analyse how it occurs in a negotiating situation and use it themselves to role play a situation.

Ⓐ

- Go through the Useful language box with the whole class. Get individual Ss to read the expressions, working on intonation.
- Explain briefly the role and importance of these expressions in structuring negotiations.

Ⓑ

- Get the Ss to read the conversation aloud in pairs, and identify signalling, checking understanding and summarising expressions.
- Ask different pairs for their findings and discuss them with the whole class.

Special requirements? What do you mean exactly? (Checking understanding)
Mmm, OK, how about this? (Signalling)
OK, so you're saying you will modify the car if we ask you to? (Checking understanding)
Right then, let's see what we've got. (Summarising)
That's it. OK, let's talk about delivery now. (Signalling)

Ⓒ 🎧 4.3

- Play the recording once right through, and then again, stopping after each item.
- Ask students to identify signalling, checking understanding and summarising expressions, so as to eliminate them.

1	checking understanding
2	signalling
3	–
4	checking understanding
5	signalling
6	summarising
7	checking understanding
8	–

So the answer is 3 and 8.

Ⓓ

- Explain the situation.
- Put the Ss into pairs and appoint the Sales Managers and Chief Buyers. Make sure that everyone knows who they are.
- Ask the Sales Managers to turn to page 153 and the Chief Buyers to turn to page 149.

- Ask the Ss to study their information carefully.
- Tell the Ss they should
  - start the negotiation with some small talk
  - get into the negotiation itself, trying to use the expressions for checking understanding, signalling and summarising, and
  - write down what they agree.
- Answer any questions the Ss may have, then tell them to do the negotiation in pairs.
- Circulate, monitor and assist. Note language points for praise and correction, especially in relation to the expressions for signalling, checking understanding and summarising.
- When the pairs have finished their negotiation, ask the different pairs what they decided. Summarise the results on the board, so that Ss can see the range of results.
- Ask one or two pairs to summarise the stages of their negotiations, the tactics each partner was using, particular difficulties and sticking points.
- Do a round-up of language points for praise and those that need correction. Focus on five or six language points, for example, in relation to expressions for signalling, checking understanding and summarising, and get individual Ss to use the correct forms.

---

1 to 1

This role play can be done between teacher and student. Don't forget to note language points for praise and correction afterwards. Discuss with the student their negotiating plan and the tactics they were using.

Case study

Camden FC

Ss study information about Camden FC and take part in the negotiations between the club and a big media company about future broadcasting rights and other issues.

Stage 1

- Divide the whole class into two halves, A and B.
- Get the Ss in Group A to read the section on Camden's background.
- Get the Ss in Group B to read about the current situation.
- Circulate and answer any queries. Discuss common queries with each half as a whole.
- Put the points in the left-hand column of table below on the board. This is a whole-class activity where individual Ss in Group B elicit information from individual Ss in Group A by asking questions based on the points on the left, for example *What has Camden's recent performance been like on the field?*
- Then, similarly, get the Ss in Group A to elicit information from those in Group B about the current situation.

Background: Camden FC

Recent performance in football	Very successful in UK and Europe
Recent performance in business	Commercially very successful
Footballing success due to	Cristos Sroda, Manager, and his strategy of promoting younger players and buying some international ones
Commercial success due to	Sophie Legrange, Commercial Director, and her strategy of increasing profits through ⊚ corporate hospitality ⊚ advertising ⊚ sponsorship ⊚ conferences and banquesting ⊚ diversification: travel agency, etc.
Turnover (= sales)	Increased four-fold to £70 million
Profits	£15 million
One lucrative source of income	TV rights

Current situation

Current sponsorship deal with	Insurance company
Possible new deal with Other income from United Media's interest in Camden due to United Media's	United Media plc other activities Potentially large audiences (advertisers will be interested – not specifically stated)
Key factors in negotiations between Camden and United Media	⊚ Camden feel they are in a strong position ⊚ Some say Camden rely too much on their star player, Paolo Rosetti and he has personal problems ⊚ Commercial Director Sophie Legrange wants a good deal and will only choose United Media if they can provide one

⊚ Check that the situation is clear to all the Ss by asking a few quick questions.

⊚ Once you are satisfied that the situation is clear, move on to Stage 2.

Stage 2

⊚ Divide the class into groups of four to six. Within each group, half the Ss will represent Camden FC and the other half, United Media plc: two to three Ss on each side.

⊚ Ask the whole class to look at the agenda for the negotiations and elaborate briefly on each point.

⊚ Before the Ss read their role cards, make it clear that each side will have to work out its objectives, priorities, strategy and tactics, and think carefully about what concessions they are willing to make.

⊚ Camden FC negotiators turn to page 147 and read their role cards.

⊚ United Media negotiators turn to page 154 and read their role cards.

⊚ Get the each team to work together to develop an effective strategy for the negotiations. Circulate, monitor and assist.

Stage 3: Task

⊚ Make sure that each side has a chief negotiator who will be the first to speak. The chief United Media negotiator will outline the purpose of the negotiations and the chief Camden negotiator will reply. The chief negotiators should make sure that the discussions move on smartly, so that participants do not spend too long on each point.

⊚ The negotiations can begin, in parallel where there is more than one group.

⊚ Circulate and monitor, noting strong points and those that need correction. Do not intervene in the negotiations themselves unless the teams are completely stuck.

⊚ When time is up, ask the Ss on different sides what happened in their particular negotiations: what their objectives were, what tactics they used, whether they achieved their objectives, etc.

⊚ Praise strong language points and correct ones that need correcting, getting individual Ss to rephrase what they said earlier, incorporating the corrections.

Stage 4: Writing

Following the negotiations, the Ss write a press release or a letter depending on the outcome of their particular session.

⊚ This writing exercise can be done as pair work in class or for homework.

⊚ Make sure that each student knows which type of writing they are going to produce: a press release from the point of view of the company they represented, or a letter, if the negotiation was unsuccessful.

 Writing file page 141.

> **1 to 1**
>
> This negotiation can be done 1 to 1. Ask the student which side they would prefer to represent. You represent the other side. Don't forget to note language points for praise and correction after. Afterwards, discuss with the student their negotiating plan and the tactics they were using. Highlight some of the language you chose to use as well.

5 Job satisfaction

At a glance

	Classwork – Course Book	Further work
Lesson 1 *Each lesson (excluding case studies) is about 45–60 minutes. This does not include administration and time spent going through homework.*	**<u>Starting up</u>** Ss discuss what motivates people at work. **Reading: Fringe benefits** Ss read about the generous fringe benefits offered by some companies and discuss them in relation to work / life balance.	**Text bank** (pages 152–155)
Lesson 2	**Listening: Motivating factors** A specialist on job satisfaction talks about the factors that most motivate different groups of workers. **Vocabulary: Synonyms and word building** Ss look at the vocabulary of motivation and job satisfaction. **Discussion: What's in a title?** Ss read a short article about job titles and discuss their importance in providing job satisfaction.	**Practice File** Vocabulary (page 20)
Lesson 3	**Language review: Passives** Ss work on the passive forms of a range of verb tenses. **<u>Skills: Handling difficult situations</u>** Ss look at the language used in tricky situations, and apply it themselves to role play a situation.	**ML Grammar and Usage** **Practice File** Language review (page 21) **Resource bank** (page 198)
Lesson 4 *Each case study is about 1¹/₂ to 2 hours.*	**<u>Case study: Office attraction</u>** A Managing Director is worried about close relationships between employees and their effect on the company. Ss suggest what action the company should take.	**Practice File** Writing (page 22)

For a fast route through the unit focussing mainly on speaking skills, just use the underlined sections.

For 1 to 1 situations, most parts of the unit lend themselves, with minimal adaptation, to use with individual students. Where this is not the case, alternative procedures are given.

Business brief

'Happiness is having one's passion for one's profession,' wrote the French novelist (and management thinker) Stendhal. The number of people in this fortunate position is limited, but there are all sorts of aspects of office and factory work that can make it enjoyable. Relations with colleagues can be satisfying and congenial. People may find great pleasure in working in a team, for example. Conversely, bad relations with colleagues can be extremely unpleasant, and lead to great dissatisfaction and distress.

Basic work on what motivates people in organisations was done by Frederick Herzberg in the 1960s. He found that things such as **salary** and **working conditions** were not in themselves enough to make employees satisfied with their work, but that they can cause dissatisfaction if they are not good enough. He called these things **hygiene factors**. Here is a complete list:

- Supervision
- Company policy
- Working conditions
- Salary
- Peer relationships
- Security

Some things can give positive satisfaction. These are the **motivator factors**:

- Achievement
- Recognition
- The work itself
- Responsibility
- Advancement
- Growth

Another classic writer in this area is Douglas McGregor, who talked about **Theory X**, the idea, still held by many managers, that people instinctively dislike work, and **Theory Y**, the more enlightened view that everybody has the potential for development and for taking responsibility.

More recently has come the notion of **empowerment**, the idea that decision-making should be decentralised to employees who are as close as possible to the issues to be resolved: see Units 8 **Team building** and 12 **Management styles**.

But where some employees may like being given responsibility, for others it is a source of **stress**. People talk more about the need for work that gives them **quality of life**, the **work-life balance** and the avoidance of stress. Others argue that **challenge** involves a reasonable and inevitable degree of stress if people are to have the feeling of **achievement**, a necessary outcome of work if it is to give satisfaction. They complain that a **stress industry** is emerging, with its **stress counsellors** and **stress therapists**, when levels of stress are in reality no higher today than they were before.

Read on

Warren Bennis et al.: *Douglas McGregor Revisited – Managing the Human Side of Enterprise*, Wiley, 2000

Wayne Cascio: *Managing Human Resources*, McGraw-Hill, 1997

Harvard Business Review on Work and Life Balance, Harvard Business School Press, 2000

Frederick Herzberg: *Motivation to Work*, Transaction, 1993

Paul Spector: *Job Satisfaction: Application, Assessment, Causes and Consequences*, Sage, 1997

Business brief

Lesson notes

Warmer

- Write *job satisfaction* and *motivation* on the board. Ask Ss, in pairs, to discuss and define each of them.
- Ask each pair for the results of their discussion, and their definition. Invite comments from the whole class. (The *Longman Dictionary of Contemporary English* defines *satisfaction* as 'a feeling of happiness or pleasure because you have achieved something' and *motivation* as 'eagerness or willingness to do something without needing to be told or forced to do it'.)

Overview

- Tell the Ss that they will be looking at job satisfaction.
- Ask the Ss to look at the Overview section at the beginning of the unit. Tell them a little about the things on the list, using the table on page 40 of this book as a guide. Tell them which points you will be covering in the current lesson and which in later lessons.

Quotation

- Ask the Ss to look at the quotation and say if they agree with it. Ask if they know who Barrie was (writer of *Peter Pan*, if they're interested).

Starting up

Ss discuss motivating factors at work, and have the opportunity to do a quiz on professional burnout.

Ⓐ

- Go through the list of words and expressions. Get individual Ss to explain the less obvious ones (there's no need for them to explain *bigger salary* for example). Explain terms that the Ss don't know. Work on pronunciation where necessary. (Share options are often given to top managers and sometimes offered to all employees in addition to salary: they make money if the company performs well and the shares therefore perform well.)

Ⓑ

- Get the Ss to discuss the questions in pairs or threes. Circulate, monitor and assist. Note language points for praise and correction.
- Get the representatives of the pairs or threes to say what their findings were. Encourage whole-class discussion, comparing the results from each group.
- Praise good language points from the discussion and work on three or four points that need improvement, getting individual Ss to say the correct forms.

- If you have time, get the Ss to look at the 'Are you in danger of burning out' quiz on page 137. They can do it in pairs in class, or for homework. In both cases, ask individual Ss afterwards for their 'profile' and ask if they agree with it. Invite comments and encourage discussion.

Reading: Fringe benefits

Ss read about the very generous fringe benefits offered by different companies and discuss them in relation to work / life balance.

Ⓐ

- Ask the whole class for fringe benefits that they know of: canteen, company car, healthcare provision, company pensions, etc. Then ask what companies should provide for their employees. Ask if they know of any unusual fringe benefits.

Ⓑ

- Go through the list of fringe benefits, explaining any that the Ss don't know. Tell them they're going to look at an article about some companies that are very generous in their provision of fringe benefits. Which ones do they think they will find mentioned (show of hands)?

Ⓒ

- Emphasise that the Ss should only skim the first four paragraphs of the article to find the fringe benefits that are mentioned from the list in Exercise B, rather than try to understand every word.
- Get the Ss to work on the article in pairs.
- Ask pairs for the fringe benefits from the list in Exercise B that they found.

> childcare   company holidays   guitar lessons   haircuts   masseurs   sushi   (Viagra, not on the list in Exercise B, is of course the well-known male potency drug.)

Ⓓ

- Go through the questions with the whole class.
- Ask the Ss, in pairs, to read the whole article, looking specifically for the answers. Circulate, monitor and assist with any difficult vocabulary.
- Get the Ss to say what their answers were. Invite comments and encourage discussion.

1 By *practising 10 specified healthy behaviour patterns*. (Ask the whole class what these patterns might be: employees should go running every day, not smoke ...)

2 The idea that employees should have a healthy balance between time spent at work and time for themselves. Companies in the article are trying to solve the problem by providing numerous benefits. They have been successful in that hardly anyone leaves, perhaps, according to the writer, because it would be daunting to leave companies that provide so much. However, the basic problem of work / life balance is not being tackled.

3 a) Everyone is extremely happy.
   b) The idea of leaving seems so difficult that employees decide to stay where they are. (Don't forget to ask the Ss which reason seems most likely.)

4 The answer is a). Explain the use and meaning of *mere*.

5 Some employers provide <u>subsidised</u> housekeepers. One company provides $10,000 <u>towards</u> the cost of adopting a child.

(E)

◎ Ask the Ss to discuss the questions in pairs or threes.

◎ Circulate and monitor.

◎ Ask the pairs or threes to present their findings to the whole class. Invite comments and encourage discussion.

◎ If the Ss ask, point out that *leisure* is pronounced like *pleasure* in British English and like *seizure* in American English.

◎ Praise good language points from the discussion and work on three or four points that need improvement, getting individual Ss to say the correct forms.

Vocabulary: Synonyms and word building

Ss look at the vocabulary of motivation and job satisfaction and also at the prefixes *un-*, *dis-* and *de-*.

(A)

◎ Go round whole class and get the Ss to read out the words and expressions. Correct stress and pronunciation where necessary, for example *auTOnomy*, *burEAUcracy*, but don't explain meanings at this point.

◎ Get the Ss to do the matching exercise in pairs. Circulate and monitor.

◎ Check the answers with whole class.

> 1 a   2 e   3 b   4 f   5 h   6 g   7 c   8 d
> (*Human resources* is the more modern term for *personnel*.)

(B)

◎ Ask the Ss to complete the exercise in pairs. Circulate, monitor and assist.

◎ Go through answers with whole class.

> 1 a) satisfied   b) <u>dis</u>satisfied   c) satisfaction
> 2 a) motivating   b) <u>de</u>motivated   c) motivation
>   (Note: not 'motivator')
> 3 a) fulfilment   b) fulfilled   c) <u>un</u>fulfilled
> 4 a) inspiring   b) inspiration   c) <u>un</u>inspiring
> 5 a) frustration   b) frustrating   c) frustrated

◎ Point out the negative prefixes underlined above. Tell the Ss that the best thing is to learn these as complete words, rather than get into the 'rules' for forming negatives, which are quite complicated.

Listening: motivating factors

A specialist on job satisfaction talks about the factors that most motivate different groups of workers in different parts of the world.

(A)

◎ Ask the whole class to look through the different groups of people mentioned. Ask them, by a show of hands, which groups they expect to be most satisfied, and which least satisfied, according to Professor Oswald. Quickly group them on the board under the two headings.

(B) 🎧 5.1

◎ Play recording 5.1 once right through and then a second time, stopping halfway through each of Professor Oswald's answers, and stopping at the end of Professor Oswald's second answer. The Ss work in pairs, putting the different groups under the two headings.

◎ Play the same section of the recording a third time if necessary for the Ss to check their answers.

> **Satisfied:** women; the highly paid; those with promotion opportunities; the self-employed; the Swiss; Americans
>
> **Dissatisfied:** those who work long hours; those in large workplaces; those without job security; those who commute long distances; Eastern Europeans; the Japanese

◎ Ask pairs if anything surprised them about the groups mentioned. Invite comments and encourage discussion, for example asking
   – if they agree with the findings on different nationalities (especially if their nationality is mentioned).
   – why they think employees in small countries are happier. (There's no clear answer to this.)

Ⓒ 🎧 5.1

◎ Get the Ss to look at the question and play Professor Oswald's third answer once or twice.

◎ Go round whole class for answers.

1	high pay
2	job security
3	opportunities for promotion

◎ If the Ss are interested, compare Professor Oswald's findings with those of Frederick Herzberg, discussed in the Business Brief on page 41. Herzberg found that pay was not enough in itself to motivate people, but could cause dissatisfaction if it was not good enough. Ask the Ss what they think.

Ⓓ 🎧 5.1

◎ Ask the Ss to look at the four points and say which they think are true before playing the recording.

◎ Play the last question and answer once or twice and ask the Ss for Professor Oswald's responses.

1	false
2	true
3	true

◎ Ask the Ss if they are surprised by points 1 and 2. Do they think this is the case in their own industry / profession? Invite comments and encourage discussion.

Discussion: What's in a title?

Ss read a short article about job titles and discuss their importance in providing job satisfaction.

Ⓐ

◎ Introduce the topic by asking the Ss about job titles in their organisation (or one they would like to join). Are they important? Do they give a good idea about what someone actually does? (Be tactful about this. Some cultures take job titles much more seriously than others.)

◎ Ask the Ss to discuss the questions in pairs. Circulate, monitor and assist. Point out that the answers to question 4 will be in the text they will soon read. You can ask your Ss to look ahead to it now, or keep them guessing for the time being.

◎ Note language points for praise and correction.

◎ Get pairs to report their responses to the whole class. Invite comments and encourage discussion.

◎ Praise good language points from the discussion and work on three or four points that need improvement, getting individual Ss to say the correct forms.

Ⓑ – Ⓒ

◎ Tell the Ss they are going to read an article about job titles, like the ones in Question 4 in Exercise A.

◎ Ask the Ss to read the article individually or in pairs and answer the questions. Circulate, monitor and assist.

◎ Ask individuals / pairs for their answers to the questions.

1 a	2 b	3 a	4 a

◎ Ask someone to summarise the article. Ask them if they think these job titles would be taken seriously in the students' own cultures.

◎ Invite comments and encourage discussion.

Ⓓ

◎ Get the Ss to quickly match the pairs.

1 c	2 b	3 d	4 a

◎ Get the Ss to suggest their own 'imaginative' job titles. Treat the exercise light-heartedly.

Language review: Passives

Ss work on the formation and use of the passive forms of a range of verb tenses.

Ⓐ

◎ Go through the three points in the Language review box with the whole class fairly quickly. Don't spend too much time on them now, but come back to them in relation to later activities in this section: see below.

◎ Ask the Ss, in pairs, to match the sentences a)–h) with the tenses. Circulate, monitor and assist, reminding them about modal verbs (*must*, *might*, *should*, etc.), and helping with vocabulary, e.g. *hampered*.

◎ Ask the pairs for their answers.

1 c	2 e	3 h	4 b	5 d	6 g	7 a	8 f

◎ Discuss the sentences with the whole class, in relation to the first of the three points in the Language review box, for example

a) We're more interested in the supervisors being trained than in the people training them.

b) We're more interested in the people being forced out than those forcing them out.

Ⓑ

◎ Explain vocabulary from the extracts that you think may be unfamiliar: *conduct*, *perceive*, etc. (without giving the answers, of course).

◎ Ask the Ss to work in pairs on the extract. Circulate, monitor and assist.

◎ Ask pairs for the answers.

1 *have been conducted*
2 *be perceived*
3 *are entered*
4 *were given*
5 *were paid*
6 *were paid*
7 *is reduced*

C

◎ Explain that the points form the basis for sentences from a report on an Employee Incentive Scheme.

◎ Explain any words that require it, for example *incentive*, *canvass*. Explain that *data* can be singular or plural.

◎ Go round the class quickly and get answers from individual Ss.

Procedure

Questionnaires were distributed to all departments.
All managers were interviewed.
A sample of workers was canvassed.
Data on similar schemes was (or were) consulted.

Recommendations

A new scheme should be introduced from 1 Jan.
A system of team bonuses should be adopted.
Other incentives beside financial ones should be investigated.
Further research should be carried out into a share option scheme.
The existing range of fringe benefits should be maintained.

◎ Relate this exercise to the initial point about the passive being used to describe processes and procedures.

Skills: Handling difficult situations

Ss look at and listen to the language used in tricky situations, and discuss what they would say in other difficult circumstances.

A

◎ Explain to Ss that they will be looking at language for dealing with tricky situations, and get them to do the exercise in pairs. Circulate and monitor.

◎ Check the answers with the whole class.

---

1 h   2 g   3 d   4 e   5 f   6 b   7 a   8 c

◎ Ss work in parallel pairs again, role playing the three situations. Circulate, monitor and assist. Note language points for praise and correction.

◎ Ask for a few performances of the situations from individual pairs in front of the whole class.

◎ Praise good language points from the discussion and work on three or four points that need improvement, getting individual Ss to say the correct forms.

---

1 to 1

These role plays can be done directly between teacher and student. Don't forget to note language points for praise and correction afterwards.

B   **5.2**

◎ Play recording 5.2, stopping after each conversation to elicit the answers.

| Apologising | Ending a conversation |
| Showing sympathy | Saying 'no' politely |

C   **5.2**

◎ Go through the Language box getting individual Ss to read the expressions with appropriate intonation. Get them to overdo it slightly, but without sounding insincere!

◎ Play recording 5.2 again. Stop after each conversation and get Ss to match an expression from each conversation to a particular heading in the Language box.

Saying 'no' politely
I'm really sorry, I really can't.

Showing sympathy
I know what you mean. You're not the only one who feels like that.

Apologising
I'm really sorry. We're going to have to …

Ending a conversation
Could we talk about this later?

D

◎ Get the Ss to discuss the expressions for the different situations in pairs. Circulate, monitor and assist.

◎ With the whole class, ask pairs for their expression. The expressions below are suggestions. Ss will certainly come up with other ideas.

---

1 That's really bad luck. I know how you must feel.
2 I don't know how to tell you this but …
3 I was thinking that it would be good to have a chance to talk about the contract over dinner.
4 I hope you don't mind me saying this, but actually it's not very comfortable. Would it be possible to move?

◎ As an additional activity, you could ask Ss to do mini role plays incorporating these expressions.

Case study

Office attraction

A managing director is worried about close relationships between employees and their effect on the company. Ss role play members of the Human Resources Department and suggest what action the company should take.

Stage 1

◎ Get the Ss to read the background section to themselves and meanwhile write the points on the left of the table below on the board. When the Ss have finished reading, elicit adjectives and expressions that describe the points on the left, and write them up.

Working atmosphere preferred by Karl Jansen, MD	relaxed
Staff rule book	slim
Company culture	casual, maybe too casual
Working hours	long
Competition with other companies and its effect	fierce, causing stress among employees
Close relationships between members of staff	increasingly common

◎ Get the Ss to read the memo and meanwhile write the points on the left of the table below on the board. When the Ss have finished reading, elicit information about the points on the left, and write them up.

Subject	Policy on office relationships
Main point	KJ's concern about relationships between members of staff
Result of three recent relationships	Damaged performance of those concerned as well as that of colleagues
Names of those involved and nature of problem	Tania Jordan – appointment John Goodman – re-assignment Derek Hartman – complaints

Stage 2: The details and specific questions 🎧 5.3

◎ Divide the class into groups of four. These groups will later form the basis of the role play groups. They represent members of the Human Resources Department. One person is Jenny Cunningham, its head, and the other three work under her. Each of them will concentrate on a particular case: that of Jordan, Goodman and Hartman, respectively.

◎ Assign the roles of Jenny Cunningham and her subordinates in each group, making clear which case each subordinate is going to concentrate on.

◎ The person in each group playing Jenny Cunningham quickly skims the different cases to get the basic facts and then reads the 'specific questions' in order to prepare for the meeting where the Human Resources Department will decide what to recommend in each case.

◎ Ask the three 'subordinates' in each group silently to read the information about their particular case and to develop the recommendations they will put forward in the meeting. Circulate, monitor and assist. In preparing the details of each case, you could suggest to your Ss that they complete information under the headings: background; problem identified; action taken; remaining problem; recommendation.

◎ The student dealing with the Derek Hartman case should leave the group after reading the section about him and come over to one corner of the classroom. In this corner, play recording 5.3, the conversation between Karl and Claudia, once or twice to all the Ss from the different groups specialising in the Hartman case and ask them to take notes. They will need this information in the forthcoming meeting. When they are ready, ask them to rejoin their respective groups.

◎ Call the whole class to order and answer any queries.

Stage 3: Task

◎ Write the agenda for all the meetings on the board, explaining as you write up the points.

Agenda

1 Tania Jordan/Marcus Ball: facts of the case and recommendations
2 John Goodman: facts and recommendations
3 Derek Hartman: facts and recommendations
4 Written policy on close relationships at work? Sanctions (= punishments)?
5 How to avoid unfair advantages through close relationships? Specific examples of bad practice to be included in written policy, if we decide to have one?

◎ Tell the whole class that Jenny Cunningham will chair the meeting in each group. The person playing her will follow the agenda. For agenda items 1–3, tell the person playing Jenny that they should ask the student working on that case to summarise what happened, make their recommendation, and then open the meeting to general discussion. (The student working on Derek Hartman's case should be sure to summarise what they heard in the recording, as well as the other information about him.)

◎ When the situation is clear to everyone, the meetings can start. Circulate and monitor, but do not intervene except if absolutely necessary. Note language points for later praise and correction.

◎ At the end of the activity, praise good language points that you heard while you were circulating and monitoring, and work on three or four points that need improvement, getting individual Ss to say the correct forms.

◎ Ask each group to summarise its recommendations. Compare those of different groups. Invite comments and encourage discussion.

Stage 4: Writing

Ss write a set of guidelines which could be used as a discussion document at the next board meeting, based on the discussion at their particular meeting.

◎ This writing exercise can be done as pair work in class or for homework.

 Writing file page 141.

> **1 to 1**
>
> The student can discuss the different cases directly with you. Don't forget to note language points for praise and correction afterwards.

Risk

At a glance

	Classwork – Course Book	Further work
Lesson 1 *Each lesson (excluding case studies) is about 45–60 minutes. This does not include administration and time spent going through homework.*	**Starting up** Ss look at different types of risk, and listen to a risk advisor talking about the risks faced by businesses. **Vocabulary: Describing risk** Verbs and adjectives used in the context of risk. **Listening: Managing risk** Ss listen to the risk advisor talking in more detail about different risks, and ways of managing them.	**Practice File** Vocabulary (page 24)
Lesson 2	**Reading: Risks from globalisation** Ss read an article about the dangers of doing business in various countries. **Language review: Intensifying adverbs** Ss look at adverbs such as *rather*, *slightly* and *extremely* and use them in a number of situations.	**Text bank** (pages 156–159) **Practice File** Language review (page 25) **ML Grammar and Usage**
Lesson 3	**Skills: Reaching agreement** Ss listen to the language of agreement in the context of a marketing team meeting. They then put this language into action to role play a situation.	**Resource Bank** (page 198)
Lesson 4 *Each case study is about 1¹⁄₂ to 2 hours.*	**Case study: A risky business** A fashion business is losing its way, and asks a consultancy for advice on possible strategies.	**Practice File** Writing (page 26)

For a fast route through the unit focussing mainly on speaking skills, just use the underlined sections.

For 1 to 1 situations, most parts of the unit lend themselves, with minimal adaptation, to use with individual students. Where this is not the case, alternative procedures are given.

Business brief

All business is built on risk. Operating in politically unstable countries is one of the most extreme examples of this. The dangers may range from **kidnapping** of managers through to **confiscation of assets** by the government. Company managers may have to face **fraud** and **corruption**. But the fact that companies want to work there at all shows that they think the **returns** could be very high. As always, there is a **trade-off** between risk and return: investing in very challenging conditions is a graphic, if extreme, illustration of this trade-off.

Companies do not have to go to unstable countries to be harmed by criminal activity. **Industrial espionage** has existed for as long as there have been industries to spy on, but this can now be carried out at a distance by gaining access to company computer networks. **IT security** specialists may try to protect their company's systems with **firewalls** (technical safeguards against such snooping by **hackers**) and against **computer viruses**.

So far, we have looked at some of the more extreme examples of risk, but even business-as-usual is inherently risky. For example, by putting money into a new venture, investors are taking serious financial risks. Most businesses fail (some put the figure as high as nine out of ten), and as the first **shakeout** of Internet start-ups showed, this can happen increasingly quickly after they are founded. **Venture capitalists** who put money into such businesses **spread their risk** so that the **payback** from one or two successful ventures will hopefully more than compensate for the money lost in the failures. For more on financial risk, see Unit 9 **Raising finance**.

There is also the risk that even apparently **well-established companies** that are seemingly in touch with their customers can easily start to go wrong: we can all think of examples in soft drinks, clothing, cars and retailing, to name a few. Here, the risk is of losing sight of the magic ingredients that make for success. Some companies are able to reinvent themselves, in some cases several times over. Others don't understand what they need to do to survive and thrive again, or if they do understand, are unable to transform themselves in the necessary ways. The things about the company that were formerly strengths can now become sources of weakness and obstacles to change. The financial markets see this, and the company's shares fall in value. Investors are increasingly quick to demand changes in top management if there are not immediate improvements. In some cases, companies that were the leaders in their industry can even go bankrupt: in airlines, think of PanAm.

And then there is the risk of management **complacency**. Take a tyre company. A few weeks of shoddy operations and enough faulty tyres are produced to put the whole future of the company at risk through **product liability claims** following accidents caused by blow-outs. **Product recalls** are the worst possible §publicity imaginable for companies, and in the worst cases, their image is so damaged that they never recover. This is a case study in **reputational risk**: the trust that customers put in a company can be thrown away overnight. Another example of a company that destroyed the trust of its clients is the well-known Internet service provider that announced free access at all times, and then immediately withdrew the offer. One commentator described this as **brand suicide**.

Read on

Peter L. Bernstein: *Against the Gods: The Remarkable Story of Risk*, Wiley, 1998

C.B. Chapman, Stephen Ward: *Project Risk Management*, Wiley, 1996

Mark Daniell: *World of Risk*, Wiley, 2000

Lesson notes

Warmer

◎ Write the word 'risky' on the left of the board and dashes indicating the number of letters in the words that come after it, like this. (The figures in brackets indicate the number of dashes to write up):

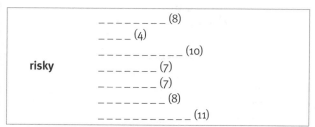

	_ _ _ _ _ _ _ (8)
	_ _ _ _ (4)
	_ _ _ _ _ _ _ _ _ (10)
risky	_ _ _ _ _ _ (7)
	_ _ _ _ _ _ (7)
	_ _ _ _ _ _ _ (8)
	_ _ _ _ _ _ _ _ _ (11)

◎ Tell the Ss that all the missing words are or can be business-related. They have to guess what they are. Tell them to shout out words they think of.

◎ If they have trouble, give them clues by showing particular letters, for example all the Es in the words, like this:

	_ _ _ _ _ e _ _
	_ e _ _
	_ _ _ e _ _ _ e _ _
risky	_ e _ _ _ _ _
	_ _ _ _ e _ _
	_ _ _ _ _ e _ _
	_ _ _ e _ _ _ _ _ _

◎ For words that the Ss still don't get, start giving other letters, or clues to their meaning, for example, the third one means 'when you put money into a business activity, or the amount of money you put in'.

◎ Ss should eventually end up with seven typical combinations, like this:

	business
	deal
	investment
risky	lending
	project
	strategy
	undertaking

◎ Point out that the last one has nothing to do with funerals, and means 'project' or 'enterprise'.

Overview

◎ Tell the Ss that they will be looking at Risk.

◎ Ask the Ss to look at the Overview section at the beginning of the unit. Tell them a little about the things on the list, using the table on page 48 of this book as a guide. Tell them which points you will be covering in the current lesson and which in later lessons.

Quotation

Ask the Ss to look at the quotation and say if they agree with it. Invite comments and encourage brief discussion.

Starting up

Ss look at different types of risk, and listen to a risk advisor talking about the risks faced by businesses.

(A)

◎ Get the Ss to work in pairs. Suggest students each come up with three risky things they have done. Circulate and monitor.

◎ With the whole class, ask pairs for their risky activities. Invite comments and encourage discussion. Who are the risk-takers in the class (show of hands)?

(B)

◎ Get the Ss to work in pairs on the different types of risk and say which thing is the riskiest in each group. Circulate and assist.

◎ Ask pairs for their findings. Invite comments and encourage discussion. (In the case of travel, don't get too bogged down in lugubrious statistics!)

◎ Ask the Ss if anything is done in their country / countries to warn of health risks and of the risks of particular types of investment.

◎ You could mention health warnings on cigarettes and, on some investment products in the UK, the 'health warning': 'The value of your investment can go down as well as up, and you may not get back the money you invested.' Point out the use of 'health warning' in this financial context.

◎ Ask if the Ss think such warnings are a) effective, b) necessary. Shouldn't people just be free to indulge in risky behaviour if they want to?

(C)–(D) 🎧 6.1

◎ Get each student to write down three types of business risk.

◎ Do a quick round-up of these risks with the whole class.

◎ Tell the Ss that they will hear a risk advisor from a bank talking about risks faced by businesses.

◎ Get the Ss to listen to recording 6.1 once or twice and note down the risks mentioned.

1	doing nothing
2	credit or guarantee risk
3	political risk
4	risk of catastrophe or disruption (= the risk of not being able to continue business as usual because of some unforeseen event)

◎ Ask the Ss for the four risks and ask which of these they had predicted hearing. If necessary, explain *disruption*. Get the Ss to give examples of each type of risk.

Vocabulary: Describing risk

Ss look at verbs and adjectives used in conjunction with *risk*.

- Do as a whole-class activity. Write the four verbs *predict*, *meet*, *assess* and *manage* on the board and get the Ss to say which heading the other verbs should come under, explaining their meanings if necessary.

Predict	Meet	Assess	Manage
foresee	encounter face	calculate estimate prioritise	eliminate minimise reduce spread

- Ask the Ss to work in pairs on the matching exercise. If they haven't done this type of exercise before, point out clues. For example, if there is *impossible to* at the end of an item on the left, look for an infinitive verb at the beginning of the item on the right. Circulate, monitor and assist. (An actuary (item 6) is a specialist who works for or advises a financial institution. For example, life insurance companies employ actuaries to calculate future mortality rates of policyholders, the payouts that will have to be made, and their timing.)
- Ask the Ss for their answers.

> 1 e   2 f   3 g   4 d   5 c   6 b   7 a

- Group adjectives on the board under the two headings with the whole class.

High: great; huge; serious; significant; substantial; terrible; tremendous	**Low:** faint; low; negligible; remote; slight

- Work on the stress of words like *sigNIFicant*, *subSTANtial*, *NEGligible* and *treMENdous*.

D

- Get the Ss to work in pairs on the three types of risk mentioned. Circulate, monitor and assist. Note language points for praise and correction, especially in relation to the verb and adjective combinations in Exercises A and C above.
- With the whole class, praise good language points from the discussion and work on three or four points that need improvement, getting individual Ss to say the correct forms.

Listening: Managing risk

Ss listen to the risk advisor they heard in the Starting up activity talking in more detail about different risks, and ways of managing them.

A 🎧 6.2

- With the whole class, ask the Ss to recap the four types of risk they heard the risk advisor mention in the Starting up section.

> 1 doing nothing
> 2 credit or guarantee risk
> 3 political risk
> 4 risk of catastrophe or disruption

- Ask the Ss to look at the questions and then play recording 6.2 once or twice. Explain any difficult words such as *flounder*, *obsolete* and *consignment*. (The speaker may be confusing *flounder* with *founder*, but unless the group is high level, do not get into this with the Ss.)
- Play the recording again, stopping after the first section. Ask the Ss for the answers to question 1.

> 1 a) true
>   b) true
>   c) false

- Continue playing the recording, stopping after each risk, and ask the Ss what is said about it.

> 2 1 The company will end up with an obsolete product in an obsolete market.
>   2 The customer may not pay.
>   3 Government actions may change the situation.
>   4 A company may encounter fraud or criminal damage.

B 🎧 6.3

- Ask the Ss to look at the points and then play recording 6.3 once or twice, explaining any difficulties, e.g. *information at your finger tips*, *harness support*. Ask Ss to answer the questions in their own words.

> 1 Companies should have good quality, up-to-date and reliable information available.
> 2 They should have a good management team in place to identify and deal with risks.
> 3 There should be good lines of communication between the people in the company who will play an important role in dealing with any risk.

© 6.4

◎ Play recording 6.4 once or twice, explaining difficult words. On the second playing, stop after each example and ask the Ss to summarise the lesson it provides for risk management, not explicitly mentioned by the speaker.

---

1 A printing press was using out-of-date technology. It had a skilled workforce, but hadn't kept up with the market and had to close down. Lesson: Companies must keep up with evolving technology and market demands or go out of business.

2 Companies sold goods on credit and were never paid. Lesson: Check the credit status of the companies you trade with, or demand payment up front.

Reading: Risks from globalisation

Ss read an article about the dangers of doing business in various countries.

Ⓐ

◎ Ask the whole class about the dangers of doing business in different parts of the world, both physical dangers and financial and political risks. Ask them to think of specific recent events or incidents to illustrate their answers.

◎ Ask the Ss, in pairs, to rate the areas given in Question 2, with a rising arrow (increasing risk), level arrow (staying the same) or a falling arrow (declining risk).

◎ Ask pairs for their answers and summarise the findings on the board, putting each pair's results against each of the four areas. For example, if there are three pairs in the class, the table might look like this:

	Pair 1	Pair 2	Pair 3
Russia	↑	↓	↔
The Middle East	↔	↑	↔
North Africa	↑	↔	↓
Latin America	↓	↔	↑

◎ Ss will get an overall picture of opinion by looking at the general direction of the arrows for a particular place. Invite comments and encourage discussion.

Ⓑ

◎ Ask the Ss to work on the exercise in pairs. Ask them to match the meanings to the words without looking at the article: they can use bilingual or monolingual dictionaries. Circulate, monitor and assist.

◎ Check answers with the whole class.

---

1 e   2 g   3 d   4 f   5 a   6 c   7 b

Ⓒ

◎ Ask the Ss to scan the article for information about risks increasing or declining in different places. Show the answers on the board.

Russia	↑
The Middle East	↔ / ↓
North Africa	↔ / ↓
Latin America	↔ / ↓

Ⓓ

◎ Get the Ss to look at the question and then read the first two paragraphs. Explain any unfamiliar vocabulary and ask the Ss to answer the question.

---

1 globalisation

2 the development of communication technologies

Ⓔ

◎ Ask the Ss to look at the question and then read the rest of the article. Circulate and assist, explaining any unfamiliar vocabulary.

◎ Get the Ss to answer the question in pairs.

---

a) terrorism, kidnapping, petty crime

b) direct action by pressure groups, consumer activism, human rights demands

c) international sanctions, currency devaluation

d) organised crime, fraud, corruption, extortion, petty crime

---

◎ Invite comments and encourage discussion. (Ss may say that in the end all risks can be classified, in some cases perhaps rather cynically, as financial.)

Ⓕ

◎ Ask the Ss to discuss in pairs and threes. Circulate, monitor and assist. Note language points for praise and correction, especially ones related to risk language.

◎ Ask groups for their findings with whole class. Invite comments and encourage discussion.

For example, the Ss might mention oil companies and environmental protest, pharmaceuticals companies and protestors against testing drugs on animals, or an economic recession that particularly affects certain types of company.

◎ Praise good language points from the pair work and whole-class discussion and work on three or four points that need improvement, getting individual Ss to say the correct forms.

Language review: Intensifying adverbs

Ss look at adverbs such as *rather*, *slightly* and *extremely* and use them in a number of situations.

◉ Go through the rules with the whole class and get the Ss to complete them.

> Most adverbs are formed by adding *-ly* to the adjective. For adjectives ending in *-ic*, for example *dramatic* or *economic*, add *-ally*.

A

◉ Ask the Ss in pairs to put the adverbs in the table. Circulate and assist.

Intensifying adverbs		
weak	**moderate**	**strong**
a bit	fairly	entirely
slightly	increasingly	exceptionally
	moderately	extremely
	quite	highly
	rather	totally
	reasonably	very
	somewhat	

B

◉ Get the Ss to complete the utterances. Ask them which adverbs are possible in each sentence and which are not. For example, in question 1, *exceptionally*, *extremely* and *very* are possible, but the other adverbs from the same group would be very unlikely. Tell the Ss there are no 'rules' about this: it's a question of learning the typical combinations.

> **Possible answers**
> 1 exceptionally, extremely, very
> 2 exceptionally, extremely, highly, totally, very
> 3 fairly, moderately, quite, rather, somewhat
> 4 entirely, totally
> 5 fairly, moderately, quite, reasonably

C

◉ Get the Ss to work in pairs, each pair working on four or five situations. (For example, half the pairs could work on the first five situations and the other half on the last five.) Each pair should make up mini-conversations like the ones in Exercise B above.

> S1: What did you think of the presentation?
> S2: Fascinating. And the speaker was incredibly well-prepared. All the equipment worked first time and the handouts were very useful.

◉ Circulate and monitor, but this time don't make notes of all language points. Concentrate on the intonation of the adverb expressions. Encourage the Ss to exaggerate slightly, but not to go too far over the top!

◉ Get pairs to give performances of the situations in front of the whole class. One performance for each situation will probably be enough. Work on intonation of adverb expressions as necessary.

Skills: Reaching agreement

Ss listen to the language of agreement in the context of a marketing team meeting. They then put this language into action to role play a situation.

A 🎧 6.5

◉ Play recording 6.5 once right through and then once or twice more, pausing at convenient points to explain any unfamiliar vocabulary and allowing the Ss to make notes to complete the table.

Ideas	Approved Yes / No	Comments
On-line promotion	yes	One of the first organisations with a website, cheap form of promotion, must be focussed
TV advertising	no	Expensive, no experience of using it, competitors use it a lot, risky to put so much money into one thing
Sponsorship	no	Could be more easily focussed on target audience, but expensive
Advertisements in journals	yes	As long as it is focussed
Using established contacts	yes	Important to build on these, not expensive
Newspapers / magazines	yes	Know the readership, successful in the past, wide audience

B

◉ Go through the expressions in the Useful language box. Get individual Ss to read them out, completing them as if they were contributing to the meeting they have just listened to, for example *Does anyone have strong feelings about TV advertising?* (They should not use exactly the same expressions as they heard on the recording.)

◉ Ask the Ss to work in pairs on expressions 1–10. Tell them they can look at the audio script on page 160 to check the context if necessary, and that some expressions go under more than one heading. Circulate and assist.

1 Disagreeing
2 Giving opinions
3 Giving opinions, Disagreeing
4 Agreeing
5 Agreeing
6 Agreeing, Emphasising
7 Giving opinions, Emphasising
8 Making suggestions
9 Giving opinions
10 Summarising

◎ Ask pairs for their answers, and to give their reasoning for them. Invite comments and encourage discussion.

Ⓒ

◎ Present the situation to the whole class and make sure they understand it.

◎ Put the Ss into threes and allocate roles. Tell the Ss to look at the information related to their role. Circulate, monitor and assist.

◎ When the Ss are clear about their roles, tell them that one of the purposes of the activity is to give them the opportunity to use the expressions they saw in the Useful language box.

◎ The activity can then begin. Circulate and monitor, noting language points for praise and correction, especially in relation to discussion language.

◎ When the Ss have completed their meetings, call the class to order. Ask each three what they decided.

◎ Praise good language points from the discussion and work on three or four points that need improvement, getting individual Ss to say the correct forms, especially for discussion language.

1 to 1

This role play can be done 1 to 1. Ask the student to choose one of the roles. You take one of the others. Don't forget to note language points for praise and correction afterwards.

Case study

A risky business

Hi-Style, a fashion business, is having problems, and asks a consultancy for advice on possible strategies.

Stage 1

◎ Tell the Ss to read the background section to themselves and meanwhile write the points on the left in the table below on the board. When the Ss have finished reading, elicit information to complete the table.

Company type	family business
Activity	makes fashionwear
Brandname	ETC
Image	fashionable clothing at competitive prices
Main products	jeans and trainers
Current consumer perceptions	products are losing their appeal
Company's current situation	Struggling, out of touch, losing direction. Management consultants, City Associates, brought in to advise.

◎ Ask the Ss in pairs to look at the financial information and then to make statements about it, with possible explanations for the changes since last year. Invite comments and encourage brief discussion.

Examples of possible explanations:
Assets, other than stock, have declined in value, by 20 per cent. Perhaps they have sold some equipment or property, or the overall value of its equipment has fallen because it is not being replaced.
Stock has more than doubled in value, perhaps indicating an increase in stock that they have not succeeded in selling.
Sales have declined by 25 per cent, and profits even more sharply, confirming the difficult situation described above.

Stage 2: Task

◎ Say that a consultancy called City Associates has been brought in to study the different options open to Hi-Style. Write points 1–5 on the board and explain that in the group activity to follow, they will have to make their first and second choice among the options.

◎ Divide the class into groups of four. Explain that each student in the group will be responsible for presenting one of the options to the other three participants.

◎ All four members of each group will then discuss the four options. Tell them to make lists of the advantages and disadvantages of each option, and to look at the areas mentioned in points 1–5 before choosing the best and second-best alternatives. Encourage the Ss to use the language from the Skills section, if they have covered it.

◎ When the Ss are clear what to do, start the discussion. Circulate and monitor, intervening only if necessary. Note language points for praise and correction.

Stage 3: Feedback

◎ Praise good language points from the discussion and work on three or four points that need improvement, asking individual Ss to say the correct forms. Refer especially to their use of the language from the Skills section if they studied it earlier.

◎ When the groups have made their choice, ask each group to make a succinct presentation of its recommendations to the whole class, based on the five points that you wrote on the board. One way of doing this is to ask a representative from each group to come to the front of the class. Invite comments and encourage discussion after each presentation, but leave time for as many groups as possible to present their findings.

Stage 4: Writing

◎ Ask the Ss to do this collaboratively in class or as homework. They should write the report as if it comes from the head of City Associates. Point out the importance of using structuring language, for example: *On the one hand ..., on the other hand ..., so our recommendation would be to ... .*

 Writing file page 144.

> **1 to 1**
>
> This case study can be done 1 to 1 as a discussion between teacher and student. Ask the student to make a formal presentation of the options and the best alternatives, as if they were a representative of City Associates.

UNIT 7 e-commerce

At a glance

	Classwork – Course Book	Further work
Lesson 1 *Each lesson (excluding case studies) is about 45–60 minutes. This does not include administration and time spent going through homework.*	**Starting up** Ss talk about their use of the Internet and experiences of e-commerce. **Listening: Trading on the Internet** The Managing Director of an e-commerce business talks about what makes e-businesses successful. **Vocabulary: Internet terms** Ss look at words related to e-commerce, and use them to describe an e-commerce service company.	**Practice File** Vocabulary (page 28)
Lesson 2	**Reading: Using the Net** Ss read about a sports goods retailer, and study the vocabulary of e-commerce in context. **Language review: Conditionals** Ss recap the different types of conditionals and use them to talk about different situations.	**Text bank** (pages 160–163) **ML Grammar and Usage** **Practice File** Language review (page 29)
Lesson 3	**Skills: Presentations** Ss listen to a senior manager of an Internet company making a presentation, and analyse the language he uses.	**Resource bank** (page 199)
Lesson 4 *Each case study is about 1½ to 2 hours.*	**Case study: KGV Europe** A traditional retailer studies the possibility of getting into e-commerce.	**Practice File** Writing (page 30)

For a fast route through the unit focussing mainly on speaking skills, just use the underlined sections.

For 1 to 1 situations, most parts of the unit lend themselves, with minimal adaptation, to use with individual students. Where this is not the case, alternative procedures are given.

Business brief

Six months in e-commerce is like six years in any other business. At least, that's the way it seems at the time of writing (mid-2000). The e-commerce landscape is still very much in its formation. Let's look at three e-commerce operations that illustrate the fluidity of the situation.

Amazon is prehistoric by Internet standards. Using its vast accumulated expertise, it has gone beyond books to sell CDs, videos and other things as well, and its site acts as a 'host' for other suppliers, too. It benefits from a very good reputation for service, especially in delivery: the massive investments in warehouse automation and dispatch seem to have paid off. But it is famous for not making a profit, and there are now reports that it risks not being able to meet debt repayments.

Lastminute.com was founded on the original and attractive idea of catering for people who'd like to do something at the last minute, even if you can buy tickets for flights, etc. several weeks ahead. Its founders are famous and feted, at least in the UK, and there has been some clever PR to build the hype. It recently sold shares to outside investors for the first time, but the timing was bad. There was increasing scepticism about the real value of companies like Lastminute.com: the multi-billion valuation implied in the share issue bore no relation to the money it actually made. Its income (commissions from selling tickets, etc.) in 1999 was less than £1 million: peanuts. People who bought its shares presumably hoped to get in early on a company that might one day be very profitable, even if no profits are forecast for several years to come.

Boo.com was one of the first major casualties of e-commerce. It sold sports goods. Development of its site took much longer than planned, because its founders 'wanted everything to be perfect'. The launch was late, and meanwhile the company had used up all its capital.

At the time you read this, how are Amazon and Lastminute doing? Are they among the major players in e-commerce? Do people remember boo.com, perhaps as an object lesson in things that can go wrong, and as a victim of one of the first **shakeouts** in the industry?

Some of the key issues for e-commerce are:

- Physical delivery of goods. Parcel-delivery companies (**old-economy** organisations par excellence) have benefited enormously from companies like Amazon, where goods have to be **physically delivered** to homes. (They are even planning to deliver in the evenings, when people might actually be at home!)

- The future of services. Some think that the real growth in consumer e-commerce is going to be in services like travel and financial products, where the value of each transaction is quite high, and goods do not have to be physically delivered. On some airlines, two-thirds of bookings are being made on the Internet.

- The frustration of using **e-commerce sites**. A recent report found that, on average, 30 per cent of purchases on the Internet are not completed. It conjured up the spectacle of hordes of **virtual shopping carts** abandoned in the **virtual aisles** of these sites – an **e-tailer**'s nightmare! This, of course, has a very negative effect on the company's brand image, and the report even found that some people who had bad experiences on a company's website then avoided its **bricks-and-mortar** stores. This is one of the problems for traditional retailers who are trying to develop an **e-tail** operation, part of the more general question of how the two types of operation are going to relate to each other.

- **Business-to-business (B2B) e-commerce.** Some say that the biggest impact of the Internet is going to be in business-to-business applications, where suppliers can competitively bid for orders. Competing companies, for example in the car industry, have set up networks where they can get suppliers to do this. Orders are placed and processed, and payment made, over the Internet, hopefully with massive cost reductions through the elimination of processing on paper.

We live in exciting times. Things will develop in ways that are difficult to anticipate. E-commerce will **mature**, settling into more established patterns. What these patterns will be like, it's too early to say. Fortunes will be made by guessing future trends. Luck will no doubt play a big role.

Read on

Because of its fast-moving nature, books are not a good source of up-to-date information on e-commerce. The *Financial Times* runs regular features on the subject under the heading 'E-business Europe'. Search for articles on the *Financial Times* archive: www.ft.com.

Lesson notes

Warmer

- Write the letter *e-* on the left of the board. On the right put the word *commerce*, and the initial letters of the second part of other words.

	1	commerce
	2	m_____
e-	3	b_____
	4	c_____
	5	t_____
	6	f_____

- Ask the Ss if they know other words beginning with *e-* (which of course stands for *electronic*). The Ss can work in pairs to find them.
- Depending on the Ss' knowledge of the Internet, give them clues about the words.
  - 2 – the sending and receiving of messages on the Internet.
  - 3 – commercial activity on the Internet, not just buying and selling.
  - 4 – is used to talk about the 'new' economy that depends on the Internet.
  - 5 – selling goods on the Internet. (It is short for 'e-retailing').
  - 6 – the activity of sending goods that have been ordered on the Internet. (This one is difficult.)
- Ask the Ss for their answers and write them on the board.

2	e-mail
3	e-business
4	e-conomy
5	e-tailing
6	e-fulfilment

- For spelling enthusiasts, point out that 6 can be spelt with two 'l's in AmE.

Overview

- Tell the Ss that in this unit they will be looking particularly at e-commerce.
- Ask the Ss to look at the Overview section at the beginning of the unit. Tell them a little about the things on the list, using the table on page 56 of this book as a guide. Tell them which points you will be covering in the current lesson and in later lessons.

Quotation

- Ask the Ss to look at the quotation and say if they agree with it. Invite comments and encourage discussion, but do not pre-empt the topics of the unit too much.

Starting up

Ss talk about their use of the Internet and experiences of e-commerce.

- If necessary, adapt the questions in relation to the Ss' knowledge of the Internet. Even if they haven't used it, they will have ideas about it.
- Ask the Ss to work on the questions in pairs. Circulate and assist.
- With the whole class, ask pairs for their answers. Invite comments and encourage discussion.

> 2 Perhaps Ss have bought things by mail order, e.g. clothes, investment products. Would they buy them over the Internet?
> 3 Some say that travel and financial products are the best things to sell on the Net. (See Business brief.)
> 4 Ss may talk about fraud, and the danger of giving your credit card number.

B

- The world of e-commerce is changing very fast. Ask the whole class what they think of this quote. Can they remember the euphoria surrounding e-commerce companies in 2000–2001, a boom that quickly turned to bust? What is the situation now?

Listening: Trading on the Internet

The Managing Director of an e-commerce business talks about what makes e-businesses successful.

A 🎧 7.1

- Ask the Ss to look at the question. The recording starts with the answer to this question. Play it once or twice, explaining any unfamiliar words. Ask students for the answer.

B 🎧 7.1

- Ask the Ss to look at the extract they will have to complete and play the recording as far as 'So I think many start-up companies in e-commerce will fail because frankly they run out of cash.' two or three times, explaining any unfamiliar words. Invite the Ss to say what they think will be in the extract, and then play the part of the recording that contains it two or three times. Ask the Ss for the exact words of the recording.

1	good business idea
2	technology idea
3	good management team
4	resources

- Ask the Ss what they understand by 'a technology idea that is looking for a business home'.

ⓒ ∩ 7.1

- Get the Ss to look at the question, play the last part of the recording two or three times and ask the Ss for the answer: the idea that people may spend a lot of time using the Internet at the expense of other pastimes.

Vocabulary: Internet terms

Ss look at words related to e-commerce, and use them to describe an e-commerce service company.

Ⓐ

- Get the Ss to work on the words in pairs, using monolingual or bilingual dictionaries. Circulate, monitor and assist.
- Ask pairs for their answers.

> **browse:** to look through a series of web pages, perhaps those of a particular site, or ones found by a search engine relating to a particular topic.
> **directories:** lists of sites of similar organisations, or of sites with information on particular topics.
> **hits:** the number of visits that a particular site receives or the sites found by a search engine that contain the key word you entered.
> **key word:** a word that you enter into a search engine in order to find sites with web pages that contain this word.
> **locate:** find information, a site, etc. that you are looking for.
> **Net:** another word for Internet.
> **on-line:** used as an adjective or adverb to talk about activities related to the Internet.
> **search:** to look for particular information or a particular site, or the act of looking for it.
> **search engines:** sites like Google, Yahoo, AltaVista, etc. that allow you to find other sites with the information you are looking for by entering key words or expressions.
> **site:** a series of related screens with information about a subject, organisation, etc.
> **surfers:** people who go and look at different sites, perhaps in a random way with no particular purpose in mind.
> **traffic:** the number of people looking at a site in a particular period.

Ⓑ

- Ask the Ss to look through the *Topsite* description and then complete it in pairs, using words from the box. Circulate and assist.
- Go through the answers with the whole class.

> 1 Net?
> 2 search engines
> 3 traffic?
> 4 site
> 5 search
> 6 site
> 7 hits
> 8 surfers
> 9 on-line
> 10 directories
> 11 search
> 12 locate

ⓒ

- Give the Ss time to scan the article about Cool Sportz in the next section. With the whole class, get the Ss to match the sentence parts.

> 1 b 2 a 3 c

Reading: Using the Net

Ss read about a (fictional) sports goods retailer, and study the vocabulary of e-commerce in this context.

Ⓐ

- Give the Ss time to scan the article in pairs if they haven't already done so, and answer the questions.
- Elicit answers from the pairs with the whole class.

> 1 extranet
> 2 Internet
> 3 intranet
> 4 extranet, Internet
> 5 intranet

Ⓑ

- Ss again work on the article in pairs in order to answer the questions.

> 1 thousands
> 2 1,200
> 3 2,500
> 4 retail stores and employees
> 5 suppliers, manufacturers, distributors, freelance product designers, lawyers, accounting firm, ad agency, bank, independent retailers
> 6 They can refer to the company handbook, they can check and change their investment and health-care arrangements, calculate their retirement benefits, and file expense claims.

- Elicit answers from pairs with the whole class.

Ⓒ

◉ Do this as a quick-fire activity with the whole class.

Examples:
◉ Cool Sportz used to send invoices by post. Now Cool Sportz sends them by e-mail.
◉ Cool Sportz used to fly marketing people to New York to discuss advertising campaigns with their ad agency. Now Cool Sportz have brainstorming sessions over the extranet.

Ⓓ–Ⓔ

Ss work in pairs. Explain *key players*: **important people and organisations.**

1	supplier	6	merchant
2	manufacturer	7	employee
3	retailer	8	buyer
4	partner	9	distributor
5	consumer	10	designer

Advantages include:	Disadvantages include:
Easier communication with everyone: things happen in 'real time'. Less danger of misunderstandings and mistakes in dealing with suppliers, manufacturers and retailers.	Things may happen automatically that Cool Sportz's managers might want more control over, for example it may pay suppliers' bills too quickly, causing cash flow problems.
Less time spent travelling to deal with lawyers, accountants and advertising agencies.	Freelance designers may feel isolated working on their own with no human contact.

◉ Elicit answers from pairs with the whole class. Invite comments and encourage discussion about the advantages and disadvantages.

Language review: Conditionals

Ss recap the different types of conditionals and use them to talk about different situations.

◉ Go through the first set of conditional sentences with the whole class.

◉ Point out the fact that the first two are 'possible' conditions, in the sense that they describe situations that are possible in the future, whereas the third conditional is 'impossible': it describes a situation in the past that it is impossible to do anything about now. The zero conditional describes a 'general truth'.

◉ In pairs, get the Ss to change the form of each sentence in the second section so it is like one of the ones in the first section. Write the first sentence on the board as an example to give them the idea.

If you (or we) lose that password, we'll never be able to access that file again.
If you tell us what you need to get the job done, you'll have it.
If you need any further information, please contact our helpline.
If the market conditions had been better, the share offer would have been a success.
If we are given time, our factory can meet all those orders.

◉ Go through the new forms of the sentences with the whole class.

Ⓐ

◉ Go through the different categories with the whole class, explaining where necessary.

◉ Ask the Ss to categorise sentences. Circulate, monitor and assist.

---
1 reflecting on the past
2 advice
3 promise
4 speculating about the future
5 bargaining
6 promise
7 speculating about the future
8 invitation / request
9 promise / bargaining
10 advice / warning / threat
11 reflecting on the past
12 request

◉ Go through the answers with the whole class. Invite comments and encourage discussion.

Ⓑ

◉ Write the following two sentences on the board as examples of different conditionals. Point out which you would use if you thought the situation was likely to happen or which if you thought it was not. Then tell the Ss to work on the situations in pairs. Circulate, monitor and assist.

If I win the lottery, I'll buy a yacht.
If I won the lottery, I'd buy a yacht.

◉ Go through the answers with the whole class.

Ⓒ

◉ Write the sentence 'If they'd set up the site properly, they wouldn't have had so many complaints.' Tell the Ss that this is an 'impossible' condition like 'If we'd prepared properly, we wouldn't have lost the contract', which they saw at the beginning of this section. Write this second sentence on the board under the first one, to show that their structures are the same.

◉ Ask the Ss to work in pairs on what went wrong with ClickShop.com. Circulate, monitor and assist.

◉ Go through the answers with the whole class.

Example answers:

If they'd set up the site properly, they wouldn't have had so many complaints.

If they'd planned more carefully, they wouldn't have had so many problems.

If they'd used an expert, their site would have been better.

If they hadn't tried to cut corners, they wouldn't have ended up in this situation.

If they'd allocated a bigger budget, they would have saved money in the end.

If they'd recognised the problems earlier, they would have been able to correct them.

If they'd listened to customer feedback, they would have some customers left today.

If they'd done more research, they wouldn't have made all these mistakes.

Skills: Presentations

Ss listen to a senior manager of an Internet company making a presentation, and analyse the language he uses.

Ⓐ 🎧 7.2

- Tell the Ss that they are going to listen to a manager at an Internet company giving a presentation to potential customers. Ask them to look quickly through questions 1–3.
- Play the first extract right through and then play it again, as far as '… a sort of quality-controlled environment', explaining anything that causes general problems. Ask the Ss for the answers to questions 1 and 2.

---

1 Smarterwork connects small business customers with providers of particular services.

2 **a)** the number of months Smarterwork has been in existence

  b) the number of registered users of its site

  c) the number of employees that it has

- Play the rest of the recording, explain any general problems and ask for the answer to question 3.

---

3 Clients, typically small businesses, and suppliers: service-providers who have been pre-screened.

- Ask the Ss to explain *pre-screened* (checked to make sure that they are competent and reliable).

Ⓑ 🎧 7.3

- Ask the Ss to look at the stages. Discuss with them what the missing stages might be, before playing the recording.
- Play the second extract two or three times, answer any general queries, and get the Ss to complete the stages. Check their answers with them.

The missing stages are:

The client evaluates the bids (with the help of one of Smarterwork's account managers).

The client assigns the project to a supplier.

The client and supplier develop the project.

The money is paid to the supplier.

Ⓒ 🎧 7.2

- Ask the Ss to look at the questions and then play recording 7.2 again.
- Get Ss to shout out the answers.

---

1 a b d

2 **1** I'm going to

  2 begin by giving you

  3 I'll go on to tell

  4 I'll explain

Ⓓ 🎧 7.3

- Ask the Ss to listen out for ways that the speaker signals stages of the process and play recording 7.3 again.
- Ask the Ss for the phrases that they noted.

Firstly, the client posts a project, …

Then the suppliers visit the site …

After that the client evaluates the bids.

At the next stage, the client assigns the project to a supplier and *then* the client transfers …

The client and supplier *then* develop the project.

Finally, the client signs off …

Ⓔ

- With the whole class, look at the expressions given and the headings in the Useful language box. Get them to match the two. You could also ask them to suggest one or two more possible expressions of each type.

---

1 Involving the audience

2 Emphasising

3 Commenting

4 Changing subject

5 Referring to visuals

Ⓕ

- Ask the Ss to prepare a three-minute presentation. The content should be interesting, but it's also important to recycle the language, structure the presentation correctly and stick to the time limit.
- Ss can prepare the presentation in pairs or threes, with one member responsible for actually giving it. Circulate, monitor and assist. Each group should prepare a list of key points that the presentation will contain. They can also prepare visuals, for example organigrams, maps, etc. If you have transparencies and overhead pens, hand them out and get the Ss to prepare their presentations using them.

- Ask the Ss to give their presentations. Note language points for praise and correction. If there are a lot of Ss, keep some presentations for a later session to avoid presentation fatigue setting in!

- Praise good language points from the presentations and work on three or four points that need improvement, getting individual Ss to say the correct forms. Concentrate on structuring language, but also comment on other points.

Case study

KGV Europe

A traditional retailer studies the possibility of getting into e-commerce.

Stage 1: Background

- Get the Ss to read the background section. Meanwhile write the points in the first column of the table below on the board. When the Ss have finished reading, elicit information to complete the table.

Company type	High-street music retailer
Stores	12 in the Netherlands, of which 3 are megastores; 65 in Europe, of which 8 are megastores
Profits	Down 35% in three years
Megastore sales	Up 8% (heavy expenditure on advertising): 55% of total turnover
Problems / Weaknesses	Fierce competition, narrow product range, lack of innovation, not exploiting Internet opportunities

Stage 2: Market study: 🎧 7.4

- Ask the Ss to go through the findings of the Market study in pairs. All pairs look at the six main findings of the study, but also specialise in the different areas. Ask half the pairs to look also at Chart 1 and the other half to look at Chart 2, in addition to Chart 3 and the six main findings.

- With the whole class, ask different pairs to summarise the information that they studied.

- Say who the people are that the Ss will hear on the recording: Michael, a director, and Hanna, the newly-recruited Financial Director. Get the Ss to listen to their conversation once or twice, explaining any difficulties. They should note down the key points.

Michael
- serious problems need radical solution
- leave high-street retailing
- sell stores and use money to set up Internet operation
- Internet: lower costs
- can't stay as they are: ageing client base, falling share price

Hanna
- no experience in e-commerce
- e-commerce businesses not doing well and not the whole answer
- must improve promotion
- outsource advertising: use agency
- learn lessons from market study and commission another on product range

Stage 3: Task

- Divide class into threes or fours. Get the whole class to look at the agenda points and go through them quickly. Say that the overall purpose of the meeting is to find a new strategy for KGV and that each group will have to make a mini-presentation of this strategy, and the way they decided on it, to the whole class after the meeting.

- When the Ss are clear about the content and purpose of the meeting, it can start. Circulate and monitor. Do not intervene unless necessary. Note language points for praise and correction.

- When the groups have finished their meetings, praise good language points from the discussion and work on three or four points that need improvement, getting individual Ss to say the correct forms.

- Get a member of each group to present the strategy the group has chosen and explain briefly how they reached their decision.

---

1 to 1

The task can be done as a discussion between teacher and student, looking at the different options. Don't forget to note language points for praise and correction afterwards.

Writing

- Ss can do this as homework or collaboratively in class. Explain the writing task. Point out that the memo should:
  - give a summary of the discussion at the meeting
  - give the decisions that were made
  - ask the director for their comments.

 Writing file page 140

Revision

This unit revises and reinforces some of the key language points from Units 1–7, and links with those units are clearly shown. You can point out these links to the Ss if you think that would be useful.

This revision unit, like Revision Unit B, concentrates on reading and writing activities. Some of the exercise types are similar to those in the Reading and Writing section of levels 2 and 3 of the Business English Certificate examination organised by the University of Cambridge Local Examinations Syndicate.

For more speaking practice, see the Resource Bank section of this book beginning on page 196. The exercises in this unit can be done in class individually or collaboratively, or for homework.

1 Communication

Adjectives

(A)–(B)

◎ These exercises look again at the vocabulary describing good communicators (page 7).

> A
> 1 persuasive
> 2 articulate, coherent, eloquent
> 3 hesitant, inhibited
> 4 succinct
> 5 lucid
> 6 responsive
> 7 fluent
>
> B
> 1 fluent
> 2 articulate
> 3 lucid
> 4 inhibited
> 5 succinct
> 6 responsive

Problem solving

◎ Ss practise problem solving with an exchange of e-mails, relating to the Problem-solving activity on page 11.

Model answer

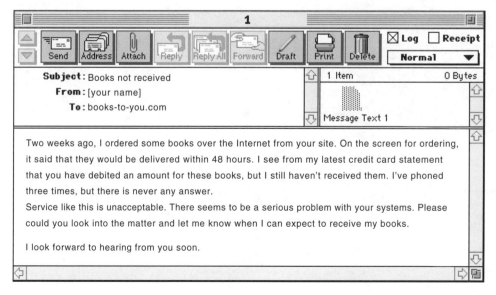

Subject: Books not received
From: [your name]
To: books-to-you.com

1 Item   0 Bytes
Message Text 1

Two weeks ago, I ordered some books over the Internet from your site. On the screen for ordering, it said that they would be delivered within 48 hours. I see from my latest credit card statement that you have debited an amount for these books, but I still haven't received them. I've phoned three times, but there is never any answer.

Service like this is unacceptable. There seems to be a serious problem with your systems. Please could you look into the matter and let me know when I can expect to receive my books.

I look forward to hearing from you soon.

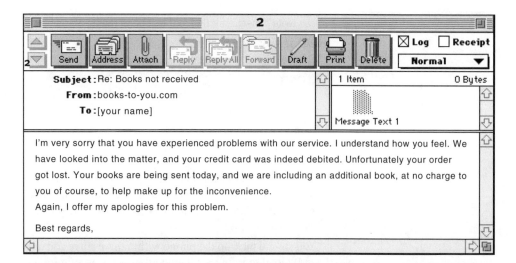

2 International marketing

Reading

◉ This reading text fits into the general theme of International marketing.

| 1 b | 2 c | 3 d | 4 c | 5 b | 6 d | 7 b | 8 c | 9 d | 10 b |

Writing

◉ Ss write about the launch plan for a new car.

Model answer

> **Positioning**
> The Lynx will be positioned as offering great luxury, but at the same time high power and performance.
>
> **The launch and advertising campaign**
> A good location for filming the advertising campaign would be Rome. The architecture there would provide a suitably sophisticated background, and reinforce that image of power and performance of the Lynx.
> I feel that an appropriate place for the launch would be the French Riviera, again because of its image of luxury and style. There are many good hotels that journalists can use, and a conference centre that is ideal.
> I suggest we use the American model Claudine Haddington in advertising and at the launch, if she is available.
>
> **Other promotional activities**
> Of course, motoring journalists go to very many car launches, and we must find new ways of impressing them. I suggest that the press pack includes luxury items such as expensive fountain pens and notepaper to reinforce the image of luxury we are trying to create. Other promotional activities could include an evening balloon-ride over the Riviera at sunset. This should impress even the tiredest of journalists!

3 Building relationships

Reading

◉ These short texts about doing business in different countries take up some of the themes introduced in the Listening section (page 24).

| 1 c | 2 b | 3 c | 4 d | 5 c | 6 c | 7 a |

Multi-word verbs

◉ This exercise practises the multi-word verbs from the Language review section on page 26. It can be quite tricky, so spend time explaining it to the Ss before asking them to do it.

1	off
2	about
3	✓
4	for
5	on

Writing a memo

◎ Ss write a memo relating to the general theme of the unit.

Model answer

MEMO

To: All receptionists
From: [your name]
Subject: Telephone answering procedure

I have had a number of complaints recently from customers who were not happy with the way their phone calls were dealt with when they phoned the company. As you know, the telephone is extremely important in maintaining good relations with our customers.

You should pick up the phone within three rings and answer with the company name and 'Good morning' or 'Good afternoon', as appropriate. Of course, courtesy and a pleasant tone of voice are also extremely important.

I hope you will pay attention to these points in future. I cannot overstate how important they are in maintaining good customer relations.

---

4   Success

Verb tenses

◎ Ss work further on present and past tenses from the Language review section of the unit (page 33).

Model answer

Texas Cake and Cookie Kings (TCCK) is a San Antonio-based cakemaker, with a 14 per cent share of the US cookie market. It has manufacturing sites in San Antonio, Buffalo (NY) and Sacramento (California). Of Americans, 64 per cent recognise the TCCK brand, but it is less familiar in the rest of the world.
Betty Brandon founded the company in 1934, using her grandmother's recipes. She succeeded in expanding the company over the next 20 years and introduced many new products. In 1955 Multilever, a large food and consumer product manufacturer, offered to buy the company, but Betty refused. In 1960, Betty retired, and the company was then headed by 'Wild' Bill Brandon, her son. Multilever finally bought TCCK in 1975, but Bill remained as head of the company.
TCCK has recently been developing its mail-order business, especially during the busy Thanksgiving and Christmas periods. Bill Brandon retired two years ago. TCCK is now managed by Laura Antonelli, a Multilever executive.
TCCK has recently been expanding its ranges and establishing an international presence. It has been working on building its brand in Europe and Asia. It has further developed the mail-order business, and promoted its sales in the fine foods sections of department stores. TCCK had sales last year of $550 million, of which 27 per cent were outside the US.

Prefixes

◎ More practice on points from the Vocabulary section (page 34).

---

1 underperforming
2 overestimated
3 outbid
4 outsource
5 undercharged
6 overextended
7 outmanoeuvred
8 overrun

---

5 Job satisfaction

Passives
- Ss look again at passives, dealt with in the Language review section on page 42.
- This type of exercise can be quite tricky, so spend some time explaining it to the Ss before asking them to do it.

> 1 ~~promotion~~ promoted
> 2 ~~isolating~~ isolated
> 3 ~~were~~ was
> 4 ~~discussion~~ discussed
> 5 ~~love~~ loved
> 6 ~~motivating~~ motivated
> 7 ~~be~~ being
> 8 ~~assess~~ assessed

Tactful and less tactful responses
- Another look at dealing with difficult situations, as in the Skills section on page 43.

The more appropriate response is underlined in each case.

> 1 c, j   2 a, <u>d</u>   3 <u>b</u>, h   4 <u>e</u>, f   5 g, <u>i</u>

6 Risk

Intensifying adverbs
- Ss revise the intensifying adverbs presented in the Language review section on page 50.

> 1 b   2 a   3 e   4 f   5 g   6 d   7 c

Writing
- Ss write a memo that involves describing and evaluating risks, and recommending the best option.

Model answer

> ## MEMO
>
> **To:** Chief Executive
> **From:** [your name]
> **Re:** New office location
>
> I have looked at Monroe, Newtown and Osborne as possible locations for our new office. Unfortunately, Newtown is not particularly stable, and the business climate is not good. Another negative factor is that communications with the rest of the region are very bad: flights are infrequent and the telephone system often breaks down. Office rents in Newtown are, unsurprisingly, very cheap, but I do not recommend locating our office there.
> That leaves Monroe and Osborne. Osborne is politically slightly less stable than Monroe, and the business climate slightly less good, but still acceptable. The quality of communications is about the same. However, office rents in Osborne are much lower, so I recommend setting up our new office there.

7 e-commerce

Conditionals
- More work on the conditionals from the Language review section on page 58.

> 1 b   2 c   3 b   4 a   5 c   6 c   7 a   8 b   9 b   10 c
> 11 a   12 c

Reading
- Ss answer questions about different types of website.

> 1 c   2 b   3 b   4 a   5 c   6 d   7 a

At a glance

At a glance

	Classwork – Course Book	Further work
Lesson 1 *Each lesson (excluding case studies) is about 45–60 minutes. This does not include administration and time spent going through homework.*	**Starting up** Ss talk about their experiences of the teams they have been in, and do a quiz about different types of team members. **Vocabulary: Prefixes** Ss look at a number of prefixes and use them in context to talk about people they have worked with and teams they have been in. **Reading: Successful teamworking** Ss read some advice about forming teams and do an exercise on fixed pairs.	**Practice File** Vocabulary (page 32) **Text bank** (pages 164–167)
Lesson 2	**Listening: Building a team** A management trainer talks about the key ingredients for teams, and the need or otherwise for leaders. **Language review: Modal perfect** Ss look at how modal perfect verbs such as *needn't have*, *may have*, *might have*, *must have*, *could have*, *should have* and *would have* are used.	**ML Grammar and Usage** **Practice File** Language review (page 33)
Lesson 3	**Skills: Resolving conflict** Techniques for dealing with disagreements: Ss apply the language for this to role play a situation in which one member of a team is causing problems.	**Resource bank** (page 200)
Lesson 4 *Each case study is about 1½ to 2 hours.*	**Case study: The new boss** There are problems when a new manager takes over a sales team. Ss role play the directors of the company in their efforts to resolve them.	**Practice File** Writing (page 34)

For a fast route through the unit focussing mainly on speaking skills, just use the underlined sections.

For 1 to 1 situations, most parts of the unit lend themselves, with minimal adaptation, to use with individual students. Where this is not the case, alternative procedures are given.

Business brief

In constructing teams, it's important not just to get talented people, but the right combination of talents. In the famous phrase, 'it's important to have a great team of minds, rather than a team of great minds'. Meredith Belbin sees these types as necessary in teams, whether in business or elsewhere:

- The **Implementer**, who converts the team's plan into something achievable.
- The **Co-ordinator**, who sets agendas, defines team-members' roles and keeps the objectives in view.
- The **Shaper**, who defines issues, shapes ideas and leads the action.
- The **Plant**, who provides the original ideas and finds new approaches when the team is stuck.
- The **Resource Investigator**, who communicates with the outside world and finds new ways to get things done.
- The **Monitor Evaluator**, who evaluates information objectively and draws accurate conclusions from it.
- The **Team Worker**, who builds the team, supports others and reduces conflict.
- The **Completer Finisher**, who gets the deadlines right.

This model lends itself better to some business situations than others, but the idea of roles and competencies in a team is important, whatever form these take in particular situations. Some organisations are more **hierarchical** and less **democratic** than others, and team members are obviously expected to behave more deferentially in the former. Senior managers there have the traditional leader's role: what they say goes. In other organisations, power is more **devolved**, and managers talk about, or at least pay lip-service to, the **empowerment** of those under them: the idea that decision-making should be decentralised to members of their teams.

In addition to the traditional organisation, we increasingly find **virtual organisations** and virtual teams. People are brought together for a particular project and then disbanded. Here, in addition to Belbin's types above, the role of the **selector/facilitator** is crucial.

Stages of team life

The typical team is said to go through a number of stages during its existence.

1 **Forming**. The group is anxious and feels dependent on a leader. The group will be attempting to discover how it is going to operate, what the 'normal' behaviours will be: how supportive, how critical, how serious and how humorous the group will be.
2 **Storming**. The atmosphere may be one of conflict, with rebellion against the leader, conflict between sub-groups and resistance to control. There is likely to be resistance to the task, and even the sense that the task is impossible.
3 **Norming**. At this stage, members of the group feel closer together and the conflicts are settled, or at least forgotten. Members of the group will start to support each other. There is increasingly the feeling that the task is possible to achieve.
4 **Performing**. The group is carrying out the task for which it was formed. Roles within the group are flexible, with people willing to do the work normally done by others. Members feel safe enough to express differences of opinion in relation to others.
5 **Mourning**. The group is disbanded; its members begin to feel nostalgic about its activities and achievements. Perhaps they go for a drink or a meal to celebrate.

All this may be familiar from the groups we encounter, and play our role in managing, in language training!

Read on

Meredith Belbin: *Management Teams: Why they Succeed or Fail*, Butterworth Heinemann, 1981

Ron Johnson, David Redmond, Meredith Belbin: *The Art of Empowerment*, Prentice Hall, 1998

The first four stages of team life above were suggested by B.W. Tuckman, as quoted in Michael Argyle: *Social Interaction*, Tavistock, 1969

Lesson notes

Warmer

- Write the word 'TEAMS' in big letters on the board. Ask Ss in pairs or threes to brainstorm all the types of team they can think of, in the business world and outside. (Point out that you are not looking particularly for words that come in front of *team*.) Circulate and monitor.
- After a few minutes, ask pairs and threes to say what they came up with. Invite comments and encourage discussion.

> **Examples:**
> sports teams
> project development teams
> sales teams
> medical teams doing operations
> management teams
> teams of ministers with their political advisers and civil servants

Overview

- Tell Ss that in this unit they will be looking at team building.
- Ask Ss to look at the Overview section at the beginning of the unit. Tell them a little about the things on the list, using the table on page 68 of this book as a guide. Tell them which points you will be covering in the current lesson and in later lessons.

Quotation

- Ask the whole class what they understand by the quotation and if they agree with it. Do they have a similar proverb in their own language(s)?

> Ss might mention that a team brings together a *combination* of different skills and talents: see Business brief on page 69. If they don't raise this point, you might want to introduce it yourself.

Starting up

Ss talk about their experiences of the teams they have been in, and do a quiz about different types of team members to see what profile they themselves have.

A

- Ask Ss to discuss the question in pairs. Circulate, monitor and assist.
- Get pairs to report their findings to the whole class.

Possible issues Advantages	Disadvantages
⊚ Things can be achieved by a team that can't be achieved by individuals working separately – some things can only be achieved by teams. ⊚ Some people prefer working with others rather than on their own. ⊚ Team-working allows everyone to feel they have something to contribute.	⊚ Explaining and organising the task can take so much time that it's easier and quicker to do it yourself. ⊚ Communication breakdowns can lead to severe problems in achieving the task. ⊚ Conflict between team members can be very destructive.

B – C

- Go through the quiz with the whole class and explain any difficulties.
- Divide the class into threes or fours. Appoint someone in each group who will record members' responses but also do the quiz themselves.
- Tell the notetakers that after the activity, they will have to give a mini-presentation about the group members' profiles as team players. Read out the text in the box below to give them the idea.

> Anita is a creative type, who values ideas over detailed planning. Bertil, on the other hand, is more interested in clear thinking. Catherine found that the quiz told her that she is more interested in details and clear planning, and she was a bit surprised by this. The quiz told me I'm more of a creative person, which I tend to agree with.

- Ss in each group do the quiz individually, finding what sort of team player they are by looking at the key on page 149 of the Course Book. Ss then tell the other members of the group what sort of team player they are and the notetaker records this. Notetakers should also record if the other Ss agree with what the quiz tells them.
- Circulate, monitor and assist. Note language points for praise and correction.
- When Ss have finished the quiz, the notetaker summarises the profile of each group member as you did in the example above.
- Praise good language points from the discussion and work on three or four points that need improvement, getting individual Ss to say the correct forms.
- Ask your Ss to work on Questions 1 and 2 in Exercise C in threes or fours. Circulate and monitor.
- Ask the groups for their answers. Invite comments and encourage discussion.

Vocabulary: Prefixes

Ss look at a number of prefixes and use them in context in a written exercise, and to talk about people they have worked with and teams they have been in.

- Go quickly through the prefixes with the whole class. Get Ss to read the words with the correct stress patterns, e.g. *misMANage*, *pro-EuroPEan*. Point out the pronunciation of *bi-* as in *buy*, not as in *bee*.
- Get Ss, in pairs, to match the prefixes to their meanings.
- With the whole class, go quickly through the answers.

1 b	2 b	3 c	4 a	5 c	6 b
7 b	8 a	9 c	10 a	11 b	12 b

- With the whole class, get Ss to give typical combinations containing the words with prefixes. Give them one or two possible combinations from the list below as examples. Do as a quick-fire activity.

> mismanage of a company, the economy
> pro-European voters, politicians
> predict events, the future
> post-industrial economies
> dishonest behaviour, politicians
> ex-President Clinton
> underdeveloped countries
> antisocial behaviour
> bilateral trade agreements
> reconnect the power supply
> irresponsible actions, behaviour
> hyperactive children

- Get Ss to work in pairs on the texts. Circulate and assist.
- Check the answers with the whole class.

1	ex-President
2	bilateral
3	predicted
4	pro-European
5	underdeveloped
6	mismanagement
7	dishonest

C

- Do add-the-prefixes as a quick-fire activity with the whole class.

uncommunicative	indecisive	inefficient
unenthusiastic	inflexible	unfocussed
unimaginative	disloyal	disorganised
unpopular	impractical	unsociable
unstable	intolerant	

- Get Ss to work, in pairs, on the questions. Circulate, monitor and assist. Treat Question 1 tactfully. Tell Ss they don't have to name the people involved.
- Each member of the pair talks about the other member's colleagues in relation to Question 1. For Question 2, one member of the pair talks about their general findings.

Reading: Successful teamworking

Ss read some advice about forming teams and do an exercise on fixed pairs.

- Get Ss to look through the paragraph headings. Clarify any difficulties. Explain that they will have to match these headings to the different sections of the article.
- Read the first four paragraphs with the whole class, explaining any difficult words. Ask for the first heading – 'Common goals with challenging targets'.
- Get Ss to read the rest of the article in pairs, finding the rest of the headings. Circulate, monitor and assist by explaining difficult words.
- Recap difficult words and expressions that more than one pair found difficult, working on meaning and, where necessary, pronunciation.
- Ask pairs for the section headings.

1	Common goals with challenging targets
2	Open communication
3	Involvement of all team members
4	Conflict resolution
5	Leadership
6	Measuring progress against goals

- Invite comments and encourage discussion of these points with the whole class.

B

- Get pairs to look at the article again and answer the questions.
- Elicit the answers from the pairs and discuss with the whole group.

1	to create something that is greater than the sum of its parts
2	synergies (line 8)
3	– meetings that overrun
	– frequent arguments between team members
	– unhealthy level of competition between individuals
	– people not completing tasks assigned to them
	– last minute panics to meet deadlines

- If there is time, get Ss to work in pairs, some pairs evaluating a project they have worked on in relation to the six points in Exercise A above. Did the project meet these criteria?
- Other pairs discuss the five points from Question 3 above in relation to a project they have worked on.

◎ Circulate, monitor and assist. Note language points for praise and correction, especially in relation to team building language.

◎ Praise good language points from the discussion and work on three or four points that need improvement, getting individual Ss to say the correct forms.

◎ With the whole class, get feedback from each pair. Invite comments and encourage discussion.

C

◎ Ask Ss to look at *nook and cranny* and the fixed pairs in the box. Say that one of their characteristics is that the order cannot vary (except for comic effect). You cannot normally say, for example, *cranny and nook* or *go and touch*.

◎ Ask Ss to work on questions 1 and 2 in pairs. Circulate, monitor and assist with the more difficult expressions.

◎ Go through the answers with the whole class.

1	**a**	
2	**a**	on and off
	b	hard and fast
	c	give and take
	d	ups and downs
	e	touch and go
	f	wine and dine
	g	by and large
	h	pros and cons

Listening: Building a team

A management trainer talks about the key ingredients for teams, and the need or otherwise for leaders.

A 🎧 8.1

◎ Tell Ss they are going to listen to Doug Cole, an expert on team building. Ask Ss to look through the points to prepare them for what they are going to hear. Explain *baseline*: the starting point for something.

◎ Play the recording once or twice, explaining anything that is unclear. Ask Ss to complete the points. (Explain *generic* as *all-purpose*: there is no single answer to this question about what makes a good team in every situation.)

◎ Play the recording again, stopping where key points occur so as to give time to Ss to write down the exact words they hear.

◎ Elicit the Ss' answers about the points.

Know what your strengths and weaknesses are.
Establish your baseline, where you are in terms of your skills, in terms of your activities, in terms of your experience.
Relate that to the task in hand.
Identify what the project is or the task is.
Build the team around what you need to complete the task.

B 🎧 8.2

◎ Ask Ss to look through the questions. Point out the pronunciation of *co-ordinate* and *co-ordination*.

◎ Play recording 8.2 once or twice, helping with any difficulties. (Explain *distinct times* as *specific times*.)

◎ Ask Ss for their answers.

1	With larger groups and more complex tasks.
2	Pulling people together, checking progress against targets and deciding what the next course of action is.
3	When there's a strict time scale.

◎ Ask Ss for their reactions. Invite comments and encourage discussion. (They may point out that most business teams are organised around leaders in the form of managers. People from some cultures may say that leaders are essential in all situations.)

Language review: Modal perfect

Ss look at how modal perfect verbs such as *needn't have*, *may have*, *might have*, *must have*, *could have* and *should have* and *would have* are used and what they mean.

◎ Go through the points in the Language review box with the whole class, inviting and answering queries.

A

◎ Ask individual Ss to read out the sentences in italics, without doing the exercise. Concentrate on stress and the correct pronunciation of contractions like *needn't* and *couldn't*.

◎ Do the exercise as a whole-class activity, elaborating where necessary.

1	no
2	yes
3	yes
4	no
5	no
6	not sure
7	not sure
8	no

B

◎ Ask Ss to work on the questions in pairs. Circulate, monitor and assist.

◎ Go through the answers with the whole class, pointing out the subtleties mentioned below, but don't make it too complicated for the Ss' level.

1 should (But you didn't and now it's too late.)

2 might or could (But it wasn't.)

3 Correct. Point out to Ss that it means the same as 'might have destroyed'. (But it wasn't.) And if you say 'may have destroyed', you don't know yet whether it was destroyed or not, because you haven't found out yet.)

4 must (We don't know for sure, but we think this is the case.)

5 Correct. (We don't know for sure what the reason was. 'He must have been delayed' would show more certainty.)

6 Correct. (You couldn't have seen him a) even if you had wanted to see him, or b) even if you thought you had seen him, mistaking someone else for Mr Lebeau.)

7 must (We're assuming he had a bad flight. 'He might have had a bad flight' would mean we are less sure about this.)

8 should (But we didn't. 'We could have …' or 'We might have made him leader' implies that this was possible to do, but lacks the idea that it would have been the right thing to do.)

C

◎ Go through the situation quickly with the whole class.

◎ Divide the class into pairs, appointing a Financial Director and a sales rep in each pair.

◎ To show the class what to do, take the part of Financial Director and ask one of the Ss to be the sales rep. Say: 'You shouldn't have stayed in a five-star hotel', to which the sales rep should reply something like: 'There was no alternative. There was a big conference on and it was the only place I could get a room.'

◎ Continue with one or two of the other points, emphasising that the sales rep should find convincing excuses each time and vary the formula, so they don't say 'There was no alternative' every time, but use sentences like 'I had no choice', and 'There was nothing else I could do.'

◎ When the whole class has understood the idea, ask them to role play the situation. Circulate, monitor and assist, especially with the modal perfect. Note language points for praise and correction.

◎ Praise good language points from the discussion and work on three or four points that need improvement, especially with the modal perfect, getting individual Ss to say the correct forms.

◎ Ask for one or two public performances of the situation for the whole class.

1 to 1

This role play can be done 1 to 1. Ask your student to be the sales rep and you take the role of Financial Director. Then change roles. Encourage imagination. Don't forget to note language points for praise and correction, especially in relation to the modal perfect.

Skills: Resolving conflict

Ss look at techniques for dealing with disagreements in teams. They work on the language for this and apply it to role play a situation in which one member of a team is causing problems.

(A)

◎ Go through the suggestions with the whole class.

Do	Don't
Be positive when handling problems. Try to see the problem from the point of view of the team. Be truthful about how you see the situation. Encourage open and frank discussion. Bring potential conflict and disagreement into the open. Persist with 'impossible people' – you may win them over. Try to find 'win–win' solutions. Make sure you know who the influential members are.	Get angry from time to time with difficult members. Delay taking action, if possible. Try to ignore tensions within the team. Give special attention to team members who are creating problems.

◎ Ask Ss to categorise statements with a show of hands for each one.

◎ Invite comments and encourage discussion. The above division is for illustration only: there may be disagreements: for example, there are those who say that there is no point in trying to win over impossible people, and that energy is best expended elsewhere. Some may say that anger also has its place.

(B)

◎ Go through the expressions already in the Useful language box and ask Ss, in pairs, to add one more expression under each heading.

◎ With the whole class, elicit expressions from the pairs. See below some possibilities: Ss will certainly have thought of others. Concentrate on the ones they produce, correcting where necessary.

73

Expressing your feelings
What's really upsetting me is …
Making suggestions
Well, what I'd like to see …
Expressing satisfaction
Yes, that would make my life a lot easier.
Agreeing action
We all seem to agree on the solution. We'll …
Expressing dissatisfaction
I don't think that will work.
Showing sympathy
That must have been awful.
Stating common goals
We're all working towards the same aim.
Identifying the real problem
What exactly is the problem?
Resolving the conflict
We need to sort this out here and now.
Reviewing the situation
Can we just check on the situation.

©

◎ Divide the class into pairs, appointing the team leader and team member in each pair.

◎ Tell Ss to turn to their particular role description. Get them to read it silently. Circulate, monitor and assist.

◎ If you think it's necessary, do a demonstration in front of the whole class of the beginning of the situation, with you as the team member and an outgoing student as team leader.

◎ When all the Ss are clear about their roles and about the situation, start the activity.

◎ Circulate and monitor but do not intervene except if absolutely necessary. Note language points for praise and correction, especially in the area of conflict-resolving language.

◎ When Ss have finished, call the whole class to order. Praise good language points and work on three or four points that need improvement, getting individual Ss to say the correct forms.

◎ Ask one of the pairs to give a public performance in front of the whole group.

Case study

The new boss

There are problems when a new manager takes over a sales team. Ss role play the directors of the company in their efforts to resolve them.

Stage 1

◎ Get Ss to read the background section and meanwhile write the points in the first column of the table below on the board. When Ss have finished reading, elicit information to complete the table.

Activity	Selling fax machines, data projectors and slim plasma screens
Sales Manager until 18 months ago	Vanessa Bryant
Present Sales Manager	Nigel Fraser
Sales targets	Increase turnover by 10%; create dynamic sales team
Sales performance	20% below target; low morale since NF arrived
Problems	Team resents closer supervision by NF More meetings, dominated by one or two people: some don't turn up Staff blame each other or other departments for problems Rivalry and dislike between some members Unable to accept new ideas or criticism NF praises previous company and colleagues; staff talk about the 'good old days' under Vanessa Bryant

Stage 2: Task preparation

◎ Divide the class into threes. Write 'ADVICE' and 'ACTION' at the top of the board in big letters. Explain that the students are groups of directors who will consider the advice to be given to Nigel Fraser and the action to take in order to solve the problem, or at least improve the situation.

◎ Tell the groups that each director in the group knows more about some of the salespeople than the others. In fact, each director knows Nigel Fraser and two members of the sales team very well.
  – Director A knows Nigel Fraser, Jean Dubot and Nina Persson
  – Director B knows Nigel Fraser, Robert Driscoll and Johan Niedermeister

    – Director C knows Nigel Fraser, Eliana Petrides and Bruna
     Tardelli.
    Write these three combinations on the board to avoid
    misunderstandings.

◉ Explain also that the descriptions here don't give the
   complete picture. The directors can give positive or
   negative interpretations to them. For example, Director A
   thinks that Jean Dubot only *seems* arrogant, but that this is
   a form of humour with him and basically he's friendly.

◉ Get the directors to read for themselves the descriptions of
   the three people they know particularly well. Circulate,
   monitor and assist.

◉ With the whole class, discuss any problems that are
   causing particular difficulty.

◉ Again with the whole class, go through the five points that
   will form the basis for discussion and answer any queries.

◉ Bring the Ss' attention back to the agenda for the directors'
   discussion: advice and action.

Stage 3: Task

◉ When the situation is clear, the discussions can begin.
   Circulate and monitor. Do not intervene unless it's
   necessary. Note language points for praise and correction,
   especially in the area of team building.

◉ When the groups have finished, with the whole class praise
   good language points from the discussion and work on
   three or four points that need improvement, getting
   individual Ss to say the correct forms.

◉ Ask the groups for the advice they would give and the
   action they would have. Note them on the board under the
   respective headings.

◉ Invite comments and encourage discussion, comparing the
   findings of the different groups.

---

1 to 1

This discussion can be done 1 to 1. Give the student plenty
of time to read and absorb the background information,
the profiles of the different salespeople and the points for
discussion. Discuss the issues with your student as if you
are both directors of BES.

Writing

◉ For the writing task you can
   – tell Ss which one to do
   – ask half to do one task and the other half the other
   – or let Ss choose for themselves.

◉ Tell Ss to look at the writing task you have assigned them.
   Or, if you are letting them choose, tell them to look at both
   tasks and ask them which one they are going to do.

◉ For the first task, say that the letter should come in the
   form of a report to the MD of BES, who was not present at
   the discussion.

◉ For the second task, say that this should be a personal
   letter from the sales manager to a member of the sales
   team. Point out that they can do this in the context of BES,

i.e. a letter from Nigel Fraser to one of his sales team, or in
the context of another company.

 Writing file page 138.

Raising finance

At a glance

	Classwork – Course Book	Further work
Lesson 1 *Each lesson (excluding case studies) is about 45–60 minutes. This does not include administration and time spent going through homework.*	**Starting up** Ss compare sources of personal borrowing and discuss some common expressions about money. **Listening: Ways of raising finance** A business owner talks about sources of business finance. **Vocabulary: Financial terms** Ss study the language of borrowing and lending.	**Practice File** Vocabulary (page 36)
Lesson 2	**Reading: Financing start-up businesses** Ss read about the different approaches to raising capital for start-up businesses in Japan and Italy. **Language review: Dependent prepositions** Ss look at the prepositions that can follow certain verbs, adjectives and nouns and use them in context.	**Text bank** pages (168–171) **ML Grammar and Usage** **Practice File** Language review (page 37)
Lesson 3	**Skills: Negotiating** Ss discuss negotiating tips, look at different techniques used in negotiations and put them into action to role play a situation.	**Resource bank** (page 200)
Lesson 4 *Each case study is about 1½ to 2 hours.*	**Case study: Vision Film Company** A film company negotiates for finance to make a feature film.	**Practice File** Writing (page 38)

For a fast route through the unit focussing mainly on speaking skills, just use the underlined sections.

For 1 to 1 situations, most parts of the unit lend themselves, with minimal adaptation, to use with individual students. Where this is not the case, alternative procedures are given.

Business brief

You have a brilliant but unusual business idea. You could put all your life savings into it, and ask friends and family to invest in it as well. But this may not be enough. Or your friends may, perhaps wisely, refuse to lend you money. You go to your local bank, but they don't understand your idea and suggest you look elsewhere.

You go to a **venture capitalist** like the one in the main Course Book unit. Venture capitalists are used to looking at new ideas, especially in hi-tech industries, and they see the potential in your brilliant idea. The venture capitalist also recommends it to some **business angels**, private investors looking for new **start-ups** to invest in. They provide you with **seed capital** to set up your business.

You launch your business, and it's a great success. But the amount of money it generates from sales is not enough to invest in it further: it's not **self-financing**, so you decide to raise more capital in an **initial public offering** or **IPO**: your company is **floated** and you issue shares on a stock market for the first time, perhaps a market or a section of one that specialises in shares in hi-tech companies.

You wait anxiously for the day of the **issue** or **float**. Interest from investors is high, and all the shares are sold. Over the next few weeks, there is a stream of favourable news from your company about its sales, new products and the brilliant new people it has managed to recruit. The shares increase steadily in value.

Now look at this process from the point of view of investors. The venture capitalists and business angels, for example, know most new businesses will fail, but that a few will do reasonably well and one or two will, with luck, hit the jackpot, paying back all the money they lost on unprofitable projects and much more. This exemplifies the classic trade-off between **risk and return**, the idea that the riskier an investment is, the more profit you require from it.

In your IPO, there may be investors who think that your company might be a future IBM or Microsoft, and they want to get in on the ground floor, hold on to the shares as they increase inexorably in value. They make large **capital gains** that can be **realised** when they sell the shares. Or they may anticipate selling quickly and making a quick profit.

Other investors may prefer to avoid the unpredictable world of **tech stocks** altogether and go for steady but unspectacular returns from established, well-known companies. These are the **blue chips** that form the basis of many conservative investment **portfolios**. One day in a few years' time, when your company is **mature** and growing at five or ten per cent a year, rather than doubling in size every six months, your brilliant business idea may have become a blue-chip company itself.

Governments increasingly depend on investment from the private sector in public projects. These **public–private partnerships** are financed by a combination of commercial investment and public money from taxation and government borrowing.

Read on

Michael Brett: *How to Read the Financial Pages*, Century Business paperback, 5th edition, 2000

Graham Bannock, William Manser: *International Dictionary of Finance*, Economist Books/Hutchinson, 1999

Mastering Finance, FT Pitman, 1997

Pocket Finance, Economist Books/Hamish Hamilton, 1994

Lesson notes

Warmer

◎ Introduce the unit to Ss by saying that you can talk about *raising finance*, *raising capital* or *raising money* for a project. They are all used to talk about obtaining money through borrowing of different kinds. (Even issuing shares in your company is a form of borrowing: the company is in effect borrowing money from shareholders.)

◎ Write the word *money* in big letters on the right side of the board, with the word *raise* on the left.

◎ Ask Ss to brainstorm in small groups the different verbs that can come in front of money. Each group should think of as many verbs as possible.

◎ With the whole class, ask how many verbs each group has found. Get Ss to shout them out and write them on the left.

> Possible verbs include:
> borrow, donate, earn, invest, lend, lose, make, obtain, provide, save, spend, transfer, waste, win

Overview

◎ Tell Ss that in this unit they will be looking specifically at borrowing, especially by businesses raising finance in order to develop.

◎ Ask Ss to look at the Overview section at the beginning of the unit. Tell them a little about the things on the list, using the table on page 76 of this book as a guide. Tell them which points you will be covering in the current lesson, and which in later lessons.

Quotation

◎ Ask the whole class what they understand by the quotation and ask if they agree with it. (Polonius seems to be criticising all borrowing: ask if Ss agree with this. For example, would businesses be able to grow and develop if they followed his advice?)

◎ To encourage discussion, write up the next line of the quote on the board:
'Neither a borrower nor a lender be ...
For loan oft loses both itself and friend';
(Explain that oft means often.)

◎ Ask Ss if this changes their interpretation of the quote. (Polonius now seems to be talking specifically about the dangers of lending money to friends.) Ask if Ss agree with this.

Starting up

Ss compare sources of personal borrowing and talk about and discuss some common expressions about money.

◎ Ask Ss to look at questions 1–4, but not at question 5 yet. Explain *loan shark* (someone who lends money at very high

rates of interest to people who aren't able to borrow from banks, and may threaten violence if it is not repaid) and *overdraft*. Discuss briefly the situation with overdrafts in the Ss' own country / countries. Do they have to be arranged beforehand or are they given automatically up to a certain limit? Introduce the expressions *in the red* and *go into the red*.

◎ Get Ss to discuss Questions 1–4 in pairs. Circulate and monitor. Note language points for praise and correction.

◎ When pairs have finished their discussion, call the class to order and praise good language points from the discussion and work on three or four points that need improvement, especially in relation to this topic, getting individual Ss to say the correct forms.

◎ Ask pairs what they came up with. Invite comments and encourage whole-class discussion.

> Possible issues:
> 1 a) Bank: Advantages include: it's a business transaction that doesn't involve friends.
> Disadvantages include high rates of interest which mean it can be expensive; all sorts of problems if you can't repay the loan such as your credit rating (explain) will be affected and it might be difficult to get loans in future.
> b) Friend or colleague: Covered in the discussion about the quotation.
> c) Member of family: Families are often the main source of borrowing for many business start-ups but they might be less willing to lend for other purposes.
> d) Loan shark: The advantage is that people with no credit history (because they have never had bank accounts or credit cards) can borrow money, but the downside is that interest rates are extortionate and they might be harmed if they don't repay.
> e) Credit card company: Easy to do (explain *cash advance*) but interest rates are very high and a bank loan would be cheaper.
> 2 Ss might mention savings accounts, shares, unit trusts (putting money into financial institutions that invest in other companies, known as *mutual funds* in the US), property. If teaching in the UK, don't get bogged down in technicalities such as those of ISAs.
> 3 This is a tricky issue. Companies obviously want to be paid as quickly as possible by customers, but to pay their suppliers as late as possible. But businesses are often in no position to threaten business customers who pay late as this will alienate the customer who will then go elsewhere. Ask Ss what the normal payment times are in their country, if interest is charged after a certain time, etc.
> 4 This may depend on cultural attitudes to personal debt in the Ss' countries. Discuss tactfully.

◎ Ask the Ss to discuss the sayings in question 5 in pairs or threes. Circulate and monitor.

Lesson notes

◎ With the whole class, ask for Ss' ideas. Invite comments and encourage discussion.

Listening: Ways of raising finance

A business owner talks about sources of business finance. Ss complete a chart and answer questions about the best methods of raising finance.

(A) 🎧 9.1

◎ Copy the version of the chart with the missing items below on the board. Ask Ss what they would expect to hear in recording 9.1 about the best ways of raising finance and how they expect the chart to be completed.

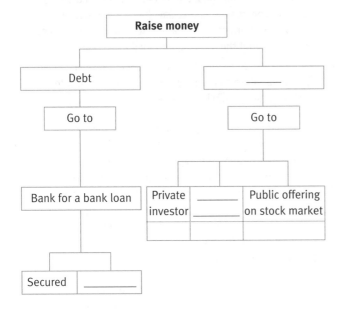

◎ Play recording 9.1 once or twice and check the answer with the Ss.

◎ You may need to explain the following to the Ss, depending on their existing knowledge.

> **Debt** is the same thing as **borrowing**. If the debt is secured on the company's assets, the lenders have the right to take those assets and sell them in order to get their money back if for any reason the borrower does not make repayments on the money borrowed.
> **Unsecured** borrowing does not give lenders this right.
> **Equity** is the same thing as **share capital**.
> **Venture capitalists** are people with access to finance who look for new business ideas to invest in. They know that many will fail or not be very successful, but they hope that the one or two that really succeed will make more than enough money to offset the failures.
> A **public offering** is when a company raises finance by selling its shares on the stock market. (An initial public offering or IPO is when it does this for the first time.)

◎ Once Ss have suggested answers to complete the table, get one or two Ss to summarise it for the whole class.

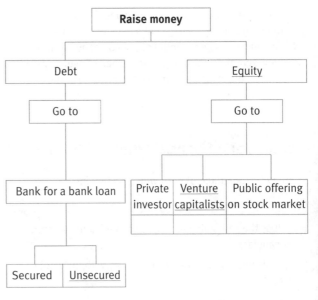

(B) 🎧 9.2

◎ Ask Ss to look at Questions 1–3. Point out the expression 'growth businesses'.

◎ Play recording 9.2 once right through. Then play it again in sections, stopping to explain any unfamiliar words.

> You may need to explain the following:
> A **financial instrument** is a particular way of raising money: for example, shares are a particular type of instrument.
> **Cash flow**, in this context, is money coming into the company from sales. Strong cash flow is needed in order to have enough money to make repayments on loans. With equity, shareholders may be willing to wait longer before the company pays out any **dividends**.

◎ After playing the first question and answer elicit answers.

> 1 It's unlikely that start-up companies will be able to get loans and finance themselves through debt. More established growth companies can finance themselves through debt.
> 2 Debt is expensive because there are regular repayments to be made to lenders. (It isn't specifically mentioned, but shareholders will be willing in some cases to wait quite a long time before they get any payback on their investment in the form of dividends.)
> 3 Equity

◎ Ask Ss to look at questions 4 and 5. Play the second and third question and answer in recording 9.2, stopping to explain any unfamiliar words. You could ask extra questions about what sort of company it is, what stage of development it's at, why they used private investors, etc.

◎ Elicit answers.

> 4 The state of the ecomony, the business concept, having the right people, having contacts with investors.
> 5 The managers kept control of the company because they were the controlling shareholders: Rosemary Leith and her business partner own the majority of the shares in the company.

Vocabulary: Financial terms

Ss study the language of borrowing and lending.

 A

- Tell Ss they are going to work on some finance-related vocabulary.
- Do this exercise as a quick-fire activity with the whole class.

> 1 e   2 c   3 b   4 d   5 a
> Point out that human capital is different in that it is not a sum of money.

 B

- Ask Ss to work on the exercise in pairs. Ss can use a dictionary, preferably a specialised one such as the *Longman Business English Dictionary*. Circulate, monitor and assist.
- With the whole class, elicit answers from the pairs. Also get Ss to discuss the meanings of the distractors and why they do not fit.

> 1 c
> 2 a   (This is more AmE. BrE speakers usually say *security*.)
> 3 c
> 4 a
> 5 b   (You could point out that this is spelt *installment* in AmE.)
> 6 a
> 7 c
> 8 b
> 9 b
> 10 a

Reading: Financing start-up businesses

Ss read about the different approaches to raising capital for start-up businesses in Japan and Italy.

 A

- With the whole class, ask Ss to recap the sources of finance from the Starting up activity, and their advantages and disadvantages.
- With the whole class, tell Ss not to read articles in great detail at this point. Explain that the idea is to scan the articles very quickly to find which statement relates to which article.

- Get Ss to start scanning the articles and to match up the statements as soon as they can.

> Article A: Statement 1
> Article B: Statement 2

 B

- Divide the class into pairs. Make sure that Ss know who is A and who is B in each pair. Student A reads article A and student B, article B. Circulate, monitor and assist with unfamiliar words.

C

- When Ss have finished, tell them to work with their partners on questions 1–5. Say that the purpose of this activity is information exchange, so that each partner can find out about the article that they did not read.
- Afterwards, go round the whole class for answers, asking Ss to elaborate on them by using quotations from the articles, rather than just saying *true* or *false*.

> 1 False. 'Only now is Japan starting to develop a business environment conducive to entrepreneurial growth'. But in Italy, 'entrepreneurship seems part of the culture'.
> 2 False. In Japan, capital was available from banks, but new companies found it hard to obtain: 'The head of a big bank … doesn't know what it's like trying to raise ¥500,000'. In Italy, 'banks have … become risk-averse and reluctant to lend'.
> 3 True. '… the country has attracted [risk capital]'. Whereas in Italy, in one study, out of 'scores of entrepreneurs' only two had obtained capital.
> 4 False. Families are not mentioned in the article about Japan. It is true of Italy, where people 'borrow from parents, other family members and friends'.
> 5 True. 'Japanese authorities have been [making] the country's legal and structural framework more venture business-friendly.' (We can assume this includes specific schemes.) In Italy, there 'is an outstandingly successful government-funded scheme to encourage young entrepreneurs'.

D

- Ask the Ss specialising in article A to find expressions 1–4 and those specialising in B to find expressions 5–8. Circulate, monitor and assist.
- Check and discuss answers with the whole class.
- Rather than asking Ss to think of sentences containing these words out of context, have a whole-class discussion about raising finance in the Ss' country / countries, talking about the issues raised in the two articles. For example, what is the role of a) government, b) banks, c) family and friends? Ss should use the answers to questions 1–8 in the discussion. Mark them up on the board and put a tick (✓) next to them each time they are used.

1   catalyst
2   foster
3   entrepreneur-friendly
4   subcontractor
5   turnover
6   equity stakes
7   unsecured loan
8   merchant bank

(E)

◉   With the whole class, write on the board:
    Only now is Japan starting to develop a business
    environment conducive to entrepreneurial growth.

◉   Elicit from Ss what the normal word order would be and
    write that sentence on the board:
    Japan is only now starting to develop a business
    environment conducive to entrepreneurial growth.
    Point out (without writing it up) that the sentence could
    also be:
    Japan is starting to develop a business environment
    conducive to entrepreneurial growth only now.

◉   Do question 1 with the whole class, writing up the answer
    on the board. Demonstrate the transformation.

◉   Ask Ss to do the others in pairs. Circulate, monitor and
    assist.

◉   Go round the whole class for the answers. Discuss and
    explain.

1   Seldom are goods returned to us because they are
    faulty.
2   At no time did he apologise for his mistake.
3   Under no circumstances must the budget be exceeded.
4   Only by spending more money on advertising will we
    increase sales significantly.
5   On no account should private calls be made from the
    office.

◉   Ask the whole class how the meanings of sentences are
    changed by putting Seldom, At no time, etc. at the
    beginning. (By doing this, these expressions are
    emphasised and underlined.) Point out also that the new
    versions are much more formal than their uninverted
    equivalents.

Language review: Dependent prepositions

Ss look at the prepositions that can follow certain verbs,
adjectives and nouns and use them in context.

(A)

◉   Tell Ss that they are going to look at prepositions following
    verbs, adjectives and nouns. Read out and comment on the
    first example from each of the three columns. (These
    patterns are often shown in dictionaries. For example, in
    Longman Dictionary of Contemporary English, the pattern
    reliance on is shown by '+ on' in front of the example. Get
    Ss to refer to their dictionaries if they have one.

◉   Discuss the verbs in more detail. The first example is a
    phrasal verb. The verb plus preposition combination brings
    a new meaning: account for. In many phrasal verbs (e.g.
    put up with something) this meaning is not clear, even if
    you know all the words individually, but here the meaning
    is fairly obvious. In many dictionaries, phrasal verbs have a
    separate sub-entry under the main verb.

◉   Get Ss to do the rest of the exercise in pairs. Circulate,
    monitor and assist.

◉   Check and discuss the answers with the whole class.

1 for	2 from	3 from	4 on	5 to	6 to
7 on	8 of	9 in			

◉   Do this exercise as a quick-fire activity with the whole
    class.

1   learn from
2   reliance on
3   dependent on
4   development of
5   difficulties in
6   Borrowing from

(B)

◉   Prepare Ss for this exercise by saying that they should try
    to anticipate the preposition that will occur at the
    beginning of the second half of each sentence. For
    example in question 1, they should be looking for in,
    thereby eliminating everything except parts d) and f). The
    sense tells you that part f) must be the right answer.

◉   Get Ss to do the exercise in pairs. Circulate, monitor and
    assist.

◉   Check and discuss the answers with the whole class,
    asking pairs how they came to their conclusions.

1 f	2 g	3 d	4 h	5 e	6 c	7 b
8 a	9 j	10 i				

(C)

◉   Refer back to the Reading section of this unit, if Ss did it.
    Here they have the chance to develop the ideas they came
    up with in the follow-up to exercise D in that section, about
    the role of a) government, b) banks, c) family and friends. If
    not, ask about this as a way of introducing the subject.

◉   Get Ss to work in threes on the main question: Why do
    people often find it difficult to get finance to start a
    business? Circulate and monitor. Note language points for
    praise and correction, especially in relation to dependent
    prepositions.

◉   With the whole class, praise good language points from the
    discussion and work on three or four points that need
    improvement, getting individual Ss to say the correct
    forms.

◉   Ask the groups what they came up with. Invite comments
    and encourage whole-class discussion.

The main idea here will probably be that most business projects fail, and that lenders / investors are right to be wary about putting up money. But Ss may also talk about how the lack of an entrepreneurial culture will mean that there are fewer institutions and individual investors with experience in this area.

Skills: Negotiating

Ss discuss negotiating tips, look at different techniques used in negotiations and put them into action to role play a situation.

(A)

◉ Tell Ss they are going to look at a number of negotiating tips, which they will discuss in pairs or threes. Tell them there are no right or wrong answers, and that the statements are designed to encourage thought and discussion.

◉ Circulate and monitor. Intervene only if necessary. Note language points for praise and correction, especially in relation to the subject of negotiation.

◉ With the whole class, praise good language points from the discussion and work on three or four points that need improvement, getting individual Ss to say the correct forms.

◉ Ask the Ss for their findings. Invite comments and encourage whole-class discussion.

1 May depend on the complexity of the negotiation. Above all, you must listen carefully to the answers. (See the Skills section of Unit 10 on active listening.)
2 Presumably there will be a point where the other side becomes irritated if they are interrupted too much.
3 This one is in a lot of text books on negotiating. Some people think that giving something away can produce a good atmosphere. Others say that it shows weakness.
4 This is really two separate points. Simple language is probably a good idea, but some might say that it's important to underplay one's high-priority objectives and over-emphasise low-priority ones.
5 Again, there will come a point where too much of this becomes irritating.
6 On the whole, negotiators probably do not do this enough, so it's worth emphasising.
7 Some might argue that this is true in an ideal world, but in practice assertiveness (rather than aggressiveness) can have its place.
8 Some people will be more comfortable with this than others. Some negotiators are good at exploiting the feelings of the other side. Showing emotions is more acceptable in some cultures than others.

(B)

◉ Ask Ss to look at expressions in the Useful language box. Go through the expressions and ask Ss to match the headings with the definitions given.

1 d	2 e	3 b	4 a	5 c

(c)

◉ Explain what Ss have to do, and then get them to work in pairs. Circulate, monitor and assist.

◉ With the whole class, go through the answers and elicit the extra expressions under each heading.

◉ Point out that Open questions often begin with *wh-* words like *what*, *why*, *when*, etc. *How* is also an honorary member of this group. Closed questions can often be answered *yes* or *no*. Point out *seems to be* a good softening phrase.

1 Closed question
2 Closed question
3 Open question
4 Softening phrase
5 Signalling phrase
6 Summarising
7 Softening phrase
8 Signalling phrase
9 Closed question
10 Summarising

(D)

◉ Explain the situation. Divide the class into threes: each three contains a Financial Manager, a Personnel Director and an observer. The job of the observer will be to note the different stages in the negotiation and the techniques and language used by each side.

◉ Make sure everyone knows which role they are taking.

◉ Give time for Ss to absorb the information needed for their role. Get the observer to skim the information for both roles. Circulate, monitor and assist.

◉ When all Ss are clear about their role and what they have to do, the activity can begin. Circulate and monitor, but do not intervene unless it's necessary. Make sure that the observer in each three is taking notes.

◉ Note language points for praise and correction, especially ones relating to the language of negotiation.

◉ When Ss have finished their negotiation, praise good language points from the discussion and work on three or four points that need improvement, getting individual Ss to say the correct forms.

◉ Ask the observer from each three to recap the different stages and point out the techniques and language used by each side in the situation they were observing. Ask the Ss playing the roles in each three to say if this is a good summary of what happened.

◉ Recap again the key negotiating phrases, and relate them, if appropriate, to those in the Useful language box.

1 to 1

This negotiation can be done 1 to 1. Ask your student which side they would prefer to represent. You represent the other side. Don't forget to note language points for praise and correction. Afterwards, ask the student about their negotiating plan, the tactics they were using, etc.

Case study

Vision Film Company

A film company negotiates for finance to make a feature film.

Stage 1: Background

With the whole class, get Ss to read the background section. Meanwhile write the points in the first column of the table below on the board. When Ss have finished reading, elicit information to complete the table.

Activity	Film making
Based	Krakow, Poland
Founded	15 years ago
Output so far	commercials and documentaries, some award-winning
Personnel	production staff plus freelancers
Current project	feature film set in post-war Europe
Finance source	European Finance Associates
Provisional finance package	$10 million
Stage in negotiations	second meeting next month to finalise
Usual investment return	sum invested + interest + share of profits

Stage 2: Executive Summary

- Divide the class into threes. Each three contains: a scriptwriter, an accountant, and a project manager
- Each person independently runs through the information that is relevant to them and should be ready to comment on it to the whole class.
  - The scriptwriter will summarise and comment, in their own words, on the story line of the film and the target audience, target market and proposed promotion.
  - The accountant will go through the budget and projected revenues, and be ready to explain the different figures.
  - The project manager will talk about the different stages of the project.
- Circulate, monitor and assist.
- When the Ss are ready, ask one scriptwriter to present their information to the whole class, one accountant to do the same with theirs, and one project manager to present theirs.

Stage 3: Task

- Divide the class into fours. In each four, there are two representatives of VFC and two from EFA, the finance company. Make sure that everyone knows who is who. (These fours have nothing to do with the threes in Stage 2 opposite.)
- Give time for Ss to read and absorb their respective information. Circulate and assist.
- Before the negotiation begins, get each side to confer about their negotiation objectives and tactics: what do they hope to get out of the negotiations and how do they hope to achieve this?
- When everyone is clear about their information, objectives and tactics, the negotiations can begin. Circulate and assist but do not intervene unless necessary.
- Note language points for praise and correction, especially in relation to negotiation language.
- When the negotiations are complete, praise good language points from the discussion and work on three or four points that need improvement, getting individual Ss to say the correct forms.
- Ask a member of each group to summarise briefly what happened and what was decided. Invite comments and encourage discussion.

---

1 to 1

This negotiation can be done 1 to 1. Ask your student which side they would prefer to represent. You represent the other side. While doing the negotiation, note language points for praise and correction. Afterwards, ask the student about their negotiating plan and the tactics they were using.

Writing

- Ss can do the writing task collaboratively in class, or for homework.

 Writing file page 139.

Lesson notes

Customer service

At a glance

	Classwork – Course Book	Further work
Lesson 1 *Each lesson (excluding case studies) is about 45–60 minutes. This does not include administration and time spent going through homework.*	**Starting up** Ss talk about what irritates them and about the place of customer care in a company's success. **Listening: New ideas in customer care** A customer service expert talks about satisfying and delighting customers. **Discussion: Customer complaints** Ss look at suggestions for ways of dealing with customer complaints and draw up a list of the best techniques for doing this.	
Lesson 2	**Reading: Customer delight** Ss read about ways of going beyond mere customer satisfaction and creating customer delight. **Vocabulary: Idioms** Ss look at words related to customer service and some common idioms, using them in context.	**Text bank** (pages 172–175) **Practice File** Vocabulary (page 40)
Lesson 3	**Language review: Gerunds** Ss study gerund formation and the way that gerunds are used. Ss then use them in drawing up guidelines about customer service. **Skills: Active listening** Ss look at listening skills in the context of customer service. They listen to interviews with satisfied and angry customers and learn some key expressions.	**Practice File** Language review (page 41) **ML Grammar and Usage** **Resource bank** (page 201)
Lesson 4 *Each case study is about 1½ to 2 hours.*	**Case study: Hermes Communications** Ss role play the handling of a range of customer complaints at a phone company.	**Practice File** Writing (page 42)

For a fast route through the unit focussing mainly on speaking skills, just use the underlined sections.

For 1 to 1 situations, most parts of the unit lend themselves, with minimal adaptation, to use with individual students. Where this is not the case, alternative procedures are given.

Business brief

Philip Kotler defines **customer service** as 'all the activities involved in making it easy for customers to reach the right parties within the company and receive quick and satisfactory service, answers and resolutions of problems'.

Customers have **expectations**, and when these are met, there is **customer satisfaction**. When they are exceeded, there may be **delight**, but this depends on the degree of **involvement** in the purchase. There is a scale between the chore of the weekly shop at the supermarket and the purchase of something expensive such as a car that, for many people, only takes place once every few years. The scope for delight and, conversely, **dissatisfaction** is greater in the latter situation.

The telephone can be used to sell some services, such as banking or insurance, entirely replacing face-to-face contact. The **customer helpline** can be a channel of communication to complement face-to-face contact. Or it can be used before or after buying goods as a source of information or channel of complaint.

The figures are familiar: 95 per cent of dissatisfied customers don't complain, but just change suppliers. As the article in the main course unit relates, customers receiving good service create new business by telling up to 12 other people. Those treated badly will tell up to 20 people. Eighty per cent of those who feel their complaints are handled fairly will stay **loyal**, and **customer allegiance** will be built. **Customer retention** is key: studies show that getting **repeat business** is five times cheaper than finding new customers. **Customer defection** must, of course, be reduced as much as possible, but a company can learn a lot from the ones who do leave through **lost customer analysis**: getting customers to give the reasons why they have defected, and changing the way it does things.

Service providers, such as mobile phone or cable TV companies, have to deal with **churn**, the number of customers who go to another provider or stop using the service altogether each year.

In many services, satisfaction is hard to achieve because the **customer interaction** is difficult to control, which is why service organisations like airlines, banks and legal firms create high levels of dissatisfaction. If a product or service breaks down, fixing the problem may build **customer loyalty**, but it will also eat into the **profit margin**. Customers must be satisfied or delighted, but **at a profit**. If salespeople or call-centre staff or hotel receptionists are over-zealous, there may be lots of satisfied customers, but the business may be operating at a loss.

Kotler says that it is not companies that compete, but **marketing networks** comprising a number of companies. For example, a PC is assembled from components made by several manufacturers, sold through a call centre which may be a subcontractor, delivered by a transport company and perhaps **serviced** by yet another organisation as part of the manufacturer's **product support**. It is the customer's total experience that counts. Making the computer is just one part of this. The **logistics** of selling and organising the services needed by each customer becomes key.

Read on

Philip Kotler: *Marketing Management*, Prentice Hall, 1999 edition, ch. 2: 'Building Customer Satisfaction, Value, and Retention'

Adrian Palmer: *Principles of Services Marketing*, McGraw-Hill, 1998

Ron Zemke, John A. Woods: *Best Practices in Customer Service*, Amacom, 1999

Lesson notes

Warmer

- Write 'CUSTOMER SERVICE' in big letters on the board. Ask the Ss, in threes, to brainstorm briefly
  - what they understand by this term
  - what their own organisation or educational institution does in this area.

> There is this definition of customer service quoted at the beginning of the Business brief on page 86: 'all the activities involved in making it easy for customers to reach the right parties within the company and receive quick and satisfactory service, answers, and resolution of problems'. This relates mainly to situations where things have gone wrong.
>
> Customer service is also used in a neutral sense to talk about normal dealings when customers are buying products or services. Ss may refer to both these senses in their brainstorming sessions.
>
> Ss working in business will have something to say about customer service, whoever their customers are, whether business-to-business or business-to-consumer. It could be interesting to see how those working for government organisations view their 'customers' and what they understand by customer service. In the case of educational institutions, do they view their students as 'customers'? How are 'customer complaints' dealt with?

Overview

- Tell the Ss that in this unit they will be looking particularly at customer service.
- Ask the Ss to look at the Overview section at the beginning of the unit. Tell them a little about the things on the list, using the table on page 84 of this book. Tell them which points you will be covering in the current lesson and in later lessons.

Quotation

- Ask the Ss to look at the quotation. Can they think of other queuing situations that can be annoying (such as supermarket checkouts, buying tickets)? Do they have particularly bad incidents to recount?

Starting up

Ss talk about what irritates them and about the place of customer care in a company's success.

(A) – (B)

- Get the Ss to discuss the different points in both exercises in pairs. Say that there is some overlap between the items, e.g. unhelpful and indifferent service personnel. The main idea is to encourage Ss to think of specific incidents they have encountered, even ones of too much customer care,

for example the waiter who asks three times during the meal if everything is alright.

- Pairs report back to the whole class. Invite comments and encourage discussion.

Listening: New ideas in customer care

A customer service expert talks about satisfying and delighting customers.

(A) 🎧 10.1

- Ask the Ss to look at the question to prepare them for the first part of the interview.
- Play the first question and answer of the interview once or twice, explaining any difficulties.
- Play the first question and answer again once or twice, pausing it in order to give the Ss time to make a note of the examples.
- Elicit answers from the Ss.
- Invite comments and encourage discussion. Have your Ss ever had a 'wow!' experience with customer service? (Ask them how they say 'wow!' in their own language(s).)

> a) Doing the right thing:
>   - Doing what we promised to do
>   - Making sure mistakes do not happen
>   - Satisfying customers
>   - Being reliable, courteous
>   - Dealing with complaints quickly
> b) Delighting customers:
>   Example: You order a book from Amazon.co.uk at 5 pm and it arrives at 9 am the next morning.

(B) 🎧 10.1

- Ask the Ss to look at the question and play the second question and answer in the same way as the first.
- Elicit the answer from the Ss.

> In e-commerce, e-mail queries often end up in the Computer Services Department. The people there care more about the website than the customer's satisfaction with the company's products. Many companies fail to answer these e-mails.

(C) 🎧 10.2

- Ask the Ss to look at question 1. Ask someone to explain what a call centre is.
- Play the first question and answer of recording 10.2 once or twice, pausing to explain any difficulties. (Point out, if the Ss comment on it, that in this context we would normally say *call up a person's details* on a computer screen rather than *dial up a person's details*.)

Lesson notes

○ Elicit the answer from the Ss. Invite comments and encourage discussion about call centres, Ss' experiences of them, etc.

---

1   Advantage: Technology can improve customer service because the person at the call centre can call up all the customer's details on their computer screen and speak to them with all the necessary information at their disposal.
Disadvantages: You don't have a personal relationship of the type that people used to have with their bank managers. Also, call centre personnel have to answer a certain number of calls an hour and may not take the time to answer all your queries to your satisfaction.

○ Ask the Ss to look at question 2. Explain that a mortgage is a loan to buy a home, and that an endowment mortgage is a particular type of mortgage, but do not go into technicalities.

○ Play the last question and answer in the interview once or twice, pausing to answer any queries.

○ Elicit the answers from the Ss.

---

2 **a** true
   b true
   c false
   d true
   e true

Discussion: Customer complaints

Ss look at suggestions for ways of dealing with customer complaints and draw up a list of the best techniques for doing this.

○ Tell the Ss that they will be drawing up a shortlist of suggestions for dealing with customer complaints, and then compiling a list of the most useful ones.

○ Get Ss to work in threes. Half the threes in the class are As, and the other half are Bs. The As discuss the list of ways of dealing with customer complaints for Group A and the Bs those for Group B. Say that each group has to decide on the five most useful suggestions in its particular list.

○ Circulate and monitor. Do not intervene unless necessary. Note language points for praise and correction.

○ When the groups have made their shortlists, praise good language points from the discussion and work on three or four points that need improvement, getting individual Ss to say the correct forms.

○ Match each Group A with a Group B, getting the Ss to change places if necessary. Tell them that each group of six (three As and three Bs) has to negotiate a final list of six suggestions from the ten suggestions that they have chosen between them.

○ Circulate and monitor again. Do not intervene unless necessary. Note language points for praise and correction.

○ When the groups have made their final list, praise good language points from the discussion and work on three or

four points that need improvement, getting individual Ss to say the correct forms.

○ Ask each group of six for its final list. Compare the lists from different groups, invite comments and encourage discussion, perhaps comparing the customer service suggestions that are suitable in different contexts and with different cultures. (For example, putting things in writing might be seen as essential in some cultures, but just an extra burden on the already irritated customer in others.)

---

1 to 1

This discussion can be done 1 to 1. Ask the student to look at and discuss each list separately, choosing five points from each list. Ask them to explain the reasons for their choice. Then ask them to choose the six most important ones from the ten they have selected and, again, to explain their reasons.

Reading: Customer delight

Ss read about ways of going beyond mere customer satisfaction and creating customer delight.

○ Prepare the Ss for the questions by asking them about the WOM (word-of-mouth) factor. Ask individual Ss for examples of times when they have bought something (or avoided buying something) following advice from a family member, friend or colleague.

○ Ask the Ss to answer the questions in pairs.

○ Ask the pairs for their answers, noting the answers of each pair on the board.

The real figures (but don't tell the Ss yet) are

1   12
2   20
3   80%

B

○ Get the Ss to read the first three paragraphs of the article in the same pairs in which they were working in Exercise A. Ask them to find what the article says about the points they looked at in Exercise A.

○ Circulate, monitor and assist by explaining any difficulties.

○ Ask the pairs for their answers, comparing them with the ones they gave in Exercise A. Were they surprised? Invite comments and encourage discussion.

○ Ask the pairs to look at questions 1–4 in Exercise B and read the rest of the article. Tell the Ss they will have to justify their answers with specific quotes from the article.

○ Circulate, monitor and assist by explaining any difficulties.

○ Elicit answers and justify quotations from the Ss.

1 **a)** True: 'customer "delight" is the stated aim for companies battling to retain and increase market share.' (lines 5–8)

   b) False: 'many people do not like talking to machines' (lines 38–39) and even if the service is fast and automated, nothing in the article indicates that people prefer this to real face-to-face service.

   c) False: 'recommended ways of inducing customer delight include: under-promising and over-delivering.' (lines 56–59)

2 Because of the number of things that can go wrong: 'delays caused by weather, unclaimed luggage and technical problems' (lines 94–97). (A more common problem than lost luggage and you might like to suggest that the author may be confusing the two.)

3 In information technology, so that 'information is available instantly on screen' (lines 109–111). In training, so that staff have 'a winning telephone style' when dealing with calls about bookings and flight times (lines 98–99).

4 Staff in different departments treat each other 'as customers requiring the highest standards of service' (lines 116–118).

◉ Invite comments and encourage discussion about points raised in the article.

C

◉ Ask the Ss for their ideas about the points in Exercise C. Ask them for any instances of this that they have encountered themselves.

A danger here is that over-delivering may be expensive. If it is not foreseen in the company's business model, over-delivering may wipe out its profit margins. Under-promising may bring about a culture among employees that it's acceptable to promise less than is really possible, with the danger that they will then perform at this level, rather than remembering that they are supposed to deliver more than they promise.

D

◉ Ask the Ss to think, in pairs, of activities where customer service is critical. (Or you could ask them to talk about the place of customer care in their own industry.) Circulate, monitor and assist.

◉ Round up the answers with the whole class.

There are many possible answers, but they might mention banking and financial services, healthcare, and traditional and on-line retailing.

Vocabulary: Handling complaints

Ss look at words related to customer service and some common idioms, using them in context.

A

◉ Tell the Ss to look through the sentence parts. Ask them to match them as a quick-fire activity. Point out the pronunciation of *rapport* with its silent *t*.

1	complaints – e)
2	rapport – d)
3	reassure – a)
4	standards – b)
5	products – c)

B

◉ Ask the Ss to work on matching the idioms in pairs. Circulate, monitor and assist.

◉ With the whole class, do a round-up of the answers and explain any difficulties.

1 c	2 d	3 f	4 e	5 a	6 b	7 g

C

◉ Do this as a quick-fire activity with the whole class. Explain any difficulties.

1	get to the bottom of the problem
2	pass the buck
3	ripped off
4	slipped my mind
5	talking at cross purposes
6	it was the last straw
7	got straight to the point

Language review: Gerunds

Ss study gerund formation and the way that gerunds are used. The Ss then use them in drawing up guidelines about customer service.

A

◉ Go through the gerunds in the Language review box with the whole class. Refer back to the article in the Reading Section where this is mentioned, even if the Ss haven't read the article in full.

◉ Get the Ss to look at the article in pairs and find gerunds. Circulate and assist.

a) <u>Averting</u> 'phone rage'... (lines 28–29)

... <u>being cut off</u> in mid-conversation or [being] <u>left waiting</u> ... (lines 31–32). Point out that *left waiting* is part of the same type of passive gerund as *being cut off*, even if the second *being* is omitted.

... (<u>saying</u> that a repair will be carried out within five hours, but getting it done within two); <u>replacing</u> a faulty product immediately; <u>throwing in</u> a gift voucher as an unexpected thank you to regular customers; and always <u>returning</u> calls, even when they are complaints (lines 60–69)

<u>Aiming</u> for customer delight is all very well ... (lines 70–71)

... <u>delighting</u> passengers is an essential marketing tool ... (lines 90–92)

b) stimulate new business <u>by telling</u> up to 12 other people (lines 14–16)

the rapid growth <u>in obtaining</u> goods and services via telephone call centres and the Internet (lines 25–28)

delays <u>in answering</u> calls (line 30)

Recommended ways <u>of inducing</u> customer delight (lines 56–57)

This can be eased <u>by coupling</u> an apology and explanation ... (lines 75–77)

is considered vital <u>in handling</u> the large volume of calls (lines 99–101)

B – C

◉ Ss can work on these exercises in pairs. Circulate and assist.

◉ With the whole class, elicit the answers from the pairs.

A

1 b   2 a   3 d   4 c

B

Possible answers. Ss may suggest others.

1 returning
2 giving
3 doing / undertaking / commissioning
4 organising / running
5 drawing up / establishing / setting up
6 drawing up / establishing / setting
7 checking / examining / monitoring
8 dealing
9 ensuring / making sure
10 learning

Check your Ss' own ideas for improving customer service.

Skills: Active listening

Ss look at listening skills in the context of customer service. They listen to interviews with satisfied and angry customers and learn some key expressions.

A

◉ With the whole class, ask about the points here. Invite comments and encourage discussion.

B

◉ Divide the class into pairs or threes. Circulate, monitor and assist. Note language points for praise and correction, especially in relation to this topic.

◉ With the whole class, praise good language points from the discussion and work on three or four points that need improvement, getting individual Ss to say the correct forms.

◉ Ask the Ss for their suggestions. Invite comments and encourage discussion. Some interesting cultural issues should emerge here.

◉ *Look people directly in the eye at all times.* But don't overdo it. It will make them feel uncomfortable. How much eye contact is appropriate in your Ss' culture(s) a) between people of the same status, b) between people of differing status?

◉ *Nod your head often to show interest.* Again, don't overdo it. Ask your Ss about nodding in general: in their culture(s) does it indicate interest, agreement, something else, or nothing at all?

◉ *Repeat what the speaker has said in your own words.* Can be useful as a way of checking key points. Another useful technique is to repeat *exactly* some of the expressions the speaker has used.

◉ *Be aware of the speaker's body language.* People will be aware of this whether they try to be or not.

◉ *Interrupt the speaker often to show you are listening.* It's good to make some 'phatic' noises such as *aha, mmm, I see, right*. Ask your Ss how much it's normal to do this in their own language, and what the equivalent of *aha* is in their own language(s).

◉ *Think about what you are going to say while the speaker is talking.* Yes, but pay attention to what they are saying as well. Some cultures, such as Japan and Finland, allow the other person time for reflecting on what the first person has said before they are expected to respond. Ask the Ss if this is the case in their culture(s).

◉ *Use body language to show you are attentive.* Again, don't overdo it. It can be intimidating.

◉ *Try to predict what they are going to say next.* But don't jump to conclusions.

◉ *Ask questions if you do not understand.* Yes, but try to avoid questions that result from not having listened properly. If someone has to answer too many questions about what they said earlier, it will undermine rapport.

◉ *Say nothing until you are absolutely sure that the speaker has finished.* Butting in is the usual habit in some places. Ask your Ss what they think about this.

C 🎧 10.3

◉ Tell the Ss that they are going to hear three customers talking about their experiences. Ask your Ss to look at Question 1.

◉ Play the recording once right through, and then once again, stopping at the end of each conversation to allow the Ss to take notes.

1

Product/service	Why good/bad
1 Wine	The customer took back some wine to the shop because they and a guest hadn't liked it. The salesman told the customer to choose two other bottles to replace it, even if they were more expensive.
2 Flight	The speaker flew to Spain with their family on a no frills airline. The service was very friendly and helpful (the speaker has small children) and the flight was punctual.
3 Printer	This customer waited in all day for a new printer to be delivered, but it never arrived. The service on the phone was very friendly and helpful, but the printer didn't turn up for the rest of the week.

◉ With the whole class, ask individual Ss to summarise each incident. Use this as an opportunity to practise summarising skills. Say they should not get sidetracked by details such as what exactly was wrong with the wine, the fact there were no meals on the plane.

◉ Ask the Ss to look at the expressions in the Useful language box. Go through them in detail, practising intonation.

◉ Play recording 10.3 again, pausing where necessary. Get your Ss to underline the expressions from the language box that they hear.

◉ Check the answers with the whole class. Then get the Ss, in pairs, to add one or two expressions of their own under each heading.

◉ Check the suggestions with the whole class.

2

Expressions heard in the recording are underlined. One other expression is suggested for each heading in italics, but your Ss may have thought of others.

Showing interest
Really?
OK / *I see*

Showing empathy
How awful!
That must have been terrible!

Asking for details
What did you do?
Tell me more!

Clarifying
When you say ..., what are you thinking of?

Summarising
(So) if I understand you correctly ...

Repetition / Question tags
See 'Fruit juice?' in conversation 1.

A *Customer satisfaction levels are increasing?*
B *Increasing? / Are they?*

D

◉ Ask your Ss to talk about excellent and poor experiences in pairs. You can show the whole class the sort of thing you are looking for by asking an individual student for one of their experiences, and using some of the expressions in the Useful language box to ask them about it.

◉ When the class has understood the idea, start the discussions.

◉ Circulate, monitor and assist if necessary. Note language points for praise and correction, especially in relation to the language in this section.

◉ With the whole class, praise good language points from the discussion and work on three or four points that need improvement, getting individual Ss to say the correct forms.

◉ Ask for one or two public performances of the situations that the Ss just talked about so that the whole class can listen.

◉ Invite comments and encourage discussion about the situations.

Case study

Hermes Communications

Ss role play the handling of a range of customer complaints at a phone company.

Stage 1: Background

◉ Read the background information with the whole class and get one student to paraphrase it in their own words. Make sure they point out that this is a simulation of training course activities for employees of a phone company: a course within a course!

◉ Divide the class into two or four groups, depending on numbers. Half the groups (A) will look at complaints 2–3 and listen to situation 6. The other group(s) (B) will look at complaints 4–5 and listen to complaint 7.

◉ Tell the Ss that they should summarise the information in each complaint. Go through complaint 1 with the whole class to give them the idea.

Communi-cation type	Brief details of complaint	Anger level*	Action/ requested response / compensation	Priority**
1 e-mail	Query on bill, but can't get through on helpline	2	Customer will call at regional office on Monday	

* Score out of 3, where 1 = unhappy, 2 = cross and 3 = furious.

** This will be judged by each group when it has looked at its four situations. 1 = top priority, 4 = not urgent.

◉ When the Ss are clear about what they have to do, get them to read the complaints they have been assigned. Circulate, monitor and assist only if necessary.

◉ When Group(s) A have finished looking at their written complaints, ask them to come to one side of the room to listen to the recording of complaint 6. Tell them to take notes and summarise the situation as with the other situations.

◉ After that, when Group(s) B have finished looking at their written complaints, ask them to come to one side of the room to listen to the recording of complaint 7. Tell them to take notes and summarise the situation as with the other situations.

◉ Bring the whole class to order. Get a student from one of the Group As to come to the board and *quickly* summarise complaints 2, 3 and 7, something like this:

Communi-cation type	Brief details of complaint	Anger level*	Action/ requested response / compensation	Priority**
2 e-mail	Customer got through to helpline but was passed from department to department and eventually gave up.	2	None	3
3 e-mail	Topped up mobile phone with credit card, but account not credited. Unable to call an important customer.	3	Wants to know how they will be compensated.	2
6 Helpline	Over-pushy sales staff in one of our shops.	2	Did not want to name member of staff. Says we should look at our training methods.	4

If there is more than one Group A, ask the other groups for the priority levels they assigned to each situation. Invite comments and encourage brief discussion by the different groups about the basis on which they assigned the priority ratings.

⊚   Then get a student from one of the Group Bs to come to the board and *quickly* summarise situations 4–6 and 8, something like this:

Communi-cation type	Brief details of complaint	Anger level*	Action/ requested response / compensation	Priority**
4 Fax	Subscribed to cheap rate calls to US for six months, but we discontinued service after three months and requested an extra £30 for it to continue.	3	None requested.	1
5 Letter	Uses phone for up to three hours a day and gets headaches.	1	Would like us to comment.	2
7 Voice-mail	Pleased with replacement phone but would also like catalogue as previously requested.	1	Send catalogue.	3

If there is more than one Group B, ask the other groups for the priority levels they assigned to each situation. Invite comments and encourage brief discussion by the different Group Bs about the basis on which they assigned the priority ratings.

Stage 2: Written responses

⊚   Explain that pairs within each group will write replies (letters or e-mails) relating to the complaints they discussed, as if they came from the Customer Services Officer at Hermes Communications. Depending on time, each pair can write two or three responses. Make sure that each pair knows which situations they are going to reply to. (With complaint 1, it's enough for the Customer Service Officer to apologise for the inconvenience and say that they are looking forward to meeting the customer when they come to the regional office the following week.)

⊚   When the Ss are clear what they have to do, the writing activity can begin. Circulate, monitor and assist if necessary.

⊚   If particular complaints are being dealt with by more than one pair, tell them to exchange e-mails so that each pair can see and comment on the written communications of other pairs from the point of view of their effectiveness.

⊚   Bring the class to order and ask Ss to comment briefly on the effectiveness of other Ss' written responses.

⊚   In the language praise and correction phase, concentrate on the written language produced by the Ss. Praise good language points from their responses and work on three or four points that need improvement.

Stage 3: Role play

⊚   Remind your Ss about complaint 1. Divide the class into pairs. Ask them to role play the meeting between the customer and the Customer Services Officer.

⊚   Circulate, monitor and assist only if necessary. Note language points for praise and correction.

⊚   With the whole class, praise good language points from the discussion and work on three or four points that need improvement, getting individual Ss to say the correct forms.

⊚   If there's time, ask one pair to do a public performance of the situation for the whole class.

Stage 4: Other role plays

⊚   If there is enough time and student interest, you could ask them to role play some of the other situations, where dissatisfied customers meet or phone the Customer Services Officer.

⊚   The activity could begin with the irate customer brandishing one of the written responses produced earlier: they could be angry about the response they received.

⊚   Get different pairs to role play different situations. (Complaint 7 is not really suitable for this, unless the Ss ham it up as a customer who has time on their hands and absolutely wants to see the Customer Services Manager, even if it's only about a brochure and / or to thank them for the excellence of the customer service.)

⊚   Circulate, monitor and assist. Note language points for praise and correction.

⊚   Praise good language points from the discussion and work on three or four points that need improvement, getting individual Ss to say the correct forms.

⊚   If there's time, ask one or two pairs to do a public performance of the situation they role played for the whole class.

---

1 to 1

These activities can be done 1 to 1, with the student analysing the information and then discussing it with you. Don't forget to note language points for praise and correction afterwards. Highlight some of the language you chose to use as well.

Writing

- Remind the Ss that they are writing as if they were native speaker participants on a training course for employees of a phone company. Ask the Ss to think of the range and type of customer complaints that a phone company would have to deal with. Their reports to the Head of Customer Services could contain these points:
  - general opinion of the course
  - realism or otherwise of the situations
  - the way it has changed their way of dealing with customers
  - suggestions for improvements
  - ideas for other courses they would like to go on.

- This written work may provide some interesting insights into what the Ss thought about the situations and the role play activity as language learners, even if they are pretending to be native speaker participants on a communications training course. Use their feedback as a guide to planning future activities of this kind!

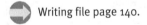 Writing file page 140.

Crisis management

	Classwork – Course Book	Further work
Lesson 1 *Each lesson (excluding case studies) is about 45–60 minutes. This does not include administration and time spent going through homework.*	**Starting up** Ss discuss the difference between a problem and a crisis, and look at the steps to take in crisis situations. **Listening: Coping with crises** An expert talks about how to deal with crisis situations, and gives some examples.	
Lesson 2	**Reading: Airline crashes** Ss read about how two airlines handled disasters in very different ways. **Vocabulary: Noun phrases with and without *of*** Ss look at these types of noun phrases and use them in context.	**Text bank** pages (176–179) **Practice File** Vocabulary (page 44)
Lesson 3	**Language review: Similarities and differences** Ss study the language for comparing things, and apply it to talk about different companies. **Skills: Asking and answering difficult questions** A chief executive answers difficult questions from journalists. Ss listen to the language used, and apply it themselves in a similar situation.	**Practice File** Language review (page 45) **ML Grammar and Usage** **Resource bank** (page 201)
Lesson 4 *Each case study is about 1½ to 2 hours.*	**Case study: Game over** Target Stores is accused of selling pirated software. Ss analyse the related information and role play Target's directors and media representatives at a press conference.	**Practice File** Writing (page 46)

For a fast route through the unit focussing mainly on speaking skills, just use the underlined sections.

For 1 to 1 situations, most parts of the unit lend themselves, with minimal adaptation, to use with individual students. Where this is not the case, alternative procedures are given.

Business brief

A crisis may well be an opportunity to test a company's capabilities, but it is an opportunity that most companies would prefer to do without. Some businesses never recover from disasters involving loss of life, such as these:

- PanAm and the Lockerbie bomb: terrorist attack;
- Townsend Thoresen and its capsized ferry off Zeebrugge, Belgium;
- Union Carbide and the Bhopal disaster: plant explosion.

Presumably, no amount of crisis management or **damage limitation** would have saved these organisations.

There are entire industries that live under a permanent cloud of crisis. For example, accidents and incidents around the world, small and large, have **discredited** the nuclear power industry and given it a permanently negative image. People perceive it as **secretive** and **defensive**. Its long-term future is uncertain.

In Britain, the beef industry has been severely damaged by the 'mad cow' crisis. This has also had repercussions for some state institutions. In future food crises, people will be less willing to believe the **reassurances** of the Ministry of Agriculture. The UK government has set up a Food Standards Agency to try and regain **credibility** in this area, but the crisis has only served to undermine confidence in the overall competence of the state.

Food and drink is a very sensitive issue. The mineral water and soft drinks companies that distribute contaminated products because of mistakes in their bottling plants know this all too well.

Even in disasters where there is no loss of life, the results can be dire, because they are situations that everyone can understand and relate to.

The new cruise ship that breaks down on its maiden voyage, or the liner that leaves on a cruise with workmen still on board because refurbishment is not finished, with passengers filming the chaos on their video cameras, scenes then shown on television, are **public relations nightmares**.

All the examples so far relate to the effect of crises on companies' external audiences: customers and potential customers. But businesses are also increasingly being judged on how well they treat their internal audience: their staff in crisis situations. Companies may offer **employee assistance programmes** to help them through difficult situations or **traumatic incidents**. For example, bank staff may be offered counselling after a bank robbery. This is part of the wider picture of how companies treat their people in general. A reputation for **caring** in this area can reduce **staff turnover** and enhance a company's overall **image** in society as a whole. This makes commercial sense too: high staff turnover is costly, and an image as a caring employer may have a positive effect on sales.

Read on

Michael Bland: *Communicating Out of a Crisis*, Macmillan, 1998

Harvard Business Review on Crisis Management, Harvard Business School Press, 2000

Robert Heath: *Crisis Management for Executives*, Prentice Hall, 1998

Mike Seymour, Simon Moore: *Effective Crisis Management*, Continuum, 1999

Lesson notes

Lesson notes

Warmer

- ◎ Write the word 'CRISIS' in big letters on the right of the board. Ask the Ss what the plural is, and write up 'CRISES' in big letters. Practise the pronunciation of both words.
- ◎ Then draw seven lines to the left of 'crisis' to represent words that can come in front of it, with the first letter of each word.
- ◎ Tell the Ss that some of the words relate to people, some to countries, and others to both. Say that you are going to give examples of each type of crisis situation, and the Ss must guess the related word.
- ◎ Read example 1 below and ask the Ss to guess the word.
- ◎ Continue with the other examples in the same way. If the Ss have trouble guessing the word, give the next letter and, if they still don't get it, one letter at a time until they do.

1 A child is ill and its parents are very worried and unable to go to work.
2 A country's money is fast losing its value in relation to the money of other countries, and the government wants to stop this.
3 A country has high unemployment, falling production and so on.
4 A country has problems in its banking system.
5 There is a border dispute between two countries, and they may go to war with each other.
6 Someone in their late 40s has feelings of uncertainty about their life and career.
7 A government cannot win votes in the country's parliament, and there may have to be an election.

1	domestic
2	currency
3	economic
4	financial
5	international
6	mid-life
7	political

Overview

- ◎ Tell the Ss that in this unit they will be looking particularly at crisis management.

  Ask the Ss to look at the Overview section at the beginning of the unit. Tell them a little about the things on the list, using the table on page 94 of this book as a guide. Tell them which points you will be covering in the current lesson and in later lessons.

Quotation

- ◎ Ask the Ss to look at the quotation. Discuss it with the whole class. If you have Chinese-speaking Ss, they may be able to write, explain and comment on the characters.
- ◎ Ask the Ss the questions:
  - What does it mean to say that a crisis can be an opportunity?
  - Is every crisis an opportunity?
- ◎ Invite quick comments and encourage brief discussion.

Starting up

Ss discuss the difference between a problem and a crisis, and look at the steps to take in crisis situations.

- ◎ With the whole class, ask the first question to one or two individual Ss to get the discussion going. Then ask the Ss to discuss Question 1 and the other questions in pairs.
- ◎ Circulate, monitor and assist if necessary. Note language points for praise and correction, especially ones relating to the pronunciation of *crisis* and *crises* and crisis language in general.
- ◎ Praise good language points from the discussion and work on three or four points that need improvement, getting individual Ss to say the correct forms.
- ◎ With the whole class, ask pairs for their answers. Invite comments and encourage discussion.

(B)

- ◎ Ask the Ss to discuss the points and complete the table in pairs. Say that they should find a logical order of presentation within each step.
- ◎ Circulate, monitor and assist.
- ◎ With the whole class, ask the pairs for their answers and write them on the board.

Before the crisis	During the crisis	After the crisis
◎ Write down and circulate your crisis management programme ◎ Try to predict what crises could occur ◎ Practise making decisions under stress ◎ Role play a potential crisis	◎ Set up a crisis management team* ◎ Inform the directors ◎ Disclose as much information as you can	◎ Find out what happened and how it happened ◎ Analyse the actions you took to deal with the situation ◎ Work out an action plan to ensure the crisis does not happen again

*Say that this step could also be done before the crisis, if the company decides to have a permanent team.

Lesson notes

Listening: Coping with crises

A crisis management expert talks about how to deal with crisis situations, and gives some examples.

Ⓐ

◎ Tell the Ss that they are going to listen to a crisis management expert. What do they think a crisis management expert does? What do they think she will say?

> Very large organisations (like BT) employ crisis management experts to plan for possible crises, give training to managers in dealing with them, etc.
> There are also consultancies that specialise in this. Firms without their own crisis management specialists go to such consultancies for advice, or bring them in to handle a particular crisis if one occurs.

Ⓑ 🎧 11.1

◎ Tell the Ss to note the crises that Jan Walsh mentions, and play the first question and answer once right through, and then again once or twice, stopping just after 'BP in Colombia'.

◎ Elicit the examples, and ask the Ss to elaborate on them if they can. If not, give them the details.

> 1 Shell 1: The Brent Spar incident
> Shell wanted to dump a disused oil rig in the Atlantic, but Greenpeace and other environmental organisations forced the company to tow it back to Norway so it could be dismantled. (1995)
> Shell 2: In Nigeria Shell has been accused of disrupting local communities and causing pollution in its drilling activities, and of failing to intervene with the Nigerian government when it sentenced to death Ken Saro-Wiwa, a novelist and political activist who had protested about the environmental damage caused by the oil industry. (also 1995)
> Nike has been accused, in recent years, of buying its trainers from sweatshop manufacturers offering very low wages and no worker representation.
> BP was accused of collaborating with the Colombian army in the suppression of political and environmental opposition to its activities there. (1996)

◎ Ask the Ss to look at question 2. Play the rest of the first answer, pausing at the end of each point to discuss these ideas.
  – reputation being like an investment from which you can make planned withdrawals. (The idea that a company can build up its reputation like money in the bank. There may be incidents that cause its reputation to suffer slightly (these are like withdrawals), but the company can make up for these in the long-term.
  – reputation seeping away or draining away. Explain these words, and ask the Ss what they understand by their use in this context.

◎ Ask the Ss to look at question 3. Play the second question and answer once or twice. Explain any difficulties and elicit the answer.

Ⓒ 🎧 11.2

◎ Ask the Ss to look at the text they have to complete. With the whole class, ask for ideas on what may be in the gaps, bearing in mind constraints of grammar and logic. Invite comments and encourage discussion.

◎ Play the first question and answer of recording 11.2 once right through, and then once or twice more, pausing to allow the Ss time to complete the gaps.

◎ Ask the Ss for answers and compare them with what they said originally.

> 1 speedily
> 2 what went wrong
> 3 communicating
> 4 loss
> 5 public confidence

Ⓓ 🎧 11.2

◎ Read out the question and play the relevant part of the recording once or twice, explaining any difficulties.

◎ Ask a student to summarise the situation without going into too much detail. Use this as an opportunity to develop summarising skills. Alternatively, get individual Ss or pairs to write one- or two-sentence written summaries. Ask Ss to read out their summaries and compare them.

Ⓔ 🎧 11.2

◎ Read out the question and play the last part of the recording once right through, and then once again, pausing to explain difficulties. Ask why Jan says 'Without being sued you mean' at the beginning.

◎ Ask a student to explain the point about ostriches. If no one gets it, draw an ostrich on the board, with its head in the sand. Ask if the Ss have heard the expression 'bury your head in the sand' in their own language(s).

Reading: Airline crashes

Ss read about how two airlines handled disasters in very different ways.

Ⓐ

◎ Ask the Ss to imagine that they are crisis management consultants. Ask them, in pairs, to draw up a list of recommendations in the form of dos and don'ts that they would give to an airline about what to do after a crash to protect its reputation.

◎ Circulate, monitor and assist if necessary.

◎ With the whole class, ask the pairs to read out their lists. Invite comments and encourage discussion.

Ⓑ
◎ Read the first part of the article with the whole class, as far as 'That is probably the only opportunity to build a trusting relationship with the family members,' he says. (line 61)

◎ Stop and explain where necessary, especially the vocabulary related to the topic, e.g. *left confidence in the airline intact* (lines 29–31), 'defining moment', '(line 37).

◎ Ask the Ss to compare the points made in the article up to this point with the lists of recommendations they came up with in Exercise A.

Ⓒ
◎ Ask your Ss to look at the table below the article and draw up and complete the information about Swissair. This should be easy, as it's exactly the same as for TWA for the first three points.

Crash site/Destination	North American coast/Europe
Casualties	No survivors
Cause of crash	Not fully explained
Public perception of airline	Earned praise for its efficiency
Effect on reputation	Increased confidence, if anything

◎ Tell the Ss to read the rest of the article in pairs and complete their tables with the missing information about Swissair.

◎ Circulate, monitor and assist if necessary.

Production of passenger list	Full manifest (list of passengers) issued within hours
Telephone communication	Fully functioning hotlines set up within hours
Treatment of relatives	Hundreds of counsellors ready to receive grieving families, immediate travel expenses covered
Political reaction	Praised by mayor
Press reaction	Favourable
Legal obligations	Legislation in force at time of crash
Agreements with other airlines	Agreement with Delta meant that Delta treated the crash as if it was itself involved

◎ With the whole class, ask pairs about what they put in their table.

◎ Ask the Ss what the *moral* of a story means (line 183). (Its overall lesson.) Ask what the *bottom line* is (last line on a company's profits). Finally, ask what the moral of this story is.

Ⓓ
◎ Ask the whole class for the answer.

> Swissair was helped by the fact that legislation was in place that forced it to have adequate procedures, and by its code-sharing agreement with Delta, which gave it more resources.

Vocabulary: Noun phrases with and without *of*

Ss look at these types of noun phrases and use them in context.

Ⓐ–Ⓑ
◎ Talk through the two types of noun phrases with the whole class. Look at the nouns and, where necessary, their pronunciation (*e.g. contingency*). Get Ss to do the two exercises in pairs.

◎ Circulate, monitor and assist.

◎ With the whole class, ask for the answers and discuss any difficulties.

Noun phrases with *of*	Noun phrases without *of*
admission of liability flow of information loss of confidence speed of response	action plan contingency plan damage limitation legal action press conference press release

> 1 speed of response
> 2 press conference
> 3 press release
> 4 flow of information
> 5 action plan
> 6 contingency plan
> 7 legal action
> 8 admission of liability
> 9 loss of confidence
> 10 damage limitation

◎ With the whole class, get individual Ss to recap the Swissair accident in the article in the reading section, using the expressions from this section.

Language review: Similarities and differences

Ss study the language for comparing things, and apply it to talk about different companies.

◎ Go through the expressions in the Language review box. The following comments may be useful for your Ss.

- *Both* – Notice that you don't say *the both*.

- *Neither* – Point out a) that it takes a singular verb, e.g. *Neither airline has* (not *have*) *a perfect safety record*, and b) that no other negatives are used with it: you don't say *Neither airline was not involved*.

- *Either* – Here, you can use another negative expression: *There were no survivors in either crash* or *There weren't any survivors in either crash*.

- *In contrast* – Point out that you can also say *by contrast*.

- With the section on modifying adjectives, adverbs and adverbial phrases, point out that you say *Swissair's response was **much faster** than TWA's*, but not *much more faster*.

Ⓐ

◎ Ask the Ss to look at the table from the reading section. In pairs, ask them to write (rather than just say) ten sentences, comparing the two airlines.

◎ Circulate, monitor and assist.

◎ With the whole class, ask pairs for their answers, writing them on the board and commenting on them where necessary.

Ⓑ

◎ Point out that some of the alternatives are grammatically impossible, for example *quite better* in question 1. Others may be grammatically possible, but are not factually true, for example 'There was a minimal difference in the way the way airlines handled the crises'.

◎ Ask the Ss to work on the exercise in pairs.

◎ Circulate, monitor and assist.

◎ With the whole class, ask pairs for their answers, discussing how they reached them.

◎ Write them on the board and underline the expressions in them as below. Tell the Ss that it's probably easier to learn and remember these expressions in blocks like this.

> 1 Swissair handled the crisis *far* better *than* TWA.
> 2 Swissair paid *much* more attention *to* people's accommodation needs.
> 3 Going by car is *nowhere near as* safe *as* travelling by air.
> 4 Some passengers feel *slightly* more confident if they can have a drink before flying.
> 5 There was a *substantial* difference in the way the airlines handled the crises.
> 6 In the 1950s, aircraft were *nothing like as* fast as they are today.

Ⓒ

◎ Ask your Ss to look at the information in Exercise C. Go through the table with the whole class and explain any difficulties.

◎ Explain that the idea is not just to repeat the information in the table, but to write a full, natural-sounding article, with information not necessarily in the form it appears here.

◎ Ask individual Ss to suggest the beginning of the article and write it on the board, something like this.

> There are some interesting lessons to be drawn from two parallel cases of contamination of drinks products last year. Clearwater had to withdraw its mineral water from all overseas markets, whereas United Drinks was forced to recall just one batch of its soft drinks from the US market. In the first case, Clearwater found that its mineral water had been contaminated at its source; in the second, United Drinks discovered that its soft drink product had been contaminated during manufacture ...

◎ Ask the Ss to complete the article in pairs, or individually for homework. If they are completing the article in pairs in class, circulate, monitor and assist. Note any strong points and any problems in writing, perhaps ones common to more than one pair.

◎ Praise good language points from the writing and work on three or four points that need improvement, getting individual Ss to say the correct forms.

◎ Get one or two pairs to read out their articles for the whole class. (If they do the exercise for homework, they can read them out in the next lesson.)

Skills: Asking and answering difficult questions

A chief executive answers difficult questions from journalists. Ss listen to the language used, and apply it themselves in a similar situation.

Ⓐ – Ⓑ 🎧 11.3

◎ Present the situation described, and tell your Ss that they are going to listen to a series of questions from journalists. Read through the questions with the whole class, explaining any difficulties. Ask if anything strikes them in the written version as being
a) neutral / polite   b) forceful / aggressive?
Emphasise that it may be difficult to judge until they hear the recording: words like *please* and *sorry* can be used quite aggressively.

◎ Write Ss' ideas on the board in note form to refer to later.

> **Possible answers**
> 1 Seems to imply that the question was not answered the first time, and may indicate forcefulness
> 2 *Please* in the middle of a question rather than at the beginning or end can imply irritation or impatience.
> 3 Like 1, seems to imply that the question was not answered the first time, and may indicate forcefulness.
> 4 Too early to say: all depends on intonation.
> 5 May be aggressive. The form *Do you deny that* ... may be designed to trip the speaker up.
> 6 Too early to say: all depends on intonation.
> 7 The form seems polite, but it might be used ironically.
> 8 The form seems polite, but again it might be used ironically: all depends on the intonation.
> 9 The double negative might trip the speaker up, as in 5.
> 10 Form seems polite, but there may be irony.
> 11 Another double negative. *Surely* is forceful.
> 12 Too early to say: all depends on intonation.

• Play recording 11.3 once right through, getting the Ss to listen particularly to the stress and intonation. Then play it again, pausing after each utterance and discussing its tone with the whole class. Compare these reactions with comments that you and the Ss made and noted on the board before hearing the recording.

1 a	2 b	3 b	4 a	5 b	6 a	7 a
8 b	9 b	10 a	11 b	12 a		

C

• Go through the answers with the whole class. Note comments on the board. A lot depends on the intonation and also on the skill of the speaker in handling difficult questions.

1 Could sound defensive in context implying that the question was aggressive.
2 Neutral / polite
3 Could be defensive, so question could have been forceful.
4 Seems neutral / but might sound defensive in context.
5 Seems neutral / but might sound defensive in context.
6 Forceful / aggressive.
7 Neutral / polite unless speaker is very skilled at handling difficult questions.
8 Speaker may genuinely not know or question was forceful / aggressive.
9 Neutral / polite.
10 Neutral / polite.
11 Seems defensive so question was probably forceful / aggressive.
12 Seems defensive so question was probably forceful / aggressive.

D

• Give the Ss the general background to the situation. Divide the class into managers from the mobile phone company and journalists.

• Ask the journalists to read their information on page 152 of the Course Book, and the managers theirs on page 148.

• Circulate and assist in the preparation of roles. Explain any difficulties.

• When the Ss have absorbed the basic information, in the managers' group, appoint a 'chief executive' who will lead the press conference. Explain to the managers that under the leadership of the chief executive, they must prepare a coherent strategy for the press conference: when to apologise, when to be defensive, etc.

• Among the journalists, appoint a senior journalist who will start the questioning. Tell all the journalists to take notes to record what the company managers say at the press conference, so as to be able to write an article about it.

• When each side has prepared, ask the managers to leave the room and come in together, sitting at the front of the room, as if at a press conference.

• Tell the lead journalist to start the questioning and then encourage the other journalists to put their questions.

• Note language points for praise and correction, especially in relation to the question-and-answer types above. Only intervene if the questioning falters.

• When the press conference runs out of steam, ask the Chief Executive to wind it up and thank the journalists for attending.

• Praise good language points from the press conference and work on three or four points that need improvement, getting individual Ss to say the correct forms.

• Ask the managers and the journalists about their relative strategies and methods. Invite comments and encourage discussion.

• As a written follow-up, you could ask
  – the journalists to write an article based on the press conference.
  – the managers to write an internal memo about what happened at the press conference and about how successful they thought their strategy was.

1 to 1

This press conference can be done as a 1 to 1 interview. Ask your student which side they would prefer to represent. You represent the other side. Give the student plenty of time to prepare and absorb the information. Afterwards, ask the student about their strategy for the press conference and the tactics they were using.

Case study

Game over

Target Stores is accused of selling pirated software. Ss analyse the related information and role play Target's directors and media representatives at a press conference.

Stage 1: Background

• Ask the Ss to read the *Euronews* article about Target Stores. Meanwhile, write the points in the first column of the table on the board.

• With the whole class, elicit the information to complete the table.

Activity	Retailing
Accusation made against the organisation	Selling pirated computer games
Number of units involved	50,000
Price	Very low
CEO's reaction	Can't be true, company known for its integrity and high ethical standards
One employee's comment	Problems in buying department recently, high staff turnover, low morale

- Ask the Ss to look at the company profile while you write the points in the first column of the next table on the board.
- Elicit information from the Ss to complete the table.

Based in	Dublin
Store locations	Most European cities
History	Started by selling stationery and books, then magazines and music products
Main product	Computer games and other software
Customers	Teens and young adults
Image	Quality products at affordable prices, high ethical standards
Slogan	'We put people first.'

- Ask the Ss to quickly look through the sales figures.
- With the whole class, ask individual Ss to summarise the information in full sentences, for example
  - Target Stores has a workforce of 8,000.
  - It had sales of 720 million euros and last year it made a profit of 90 million euros.
  - Computer software and games make up 30% of Target's sales revenue, followed by stationery and cards, with 24% ... etc.

Stage 2: Listening 🎧 11.4

- Play recording 11.4 once right through.
- Explain any difficult language.
- Play the recording again, stopping frequently to ask quick-fire questions. For example, play as far as *Well, yes there is unfortunately* and ask if the accusation is true. Elicit the answer. Play the recording as far as *wouldn't accept any responsibility for them* and ask if the supplier knew the games were pirated, etc.
- At the end, get an individual to summarise the situation.

Stage 3: Press conference preparation

- Divide the class into two groups. Explain that there will be a press conference where journalists will question Target's management of the situation. Two to six students will role play Target's management team (see below). The other Ss will play journalists. The two groups will prepare for the role play separately.
- Ask the journalists to look at their information on page 151 of the Course Book, looking at their objectives and then the results of their enquiries. If there are more than about four journalists, ask them to prepare questions for the press conference in sub-groups, afterwards choosing the best questions to ask in one group.

- Ss who will role play Target's management team include
  - Chief Executive
  - Director of Public Relations
  - Director of Human Resources
  - Head of Legal Department
  - Marketing Director
  - an outside consultant from a crisis management firm.
  (It's enough to have Ss playing the first two or three roles if the class is small.)
- Ask the Ss role playing the management team to look at their information on page 146 of the Course Book, looking at their objectives a–c and then the results of their enquiries.
- Circulate, monitor and assist with both groups if necessary. Tell Target's Chief Executive that he / she will make a brief opening statement about why the press conference has been called and then invite questions from the journalists.

Stage 4: The press conference

- When the Ss are ready, the press conference can begin. Ask the managers to go out of the room and then come in again and sit at the front of the class. The Chief Executive makes the opening statement and then invites questions.
- Note language points for praise and correction.
- Do not intervene unless necessary, but make sure that journalists are asking follow-up questions if the answers to their original questions are not satisfactory.
- Give yourself enough time to discuss the language and other points arising at the end of the session, and ask Target's Chief Executive to wind up the press conference.
- Praise good language points from the role play and work on three or four points that need improvement, getting individual Ss to say the correct forms.
- Ask Target's management team and the journalists how they thought the press conference went.

---

1 to 1

This case study can be done 1 to 1. Instead of the press conference, you can be a journalist interviewing Target's CEO. Don't forget to note language points for praise and correction afterwards. Highlight some of the language you chose to use as well.

Writing

- Go through the information with the Ss, making clear what they have to do.
- Ask the Ss to write their report collaboratively in class or as homework.

 Writing file page 144.

Management styles

At a glance

	Classwork – Course Book	Further work
Lesson 1 *Each lesson (excluding case studies) is about 45–60 minutes. This does not include administration and time spent going through homework.*	**Starting up** Ss comment on some statements about management style and talk about the management style of parents. **Vocabulary: Management qualities** Ss look at vocabulary relating to management qualities and use it to discuss different management styles. **Listening: Management styles and qualities** Ss listen to an expert talking about the qualities of good managers and the range of management styles found in companies.	**Practice File** Vocabulary (page 48)
Lesson 2	**Reading: Who would you rather work for?** Ss read two contrasting articles about women as managers, and say which ideas they agree with. **Language review: Text reference** Ss look at the ways texts are held together by words like *it*, *this* and *they*.	**Text bank** pages (180–183) **Practice File** Language review (page 49) **ML Grammar and Usage**
Lesson 3	**Skills: Putting people at ease** Ss look at the language for small talk and use it in a number of situations.	**Resource bank** (page 202)
Lesson 4 *Each case study is about 1½ to 2 hours.*	**Case study: Zenova** Ss analyse an international group where management style is causing problems, and suggest ways in which it could be improved and made more consistent.	**Practice file** Writing (page 50)

For a fast route through the unit focussing mainly on speaking skills, just use the underlined sections.

For 1 to 1 situations, most parts of the unit lend themselves, with minimal adaptation, to use with individual students. Where this is not the case, alternative procedures are given.

Business brief

Traditionally, the model for **leadership** in business has been the army. Managers and army officers give orders, and their **subordinates** carry them out. Managers, like army officers, may be sent on leadership courses to develop their **leadership skills**. But some would say that leaders are born, not made, and no amount of training can change this. The greatest leaders have **charisma**, a powerful, attractive quality that makes other people admire them and want to follow them. A leader like this may be seen as a **visionary**. Leaders are often described as having **drive**, **dynamism** and **energy** to inspire the people under them, and we recognise these qualities in many famous business and political leaders. The leadership style of a company's boss can influence the management styles of all the managers in the organisation.

In some Asian cultures, there is management by **consensus**: decisions are not **imposed** from above in a **top-down approach**, but arrived at in a process of **consultation**, asking all employees to contribute to decision making, and many western companies have tried to adopt these ideas. Some commentators say that women will become more important as managers, because they have the power to build consensus in a way that the traditional **authoritarian** male manager does not.

One recent development in consensual management has been **coaching** and **mentoring**. Future senior managers are 'groomed' by existing managers, in regular one-to-one sessions, where they discuss the skills and qualities required in their particular **organisational culture**.

Another recent trend has been to encourage employees to use their own **initiative**: the right to take decisions and act on their own without asking managers first. This is **empowerment**. **Decision making** becomes more **decentralised** and less **bureaucratic**, less dependent on managers and complex formal management systems. This has often been necessary where the number of management levels is reduced. This is related to the ability of managers to **delegate**, to give other people responsibility for work rather than doing it all themselves. Of course, with empowerment and delegation, the problem is keeping control of your operations, and keeping the operations profitable and on course. This is one of the key issues of modern management style.

Empowerment is related to the wider issue of company **ownership**. Managers and employees increasingly have shares in the firms they work for. This of course makes them more **motivated** and **committed** to the firm, and encourages new patterns of more responsible behaviour.

Read on

Robert Benfari: *Understanding and Changing Your Management Style*, Jossey-Bass, 1999

Gareth Lewis: *The Mentoring Manager*, Financial Times Prentice Hall, 1999

Eric Parsloe: *The Manager as Coach and Mentor*, Chartered Institute of Personnel and Development, 1999

Role of the Manager, Financial Times Prentice Hall (Heriot-Watt BA course), 1998

John Wilson: *Management Style*, Hodder & Stoughton, 2000

Lesson notes

Warmer

◎ Write 'MANAGEMENT STYLE' in big letters on the board. Ask the Ss to brainstorm what they understand by this term.

◎ Ask them for their definition ('the way that managers relate to and deal with the people under them' or something similar, if your Ss are stuck). Invite comments and encourage brief discussion to arouse interest, without pre-empting the topics in the unit.

Overview

◎ Ask the Ss to look at the Overview section at the beginning of the unit. Tell them a little about the things on the list, using the table on page 102 of this book as a guide. Tell them which points you will be covering in the current lesson and in later lessons.

Quotation

◎ Read out the quotation and ask the Ss to comment. (This quotation should not be too controversial!)

◎ Write 'MANAGEMENT IS …' on the board, adding 'tasks' and 'discipline' one above the other on the right of the board. As a quick-fire, whole-class activity, get the Ss to give you other words that could follow 'Management is …'. Ss might say 'structure' and 'organisation' but also encourage more unexpected words like 'imagination', 'vision' and 'creativity'.

Starting up

Ss comment on some statements about management style and talk about the management style of parents.

Ⓐ

◎ Ask the Ss to comment on the statements in pairs. Circulate and assist with any difficulties.

◎ With the whole class, discuss the pairs' findings. If there are Ss from more than one country, obviously be tactful and do not disparage any particular style. However, there should be some interesting material for cross-cultural comparisons, even if the Ss are from the same country, but thinking about different companies with different management styles.

Emphasise that there are no 'right' answers, but here are some ideas:

1 A good idea if the department is small enough (but be careful with people who dislike mixing their personal and professional lives).

2 This could seem intrusive, but was for a long time seen as a manager's prerogative, and may still be in some places.

3 Most people enjoy occasional praise. Criticism must be constructive, and not degenerate into bullying.

4 Most employees would probably like managers to arbitrate in at least some disputes.

5 People with specific, hard-earned skills may be happy to be able to do things that their managers are unable to do.

6 Some companies have an 'open-door' policy, and encourage employees to take comments and pursue grievances to the highest level. Others would not encourage this. 'At all times' might mean being able to phone your manager at home until late in the evening, but in many places there is a strict division between home and work and you would not be able to do this.

7 There are probably two basic types of manager here, those who do get involved in socialising with staff, and those that find it easier to manage by staying clear. Again, this can be a cultural issue.

8 Probably a good idea in theory, but many organisations are known for profane language between employees when away from customers with, at times, highly-developed in-house slang. Racist or sexist comments should not be tolerated, of course.

9 True in many, if not most cultures. But there are managers who pride themselves on finishing the day on time, for example by refusing to be distracted from the tasks at hand, and gain the admiration of their less organised employees for being able to do this.

10 Staff with customer contact would probably expect to be commented on if their appearance is not up to scratch. Others might find it more difficult to accept this. There are many employer–employee disputes in this area, of course.

Ⓑ

◎ Again, be tactful. Ask the Ss to comment on the statements in pairs and then ask the pairs to report to the whole class. Invite comments and encourage discussion.

Vocabulary: Management qualities

Ss look at vocabulary relating to management qualities and use it to discuss different management styles.

 A

⊚ Ask your Ss to work in pairs to complete the table. Point out that in some places there can be more than one form. Circulate and assist with the meanings and pronunciation of unfamiliar words. You could ask the Ss to use a dictionary such as the *Longman Dictionary of Contemporary English*.

1 Adjective	2 Opposite adjective	3 Noun form
considerate	inconsiderate	consideration / considerateness
creative	uncreative	creativity / creativeness
decisive	indecisive	decisiveness
diplomatic	undiplomatic	diplomacy
efficient	inefficient	efficiency
flexible	inflexible	flexibility
inspiring	uninspiring	inspiration
interested	disinterested / uninterested	interest
logical	illogical	logic / logicality
organised	disorganised	organisation
rational	irrational	rationality
responsible	irresponsible	responsibility
sociable	unsociable	sociability
supportive	unsupportive	support

> Where there is more than one form:
> *Disinterested* means 'able to judge a situation fairly because you will not gain any advantage from it'. But tell the Ss that it is now also being used with the same meaning as *uninterested* and, even if some native speakers disapprove of this, they will certainly hear or see it being used this way.
> Where there are alternative forms for nouns, say that they are more or less interchangeable when talking about people, though some forms (such as *creativity*) are more frequently used than the other.

⊚ Discuss the answers with the whole class, but don't get bogged down talking about the alternative forms.

B – **C**

⊚ First of all, check that your Ss have understood the words by going round the class and getting the Ss to start sentences with 'A manager should be ...' followed by the different adjective forms and a potted definition. For example
  – A manager should be inspiring. They (avoid clumsy *He or she*) should give people energy and the feeling that they can achieve something.
  – A manager should be sociable. They should be friendly and easy to talk to.

⊚ When you have done one or two as examples, ask your Ss to prepare the remaining words in pairs.

⊚ With the whole class, ask the Ss to read out their definitions and correct any misunderstandings.

⊚ Then ask the Ss to work in pairs on their four top qualities and their four worst ones, adding one more quality and weakness of their own. Circulate and monitor.

⊚ With the whole class, write up the scores given by each pair to each quality and each weakness, and calculate scores to find the most 'popular' qualities and weaknesses. Invite comments and encourage discussion.

D

⊚ Do as a quick-fire activity with the whole class. Explain the meanings of unfamiliar words and practise pronunciations.

1 d	2 c	3 a	4 b	5 f	6 e

E

⊚ Rather than discussing this topic in the abstract, get the Ss to talk in pairs or threes about particular work situations in their organisation and the appropriate style for each situation. With the whole class, ask the pairs and threes for their comments and encourage discussion. (If your Ss are pre-work, they may find it difficult to talk about this. If so, move on to the next exercise.)

F

⊚ Get Ss to talk about these points in pairs and threes and then report back to the whole class. The answers to this will depend to a certain extent on cultural expectations. Treat tactfully.

Listening: Management styles and qualities

Ss listen to an expert talking about the qualities of good managers and the range of management styles found in different companies.

A 🎧 12.1

⊚ Tell the Ss they have to listen out for five qualities of good managers. Play the recording once right through, then once or twice more explaining any difficulties.

⊚ Elicit answers from the Ss. Play relevant parts of the recording again if anything is still unclear. Invite comments and encourage discussion.

1	time-management
2	dealing with complexity
3	dealing with uncertainty
4	dealing with people
5	flexibility

Lesson notes

Ⓑ 🎧 12.2

◎ Ask the Ss to look at the five company names to prepare them for what they are going to hear about each company. Play recording 12.2 once right through, then once or twice more explaining any difficulties.

◎ Elicit answers from the Ss. Play relevant parts of the recording again if anything is still unclear. Invite comments and encourage discussion.

---

1 **General Electric:** Jack Welch has re-energised the company – ability to change and keep changing – was Neutron Jack (explain *decimate* as *destroy* in the sense of completely reorganising or selling off certain parts of the company) – now into training people for the future and into communication. (Welch has now retired.)

2–3 **Virgin and Body Shop:** Management led by sound values (under Richard Branson and Anita Roddick respectively).

4 **IKEA:** Brilliantly managed, networked organisation. (Ask the Ss what they understand by this: that communication between all parts of the organisation is good.)

5 **Nokia:** Innovative and imaginative – out of wood products and into mobile phones.

(Ss might notice that the heads of IKEA and Nokia are not named, and that their management style seems to be embodied in the organisation rather than a particular person. Ask them if they know anything about their leaders. IKEA developed under its founder Ingvar Kamprad, who was responsible for encouraging informality as the company style, a style that has continued without him. Anders Dahlvig is its current head. Nokia is currently managed by Jorma Ollila: see the Reading section of Unit 4 Success.)

Ⓒ 🎧 12.3

◎ Play recording 12.3 once or twice. You may have to explain *reconcile*. Ask the Ss to guess the meaning of *echelons* (= levels).

◎ Ask a student to paraphrase what they have heard, and if they agree with the ideas. Invite comments and encourage discussion.

Reading: Who would you rather work for?

Ss read two contrasting articles about women as managers, and say which ideas they agree with.

Ⓐ

◎ Tell the Ss that they are going to read an article about women as bosses. Ask them if they would prefer a man or a woman as a manager, and note the results on the board in a table like the one opposite:

	Male class participants	Female class participants
would prefer a male boss		
would prefer a female boss		
no preference		

◎ Compare responses, and encourage (tactful) discussion.

Ⓑ

◎ With the whole class, read the first paragraphs of the two articles aloud, explaining any difficulties.

◎ Ask individual Ss for the main point of each paragraph. (Article A: the best managers are women; article B: the best managers are men.)

Ⓒ

◎ Divide the class into pairs and ask one member of each pair to read article A and the other article B. Tell them to read the whole article right through once and then again, writing a summary (of 15 words or less) of each paragraph as they read.

◎ Circulate, monitor and assist with any difficulties. Check that the Ss are on the right lines in their written summaries.

◎ With the whole class, ask individual Ss to read out their summaries. Write a summary for each paragraph on the board and discuss how they can be improved.

Suggested summaries

Article A

1 Women are better managers than men, according to a recent report.

2 The report criticises men's abilities as managers in business today.

3 The report found women have better attitudes towards others and men are more selfish.

4 Women are now seen as natural managers and can show their true nature.

5 The findings were the same in another report in the US.

6 The UK report found that women organise their time better.

7 Women may save their companies money because people prefer to ask men for a rise.

8 If men want to succeed as managers, they should behave more like women.

Article B

1 Men are better managers than women.

2 A recent report found more secretaries prefer a male boss to a female one.

3 This goes against the idea that today women are better suited to be bosses.

4 One psychologist disagrees: he thinks women are better than men at many business tasks.

5 The number of women directors is increasing.

6 One woman interviewed said that women are more personal in their criticism.

7 Another said that there are status problems when women work for other women.

D – F

- Ask the Ss to work, in pairs, on both articles to find the words in Exercise D, and the female characteristics in Exercise E.

- With the characteristics, tell the Ss to note also the characteristics that are mentioned more in relation to men to emphasise how women are different: see the list below, e.g. *less egocentric, less likely to steal credit for others' work*.

- Circulate, monitor and assist.

- With the whole class, ask for the words and discuss their meanings and use if necessary.

- Then discuss women's characteristics, clarifying any difficulties. Tactfully ask the Ss for their own opinions. Invite comments and encourage discussion.

Exercise D

1 counterparts
2 indictment
3 egocentric
4 autocratic
5 aspired
6 traits
7 emphatic
8 anecdotal
9 disparity
10 assert

Exercise E
Article A

efficient
trustworthy
better understanding of the workforce
generous with their praise
more modern outlook
more open minded
more considerate
less egocentric
less likely to steal credit for others' work
less self-obsessed
less autocratic
good at teamwork
good at communicating with their staff
use time more effectively
able to juggle commitments

Article B

(The article starts by saying that ideally managers should be sympathetic, empowering, able to delegate and interested in the career development of those who work under them, but it doesn't say that these characteristics are specifically masculine or feminine; the article only perhaps later implies that some people think they are more common in male managers, but this is not explicitly stated.)
Characteristics that women do have, according to the article, are
listening skills
flexibility
more empathetic manner
less status-conscious
conduct crisper (more efficient) meetings
more effective negotiators
greater flexibility
more personal in their criticism
more status-conscious in relation to other women

Language review: Text reference

Ss look at the ways texts are held together by words like *it*, *this* and *they*.

- Go through the points in the Language review box with the whole class, explaining any difficulties.

- Do question 1 with the whole class to give the Ss the idea.

- Then ask them to answer questions 2 and 3 in pairs.

1   They will be aware of the pressures of your job, but delegate responsibility where appropriate. They will be interested in your career development. Oh, and, preferably, they will be male. (lines 3–8)

2   They listen more, are less status-conscious, … (lines 40–41)
    They are also considerably more common than they used to be. (lines 45–46)
    … they occupy a third of the seats round the conference table. (lines 50–51)
    When they are critical they are much more personal …
    … or they try to assert themselves by giving you really menial tasks. (lines 65–68)

3   a) (empty subject)
    b) the Royal Mail report
    c) people
    d) John Nicholson
    e) the reason women don't like to work for other women
    f) the reason women don't like to work for other women
    g) the situation of giving work to other women
    h) try to assert themselves by giving menial tasks

 B

◎   Point out that the extract is a continuation of article B above. Do the exercise as a quick-fire activity with the whole class.

1	them
2	they
3	it
4	they
5	we
6	their
7	they

Skills: Putting people at ease

Ss look at the language for small talk and use it in a number of situations.

 A

◎   Discuss question 1 with the whole class. Ask the Ss if there is an expression in their own language(s) for *small talk* and ask them to translate it into English.

◎   Go round the whole class and get lists of suitable and unsuitable topics from the Ss and write them up on the board. If your Ss are from more than one country, write up the different lists.

◎   Treat the subject tactfully, especially the hot potatoes of politics and religion. (You might want to teach the expression *hot potato*.)

B

◎   Ask the Ss to work on the possible questions in pairs. Circulate and monitor.

◎   Then get the pairs to integrate the questions and answers into a longer, natural-sounding conversation. Point out that the phrases do not have to be used in the same order as in the Course Book, and can be adapted. The Ss can use extra phrases as well. Circulate, monitor and assist, especially with intonation.

◎   Ask one or two pairs to give performances for the whole class.

Example conversation (with expressions from the Course Book underlined):

Host: How was the flight from London?
Visitor: Terrible. There was a lot of turbulence and several people were sick. It was a nightmare. Anyway, I'm here now. Good to be here!
Host: Have you been to Rome before?
Visitor: Yes, several times. I've been on a couple of business trips. And I came on a school trip back in 1968. A long time ago, but very memorable!
Host: Really! That was quite a year here! What's it like being back?
Visitor: I'm really impressed. The architecture is fascinating. I hope I have time to take it all in. I want to go back to all the old sites: the Pantheon, the Coliseum, the Vatican … I'm going to stay on here over the weekend and do a bit of sightseeing!
Host: Excellent! Where's your hotel?
Visitor: Right in the centre. The Grand.
Host: What's it like? Not too much noise from the traffic I hope. Rome's a very noisy city, as you probably remember.
Visitor: No, actually my room's very quiet. The Grand's very comfortable, and the service is first class.
Host: How's the family?
Visitor: They're all well, thanks very much. My son's just about to go to university, so there's a lot of excitement in the house.
Host: Which university? What's he going to do?
Visitor: He's applied to do economics at Oxford.
Host: Oh yes? My daughter did a year at Oxford as part of her English degree. She loved it! … Had time to do any sport recently?
Visitor: I enjoy tennis, when I get the time. But you know the problem with time!
Host: Yes, everyone's working harder and harder these days. It's the same everywhere! Anyway, talking of work, shall we make a start?
Visitor: By all means.

C

◎   Ask the Ss to discuss the questions in pairs or threes. Circulate, monitor and assist.

◎   With the whole class, ask the pairs or threes to talk about their conclusions.

◎   Invite comments and encourage discussion with the whole class.

1 The Ss may mention it themselves, but you could bring up ways of socialising in specific parts of the world, for example being taken to restaurants for long lunches in Paris, sporting events or concerts in the UK (corporate hospitality) or karaoke bars in Japan. You could discuss whether or not business visitors and colleagues are invited to people's homes.

2 Ask your Ss about the acceptance (or otherwise) of silence in their own cultures. They may refer to the importance of silence in meetings in places such as Finland and Japan as a sign of respect, showing that you are giving thought to what the other person has said.

3 Answers to this question will be more personal, but there may be cultural differences between Ss from different places. If so, treat with tact.

(D)–(E)

◎ Do Exercise D as a quick-fire activity with the whole class.

| 1 c | 2 e | 3 a | 4 b | 5 d |

◎ Ask the whole class what they think about this advice and about what they would say themselves to put people at their ease.

One of the issues here will be the use of names. Ask the Ss about what is usual and acceptable in their own countries. Ask them whether the situation is changing.
The appropriateness of asking about personal problems and family could also be discussed.

(F)

◎ Underline that the idea here is that the Ss are meeting someone for the first time. They have to choose four subjects to talk about.

◎ Say that for the purposes of this activity, they are in a culture where silences are embarrassing and to be avoided, and tell the Ss that they should try to make graceful transitions between the subjects!

◎ Circulate, monitor and assist only if necessary. Note language points for praise and correction, especially in relation to small talk.

◎ Praise good language points from the activity and work on three or four points that need improvement, getting individual SS to say the correct forms.

◎ Ask one or two pairs to give performances for the whole class.

Case study

Zenova

Ss analyse an international group where management style is causing problems, and suggest ways in which it could be improved and made more consistent.

Stage 1: Background

◎ Ask the Ss to read the background information about Zenova Industries. Meanwhile, write the points in the first column of the table on the board.

◎ With the whole class, elicit the information to complete the table.

Activity of company	Multinational pharmaceuticals, health and beauty products manufacturer
Project team working on	Implementation of global Customer Care Policy (CCP)
Current approach	Project team – 250 staff from different subsidiaries in Europe, America, Asia – working on implementation of CCP
Structure of team	12 managers each with 10–30 staff
Current problems caused by	Different management styles within team
State of staff	Unhappy; poor morale
Risk	Project won't be completed on time
Current solutions	Questionnaires to and interviews with staff

Stage 2: Analysing the questionnaire findings

◎ Depending on time, the questionnaire and the interviews can be analysed in parallel by different groups who then report back to each other, or all the groups can work on the questionnaire findings and then work on the interviews. The second approach is the one described here.

◎ Divide the class into threes or fours to analyse the questionnaires.

◎ Get your Ss to relate the figures in the questionnaires to the points under 'Evaluation of findings: Checklist'.

◎ Explain anything that may cause problems, e.g. troubleshooting.

◎ Get the groups to give a score out of 10 to each point analysed in the questionnaire:
10 = Zenova Industries is doing very well in this area, 1 = very badly.

- Groups may come up with different scores, but this doesn't matter.
- When the groups have discussed each issue and decided on a score for it, call the class to order and write the scores of the different groups on the board.
- If you have four groups, the results for the first two issues might look like this:

	Group 1	Group 2	Group 3	Group 4
Delegation	6	7	5	6
Feedback	4	3	3	2
Briefing				
Troubleshooting				
Teambuilding				
Coaching				
Motivation				

- Complete the table. Invite comments and encourage brief discussion by asking each group to explain how they arrived at their scores, but don't pre-empt the meeting in Stage 4 below. (For example, some groups may be more encouraged than others by the scores for *sometimes* and give them more importance.)

Stage 3: Analysing the interviews 12.4

- Play the interviews to the whole class, once right through and a second time explaining any difficulties. Ask Ss to make notes about the points on the Evaluation of findings checklist.
- Alternatively, if the room is big enough and you have more than one cassette / CD player, different groups can listen to the recordings separately, each with its own player, and make notes. In this case, circulate, monitor and assist.
- Ask the groups to give scores to the points on the checklist, this time in relation to what they heard in the interviews.
- Then get the Ss to combine the scores from the questionnaires and the interviews to get the overall picture. Invite comments and encourage brief discussion, but don't pre-empt the meeting in Stage 4 below.

Stage 4: The meeting

- When the whole class has got the overall picture, divide it into small groups again: the same threes and fours as earlier.
- Each group must review its findings and, above all, suggest solutions to achieve a more consistent management style and improve the team's morale and efficiency. Emphasise this by writing an agenda for the meetings.

Agenda
1 Review your findings.
2 How can Zenova Industries achieve a more consistent management style?
3 How can the CCP project team's morale and efficiency be improved?

- Get each group to appoint someone to take notes about who says what and about the group's recommendations. The notes must be particularly clear if you are going to ask the Ss to do the follow-up writing task: see below.
- When the Ss are clear what they have to do, the meetings can begin. Circulate, monitor but do not intervene unless necessary.
- Note language points for praise and correction, especially in relation to management styles.
- When the groups have finished, call the class to order.
- Praise good language points from the discussion and work on three or four points that need improvement, getting individual Ss to say the correct forms.
- Ask the groups for their recommendations on points 2 and 3 of the agenda, and write them on the board. Invite comments and encourage discussion from the whole class.

If the groups find it difficult to come up with ideas for improving the situation, you could mention and get the Ss to discuss the following.
- Write a **mission statement** about the kind of management qualities the company wants.
- Organise **residential training** to bring managers and staff together outside the workplace in **team-building exercises**. Training could be a physical activity such as canoeing or rock climbing.
- Organise **specific training** for managers on people management issues, including assertiveness training and communication skills training.
- Institute regular **360-degree performance appraisal sessions** for everyone. Managers and employees are appraised by their superiors, colleagues and subordinates.
- Get **senior managers to take a leading role** in showing other managers how to 'lead from the front'.
- Organise **regular mentoring sessions** where managers discuss employees' progress, careers and company strategy.
- Organise **reverse mentoring sessions**, where junior staff give training and guidance to older managers in how to use computer applications and the Internet. (This is a recent development in the business world. See how your Ss react to it, and whether they think it is practical and realistic.)

1 to 1

This case study can be done 1 to 1, with the student analysing the information and then discussing improvements to Zenova Industries' management style. Don't forget to note language points for praise and correction afterwards. Highlight some of the language you chose to use as well.

Writing

- Ask the Ss to base their writing on the notes taken in their group during the simulated meeting.
- The writing can be done collaboratively in class or as homework.
- If your Ss are doing the writing task individually for homework, you may want to photocopy the notes made by the notetaker in each group so that each student has a record of what was said and decided in their group.

 Writing file page 143.

UNIT 13 Takeovers and mergers

At a glance

	Classwork – Course Book	Further work
Lesson 1 *Each lesson (excluding case studies) is about 45–60 minutes. This does not include administration and time spent going through homework.*	**Starting up** Ss talk about recent takeovers and mergers, their effect and why most mergers do not produce the results expected. **Vocabulary: Describing takeovers and mergers** Ss study words and expressions related to different types of takeover and merger. **Listening: Making acquisitions** Ss listen to the head of a large media group talking about acquisitions and their results.	**Practice File** Vocabulary (page 52)
Lesson 2	**Reading: Why mergers fail** Two-thirds of takeovers do not benefit the shareholders of the acquiring company. The article looks at the reasons for this. **Language review: Headlines** Ss look at the particular features and vocabulary of newspaper headlines.	**Text bank** pages (184–187) **Practice File** Language review (page 53) **ML Grammar and Usage**
Lesson 3	**Skills: Summarising in presentations** Ss analyse different ways of summarising the points of a presentation, and put them into action.	**Resource bank** (page 202)
Lesson 4 *Each case study is about 1½ to 2 hours.*	**Case study: Group Bon Appetit PLC** A restaurant group takes over a chain of cafés, but gets into difficulty. Ss study the reasons for this, and make recommendations.	**Practice File** Writing (page 54)

For a fast route through the unit focussing mainly on speaking skills, just use the underlined sections.

For 1 to 1 situations, most parts of the unit lend themselves, with minimal adaptation, to use with individual students. Where this is not the case, alternative procedures are given.

At a glance

Business brief

'Magnetic's board rejected TT's bid as "derisory, unsolicited, unwelcome and totally inadequate".' This is a familiar refrain from the board of a company that is the **target** of a **hostile bid**, one that it does not want, for example because it thinks that the **bidder** is **undervaluing** its shares: offering less for the shares than the target thinks they are worth in terms of its future profitability. A bid that a target company welcomes, on the other hand, may be described as **friendly**.

Bidders often already have a **minority stake** or **interest** in the target company: they already own some shares. The bid is to gain a **majority stake** so that they own more shares than any other shareholder and enough shares to be able to decide how it is run.

A company that often takes over or **acquires** others is said to be **acquisitive**. The companies it buys are **acquisitions**. It may be referred to, especially by journalists, as a **predator**, and the companies it buys, or would like to buy, as its **prey**.

When a company buys others over a period of time, a **group**, **conglomerate** or **combine** forms, containing a **parent company** with a number of **subsidiaries** and perhaps with many different types of business activity. A group like this is **diversified**. Related companies in a group can have **synergy**, sharing production and other costs, and benefiting from **cross-marketing** of each other's products. Synergy is sometimes expressed as the idea that two plus two equals five, the notion that companies offer more **shareholder value** together than they would separately.

But the current trend is for groups to **sell off**, **spin off** or **dispose of** their **non-core assets** and activities, in a process of **divestment** and **restructuring**, allowing them to **focus on** their **core activities**, the ones they are best at doing and make the most profit from. Compare an old-style conglomerate like GEC in the UK, with a wide variety of sometimes unrelated activities, and a group like Pearson, which has decided to concentrate on media, in broadcasting, publishing and now Internet ventures.

Companies may work together in a particular area by forming an **alliance** or **joint venture**, perhaps forming a new company in which they both have a stake. Two companies working together like this may later decide to go for a **merger**, combining as equals. But as the main Course Book unit points out, mergers (like takeovers) are fraught with difficulty and for a variety of reasons often fail, even where the merger involves two companies in the same country. One of the companies will always behave as the dominant partner.

Take the scenario where one company's base is used as the headquarters for the merged company. The other company's office closes, and many managers in both companies lose their jobs. Those remaining feel beleaguered and under threat of losing theirs later. They may dislike the way the managers from the other company work. In **cross-border mergers**, these difficulties are compounded by cross-cultural misunderstandings and tensions. Problems such as these explain why merged companies so often fail to live up to the promise of the day of the press conference when the two CEOs vaunted the merger's merits.

Read on

John Child, David Faulkner: *Strategies of Co-operation: Managing Alliances, Networks and Joint Ventures*, OUP, 1998

Timothy Galpin, Mark Herndon: *The Complete Guide to Mergers and Acquisitions*, Jossey Bass Wiley, 1999

Hazel Johnson: *Mergers and Acquisitions*, Financial Times Prentice Hall, 1999

J. Fred Weston: *Mergers and Acquisitions*, McGraw-Hill, 2000

Business brief

Lesson notes

Special note

Teaching this unit will be much easier if you read it right through from beginning to end before the first lesson, as familiarity with later parts of the unit will be of great help in teaching the earlier parts.

Warmer

◉ Write TAKEOVERS AND MERGERS in big letters on the board. Ask the Ss to say what the difference is between a takeover and a merger.

> A takeover is when one company buys more than 50% of the shares in another from its existing shareholders and thereby obtains a controlling interest. A merger is when two companies combine as equals, by mutual agreement. For more on this, see the Business brief on page 112.

Overview

◉ Ask the Ss to look at the Overview section at the beginning of the unit. Tell them a little about the things on the list, using the table on page 112 of this book as a guide. Tell them which points you will be covering in the current lesson and in later lessons.

Quotation

◉ Read out the quotation and ask the Ss to comment. What did Goldsmith mean exactly?

> New owners may not fully understand how the company they're buying works, especially if they are unfamiliar with the industry it is in. You can buy the shares, but that doesn't change the 'culture' of the company.
> New owners may damage the morale of previously motivated managers and employees, perhaps by putting their own senior managers in charge of the company, or by undervaluing the skills and experience of the existing staff.

Starting up

Ss talk about recent takeovers and mergers, their effect on consumers, and why most mergers do not produce the results expected.

Ⓐ–Ⓒ

◉ Ask Ss to discuss these questions in pairs or threes. Circulate and assist. Ss' contributions to the Warmer and Quotation-related activities above will have shown if they have the knowledge and interest to do this independently. If you think they don't, discuss the points as a whole-class activity.

See the Business brief for general background. You could also look through the rest of the unit before the class (or before the remaining classes on this topic) to garner some other ideas.

Exercise A

Prepare to talk about recent takeovers and mergers by looking at publications such as the *Financial Times* or *The Economist*. They can be found on the Internet at www.ft.com and www.economist.com respectively. (Alternatively, if your Ss have access to the Internet, ask them to do some research and report back on it in the next session.)

Exercise B

Here are some specific points, if your Ss are lacking ideas. (These lists are by no means exhaustive.)

Advantages of takeovers: One advantage for the existing owner of a takeover target (for example the founder of the company) is that they can realise the value of the company by selling it and use the proceeds to start another company (or to retire).

A company taken over may get a new lease of life in the form of new management and access to new markets: ones that the acquiring company is in. It may gain better access to investment finance because of the increased size of the new company, making it more attractive for investors. The acquiring company may gain new products to sell, and new markets to sell them in, ones where the company taken over is already present.

Benefits promised to shareholders often include lower costs, for example, lower overheads. For instance, the human resources department of a company of 5,000 employees does not need to be much bigger than one of 3,000 employees, so the same general costs can be spread wider, meaning increased profitability.

The companies involved in takeovers and mergers will talk about new products, lower prices and so on, but the authorities often intervene to see if the consumer will really benefit. There may a long approval process. The US, the EU and individual countries all have bodies to decide if mergers should go ahead. They may stop a takeover or merger going ahead because they believe that the industry will end up being dominated by one or two very large companies in a quasi-monopoly situation.

Disadvantages of takeovers: Employees of a company that is taken over might benefit from an increased number of career opportunities in the larger company, but usually the story is one of redundancies through cost-cutting. To go back to the human resources department example, the new owners might close the department of the company being taken over, with the personnel being administered by its own human resources department. The people in the human resources department of the takeover target will probably lose their jobs.

For other disadvantages, see the points above under 'Quotation'.

Advantages and disadvantages of mergers: Many of the points above also apply to mergers. The word *synergy* may be bandied about by the partners (see the Business brief) but the partnership will almost always be unequal, and the dominant partner will often behave like an acquiring company.

Exercise C

Again, see the Business brief. The main problem is often cultural. The two organisations do not blend because of incompatible ways of doing things or because of personality clashes between key managers from the two companies.

Vocabulary: Describing takeovers and mergers

Ss study words and expressions related to different types of takeover and merger.

A

◎ Tell your Ss they are going to look at the language of takeovers and mergers, and to work in pairs on matching the expressions with their meanings. Circulate and assist if necessary.

◎ With the whole class, ask for the answers and explain anything that is unclear.

1 f	2 c	3 e	4 d	5 b	6 a

B

◎ Do as a quick-fire activity with the whole class and write the results on the board.

acquisition bid
bid target
hostile acquisition
hostile bid
hostile takeover
hostile takeover bid
takeover bid
takeover target
launch a bid
launch a hostile bid
launch a hostile takeover
launch a hostile takeover bid
make a bid
make a hostile bid
make a hostile takeover bid
make an acquisition
take a stake

C

◎ Ask the Ss to complete the extracts in pairs and then elicit and discuss the answers with the whole class. (Point out that each answer line stands for one missing word.)

1 takeover bid, hostile bid, acquisition bid (sounds odd, but it's possible)
2 merger
3 joint venture; take a stake

Listening: Making acquisitions

Ss listen to the head of a large media group talking about acquisitions and their results.

A

◎ Tell Ss that this exercise will prepare them for what they will hear in the recording. Ask them to do it in pairs. Circulate and assist.

◎ With the whole class, elicit the answers.

◎ Work on the stress of words like *inteGRAtion* and *moMENTum*.

1 d	2 a	3 e	4 f	5 c	6 b

B 🎧 13.1

◎ Introduce Nigel Portwood and point out that Pearson Education is the publisher of *Market Leader*. Ask the Ss to look at the question and play the first part of the interview once. Get Ss to put up their hands every time they hear one of the expressions in Exercise A above.

◎ Play the recording a second time, explaining any difficulties but without directly answering the question.

◎ Play the recording again, pausing after each step in the acquisition process to give time for the Ss to note it down.

◎ Ask the Ss for their answers, invite comments and encourage discussion.

Lesson notes

– Ensure you have a clear strategy: this will help you understand which companies are the most suitable targets for acquisition.

– If there is a suitable candidate, analyse its products, customers, sales and cost structure. Think about how you will invest in the company if you buy it, and what the financial consequences will be.

– Work out how much the company is worth to you and to its current owners. Work out how much more it will be worth to you because of the synergies you see (the benefits, not available to its current owners, that will result when it is combined with your own company).

– Work out the tactics of how to buy the company, including how to approach the owners and what price you will offer.

Ⓒ 🎧 13.2

◉ Follow a similar procedure to the one in Exercise A for the second part of the interview.

– Plan what you are going to do when you actually take ownership of the acquired company: how you are going to combine it with your own company in relation to its people (= managers and employees), facilities, its (other) assets and its customers, paying great attention to detail.

– Keep the most important managers and staff in the acquired company on your side.

– Move quickly and don't lose momentum, because this creates uncertainty.

Ⓓ 🎧 13.3

◉ Follow a similar procedure for the last part of the interview.

1 Did the things that you expected to happen actually happen?

2 Do you have a stronger competitive position as a result of the acquisition?

3 Did you get the cost savings that you expected?

4 Did the sales of the company continue as you had projected?

5 Did you pay a sensible price?

Reading: Why mergers fail

Two-thirds of takeovers do not benefit the shareholders of the acquiring company. The article looks at the reasons for this.

◉ If your Ss are of a literary bent, point out that the quotation alluded to in the title of the article is from a play called *The Old Bachelor*, by William Congreve (1670–1729):

'Thus grief still treads upon the heels of pleasure: Married in haste, we may repent at leisure.'

◉ Explain that the language of betrothal and marriage is often used by journalists to talk about mergers, as the article will mention.

◉ Discuss the two questions with the whole class.

1 As your Ss will see, the shareholders who benefit most are those of the company that is being acquired. This may be counter-intuitive. Leave the answer to this question open until they read the first part of the article.

2 Culture is famously 'the way we do things round here' whether the 'here' in question is a country, a region, a social class or a company. The article will explain that blending the cultures of two companies in a merger is not easy.

Ⓑ

◉ Read aloud the sentence immediately following the headline and explain any difficulties (e.g. *continue apace*). Then ask one of your Ss to paraphrase the sentence. This is important, as it will prepare Ss to understand the whole article.

◉ Read the first two paragraphs with the Ss, explaining difficulties. Bear in mind that Ss are asked to choose definitions for some of these words (e.g. *tarnished*) in Exercise C. Either explain them now and see if Ss pick up your explanation so as to be able to answer the questions later, or ask Ss to try to work them out from the context and let them answer the questions in Exercise C by themselves. (If a company's shares underperform its sector (lines 34–35), they increase in value less quickly and pay lower dividends than those of other companies in the same industry.)

◉ Ask Ss to answer question 1 in Exercise A above, (which is also Question 1 after the article): about 65% of takeovers fail to benefit the acquiring company. (Point out that *merger* is being used here as a variation for *takeover*, and that the writer must be referring to takeovers because he talks of acquiring companies. Mergers are combinations of theoretically equal partners.)

◉ Ask 'Why do so many mergers fail?' (question 2) and get the Ss to read the next five paragraphs in pairs. Circulate and explain any difficulties (e.g. 'implementation' (lines 45–46) and 'meld' (line 51), again bearing in mind that some of these words will come up in Exercise C.

- With the whole class, ask Ss for their answer to the question. Invite comments and encourage discussion.
- Ask the question 'What do acquiring companies need to do in order to ensure success?' (Question 3).
- Ask the Ss to read the final three paragraphs in pairs. Circulate and assist.
- With the whole class, ask for the answer to the question.
- Invite comments and encourage discussion, for example in relation to a merger that has recently been announced.

> 1 The shareholders who benefit most are those of the company that is being acquired.
> 2 Because of
>   – poor implementation
>   – incompatible cultures.
> 3 They need to
>   – define how success will be measured
>   – decide in advance which partner's way of doing things will be adopted by the merged company
>   – identify the advantages that the merged company has, ones that competitors will find it hard to copy
>   – move quickly so that competitors do not have time to catch up and overtake.

Ⓒ

- Do as a quick-fire activity with the whole class, especially if you have already explained these words to your Ss as they were reading the article.

> 1 b   2 b   3 a   4 a   5 a   6 b   7 b

Ⓓ

- Ask Ss to do the gap exercise in pairs or as a whole-class activity.

> 1 compatible
> 2 odds are stacked against
> 3 complementary
> 4 replicate

- Rather than asking Ss to make up sentences on the spur of the moment, get them to use the words to talk or write about a recent merger (proposed or completed). For example,
  – The merger between Company A and Company B will only work if implementation is good.
  – Company A has paid a premium for Company B, because it believes Company B has unique potential for development.

Language review: Headlines

Ss look at the particular features and vocabulary of newspaper headlines.

- Go through the points in the Language review box with the whole class. (If you have time before the class, find recent press headlines that have some of the same features, and show them to and discuss them with the Ss.)
- Say that, for the purposes of Exercise A, *several nouns* in point 1 means two or more nouns.

Ⓐ–Ⓑ

- Ask Ss to look at Exercises A and B together. Do the first headline with the whole class to give Ss the idea, then get them to do the rest in pairs. Circulate and assist. Discuss the answers with the whole group.

1	2	Renault is on the brink of two alliances.
2	1, 2	Moulinex and Brandt are near a merger deal.
3	2, 3, 4	Austin Reed rejects an offer as unwelcome.
4	1, 2, 3	Some biotech groups have agreed a merger.
5	2, 4	Wal-Mart is in a £6.7bn bid for Asda.
6	1, 2, 5	Melrose is to raise £5.8m via a London flotation.*
7	1, 2, 4	Rivals are in a final fight for United Biscuits.
8	1, 2, 3	The takeover target Esat has hinted at a white knight.*
9	1, 2, 3	The AOL deal has called rivals' web plans into question.
10	2,5	United News is to dispose of its US magazines.*

* Explanations

6 Melrose is to raise £5.8 million in capital by issuing shares on the London Stock Exchange.

8 Esat is in danger of being taken over against its will, and has said that there may be another company willing to take it over on better terms.

10 United News is to sell its US magazine titles to another company / other companies.

Ⓒ

- Explain why short words are used in headlines and do the exercise as a quick-fire activity with the whole class.

> 1 d   2 f   3 g   4 l   5 c   6 b   7 j
> (Check Ss' pronunciation of *row* in this context.)
> 8 a   9 k   10 i   11 e   12 h

Lesson notes

Skills: Summarising in presentations

Ss analyse different ways of summarising the points of a presentation, and put them into action.

Ⓐ

◎ Explain the context of the presentation that the Ss are about to hear: a management consultant talking to a Board of Directors involved in a takeover.

◎ Tell them that some of the words he uses are quite difficult. This exercise covers some of them.

◎ Go through words 1–8 with the whole class, practising their pronunciation. (Practise *thorough* in b) on the right as well.) Point out that *sycophant* is pronounced *sicker-fant*, or, as they will hear in the recording, *sigh-co-fant*. (Some native speakers may not agree with the second pronunciation.)

◎ Ask Ss for the meanings of the words.

1 d	2 b	3 a	4 g	5 h	6 e
7 f	8 c				

Ⓑ 🎧 13.4

◎ Play the recording once right through and ask Ss to put up their hands when they hear the words 1–8 in Exercise A above being used.

◎ Then tell the Ss they should listen out for the points Jeremy Keeley makes in his presentation, ready to summarise them, and name the pitfall listed here that he does not refer to.

◎ Play the recording again, explaining any remaining difficulties. Stop at the end of each of the main points he makes and ask Ss to summarise it. (Stop at *the basis of managing the change moving forward, so they can take it forward* and at the end of the recording.)

◎ Ask Ss for the point that was not mentioned: 'Pay attention to the cultural differences'.

Ⓒ 🎧 13.4

◎ Ask Ss to look at the Useful language box and ask individual Ss to read out the utterances, with convincing stress and intonation. Explain what a rhetorical question is.

◎ Play the recording again and get the Ss to identify the utterances that they hear.

Referring back
So as you were saying a few minutes ago …
Making points in threes
You really have to plan carefully, be rigorous in your analysis and be flexible …
It's a long process. It's expensive. It can also be very profitable.
Asking rhetorical questions
But what are the sort of things that the experts forget generally?
Ordering
There are three things in my mind and the first thing is …
Using emotive language
Beware of the sycophants in your organisation …
Repetition
They're going to be saying Yes! Yes! Yes!
Exemplifying
… for example, caring as their primary task.
Asking for feedback
What's missing?

Ⓓ

◎ Tell Ss that they will be discussing the advantages and the problems associated with takeovers and mergers. Ask them to think about some of the issues they have encountered so far. In the discussion, they will be able to talk about these and add some of their own.

◎ Divide the class into two groups, A and B. (If the class is large, you could have two Group As and two Group Bs.)

◎ Group A discusses the advantages and Group B the problems. Tell everyone to make notes of their discussion as the basis for the pair work activity below.

◎ Circulate and monitor, but do not intervene unless necessary. If they are short of ideas, you could remind them of some of the points from the Starting up section at the beginning of this unit. Note language points for praise and correction.

◎ Call the class to order. Praise good language points from the discussion and work on three or four points that need improvement, getting individual Ss to say the correct forms.

◎ Then form pairs each with one student from Group A and one from Group B. The members of each pair summarise the discussion of the group they were in.

◎ Bring the class to order. Ask one of the pairs to repeat their presentations to each other for the whole class.

◎ Invite comments and encourage brief discussion.

Case study

Group Bon Appetit PLC

A large restaurant group takes over a chain of cafés, but the group's share price then falls dramatically. Ss study the reasons for this, and make recommendations.

Stage 1: Background

- Ask the Ss to read the background information about Group Bon Appetit. Meanwhile, write the points in the first column of the table on the board.
- With the whole class, elicit the information to complete the table.

Nature of takeover	Bitterly fought
Shareholders' premium over market price	20%
Bon Appetit's share price since the takeover	Peaked at 400p, fell to less than 50p, now 80p because of possible takeover of Bon Appetit by Icarus, a predator*

- *Talk about the way that journalists describe companies that are looking to take over others as predators, and the companies that they take over, or would like to take over, as their prey, explaining the animal connotations of these words.
- Divide the class into two groups, A and B. (If the class is large, you could have more than one of each group.)
- Tell the Ss in Group A that they will analysing the market and financial information on page 114.

  The Ss in Group B that they will be analysing and summarising the extract from Bon Appetit's annual report on page 115 in the light of the financial results on page 115, and the recent developments on page 115.
- Representatives of each group will then explain their findings to the other group(s) in front of the whole class.

Stage 2: Analysing the information

- Tell members of Group A that they should summarise their analysis under these headings:

1 **Group Bon Appetit's chains**

Its existing chains, including for each chain
- clientele profile
- type of food
- average amount spent in each

Planned expansion

2 **Turnover and profits**

Figures for each chain
- turnover (= sales) in last three years
- pre-tax profits over last three years

If your Ss like to work with figures, you could ask them to work out (using calculators, of course)
- the percentage increase in turnover each year for each chain
- the percentage increase in profit each year for each chain
- profit as a percentage of turnover for each year for each chain
- total profit as a percentage of total turnover for each year for all three chains

Even if your Ss don't go into this detail, they should be able to spot and talk about major trends.
- Turnover of the Bon Appetit chain itself has increased very quickly, with profit as a percentage of sales increasing even faster.
- Turnover has more than doubled at Innovia but its profit margin has fallen away very sharply.

3 **Debt and major shareholdings**

The representative from this group should be ready to talk about
- the increased indebtedness of Group Bon Appetit and the reasons for it
- the various shareholdings.

- Circulate and assist with all the above.
- Ask Group(s) A to nominate the representatives who will talk about these issues with the whole class. There should probably be three representatives, one talking about each of the three points 1–3 above.
- Meanwhile, Group B should be studying its information.

1 **Annual Report extract**

The main point here is to make sure that the Ss reinterpret these statements in the light of the financial information for the three chains on page 114. (This is the same information as for Group A, of course. It's the only financial information that Group B should look at for the time being. See the notes above on how Ss should approach it.)

2 **Recent developments**

Ss should boil down the points here into note form, as the basis for a succinct presentation to the whole class, for example:

1 Bon Appetit and the Seashell doing well, but Innovia in trouble – strong competition from Starbucks and others.

2 Innovia's managers complain about Bon Appetit's *bureaucratic* management style – many have left.

Lesson notes

◎ Circulate and assist.

◎ Ask Group(s) B to nominate the representatives who will talk about these issues with the whole class. There should probably be two representatives, one each for points 1 and 2 above.

Stage 3: Pooling the information

◎ Ask the representatives of each group to come to the front of the class one by one and summarise their conclusions.

◎ Invite comments and encourage brief discussion, especially about the conclusions that each group drew about the turnover and profit information, but do not pre-empt the meeting.

Stage 4: Preparing for the meeting

◎ Divide the class into groups of four or six, constituted differently from the groups in Stage 2. Half the members of each group are directors of Bon Appetit, the other half are directors of Weinburg Investments.

◎ Ask each half of the group to confer separately about the four points to be discussed at the meeting.

◎ Circulate and assist.

Stage 5: The meeting

◎ Appoint a chair from among the Weinburg directors. This person should control the meeting, using the four points as an agenda.

◎ Appoint one of the participants *on each side* to be a notetaker who will take coherent and legible notes that can later form the basis for the writing task.

◎ Circulate and monitor, but do not intervene unless necessary. Note language points for later praise and correction.

◎ When the meeting(s) end(s), praise good language points and work on three or four points that need improvement, getting individual Ss to say the correct forms.

◎ Discuss the meeting(s) with the whole class, getting each group to explain what happened.

> **1 to 1**
>
> This case study can be done 1 to 1, with your student analysing the information and then discussing recommendations. Don't forget to note language points for praise and correction afterwards. Highlight some of the language you chose to use as well.

Writing

◎ Ask the Ss to base their writing on the notes taken by the member of their team during the meeting.

◎ The writing can be done collaboratively in class or as homework.

◎ If your Ss are doing the writing task for homework, you may want to photocopy the notes made by the notetakers on each side so that each student has a record of what was said and decided in their group.

 Writing file pages 144–145.

The future of business

At a glance

	Classwork – Course Book	Further work
Lesson 1 *Each lesson (excluding case studies) is about 45–60 minutes. This does not include administration and time spent going through homework.*	**Starting up** Ss comment on a range of social and technological predictions and the likelihood of them coming about. **Listening: Changing customer needs** The Business Director of an advertising agency talks about changing customer needs. Ss correct a summary of the interview and discuss some of the issues raised.	
Lesson 2	**Vocabulary 1: Expressions about time** Ss study expressions used to talk about things from the past, present and future. **Reading: Products and services of the future** Ss read some predictions for the decades ahead, and the effect they will have on business. **Vocabulary 2: Describing the future** Ss look at the adjectives that can be used to talk about the future and use them in combination with particular adverbs.	**Practice File** Vocabulary (page 56) **Text bank** pages (188–191) **Practice File** Vocabulary (page 56)
Lesson 3	**Language review: The language of prediction** Ss look at verb tenses such as *will*, *going to*, *might* and *may* used to talk about the future, and put them into action to make their own forecasts. **Skills: Getting the right information** Ss listen to situations where there are breakdowns of communication, look at language that can remedy these, and apply it to role play situations.	**Practice File** Language review (page 57) **ML Grammar and Usage** **Resource bank** (page 203)
Lesson 4 *Each case study is about 1½ to 2 hours.*	**Case study: Yedo Department Stores** A chain of Japanese department stores is in trouble, in the face of social changes and foreign competition. Ss suggest some solutions.	**Practice File** Writing (page 58)

For a fast route through the unit focussing mainly on speaking skills, just use the underlined sections.

For 1 to 1 situations, most parts of the unit lend themselves, with minimal adaptation, to use with individual students. Where this is not the case, alternative procedures are given.

Business brief

In the 1960s, we imagined a future of public transport based on elevated monorail systems, and private transport with personal helicopters, or even spacecraft, for everyone. Today, the future looks more like the past than we imagined it would. Development has been **continuous** in many ways. For example, the car has become a mundane object, but with technology far in advance of that available even 20 years ago. However, its future source of power, a **discontinuous** development that will replace petrol, is still uncertain.

Futurology, with its **futurologists** or **futurists**, is a haphazard activity, despite attempts to formalise it. There is the **Delphi method**, where experts make their forecasts about a subject independently, and a referee circulates each forecast to the other members of the group, who comment on each other's observations until they reach a consensus.

This can be one element of **strategy**, where companies make long-term plans about future activities. Here, they have to anticipate competitors' activities as well as trends in the general **economic environment**. Very large companies work on **scenario planning**, imagining different ways in which the current situation may evolve, and their place in it, including ways in which they may 'encourage' it to develop in their favour.

The main course unit makes a number of social and economic predictions. As the **Success** business brief mentions (see Unit 4), future successful products are notoriously hard to predict, as are the subtle combinations of social, cultural and technological circumstances that mean that something may succeed at one time but not another. The **E-commerce** business brief (Unit 7) looks at some of the trends in e-commerce and Internet use in this context.

One of the social predictions made 30 years ago was that people would work less and have more leisure time, but the opposite has occurred. No one foresaw how the computer would evolve away from the mainframe and facilitate a social development like working from home and while on the move, thanks to laptops and, in a parallel development, mobile phones. Similarly, the Internet may have social effects that we cannot envisage, let alone predict.

A powerful force 30 years ago was **protest** at the way society and the economy were organised, for example against 'faceless multinationals'. After a long period where youth shed its rebellious reputation, in this context at least, there are signs that **activism** outside traditional political parties is re-emerging as a social force, this time organised on a global level – witness the regular violent demonstrations against recent meetings of the International Monetary Fund and the World Trade Organization, with planning of protests co-ordinated over the Internet. This trend may intensify.

Another factor that will certainly affect the way the future of business develops is **global warming**, which is now, after ten years of debate over whether it is happening or not, an incontrovertible fact. Some possible consequences of the greenhouse effect have been predicted, but there will certainly be others we cannot even imagine.

Read on

Charles Grantham: *The Future of Work*, McGraw-Hill, 1999

Hamish McRae: *The World in 2020*, HarperCollins, 1995

Jonathan Margolis: *A Brief History of the Future*, Bloomsbury, 2000

Michael Zey: *Future Factor*, McGraw-Hill, 2000

Lesson notes

Warmer

- Write 'The future is ...' in big letters on the board. Add the word 'bright' and then ask your Ss to brainstorm other words that could follow the phrase and shout them out. (They do not all have to be adjectives.)

> **Possible answers**
> mobile
> crowded
> knowledge
> healthy
> efficient
> our children
> going to be more like the past than we think

- Invite comments and encourage discussion, but don't pre-empt the topics of the unit too much.

Quotation

- Ask Ss to look at the quotation and ask if they agree with it. Ask them for any famously inaccurate predictions from the past, e.g. the idea that we would all have so much leisure time that we wouldn't know what to do with it.

Starting up

Ss comment on a range of social and technological predictions and the likelihood of them coming about.

(A)–(B)

- Ask Ss to discuss the predictions in Exercise A in pairs, emphasising that they should concentrate on the next 20 years, and come up with other changes that are likely.
- With the whole class, get the pairs to report on their findings. Invite comments and encourage discussion.

(C)

- Again in pairs, ask Ss to comment on
  - the immediate future of business and the economy in their country
  - the longer-term prospects.
- Point out that the adjective is *optimistic*, the related noun is *optimism* and the person is *an optimist*. Do not allow Ss to say *I'm optimist* or *I'm pessimist*.
- With the whole class, ask the pairs for their findings, asking Ss to justify them. Where different Ss from the same country have different ideas about their country's future, encourage debate, but be tactful.

Listening: Changing customer needs

The Business Director of an advertising agency talks about changing customer needs. Ss correct a summary of the interview and discuss some of the issues raised.

(A) 🎧 14.1

- Ask the Ss to read through the summary. Explain any difficulties.
- Play the recording once right through.
- Tell Ss they should start thinking about the errors in the summary and play the recording again, stopping to explain any difficulties.
- Play the interview again, either stopping occasionally and asking Ss for the factual errors, or playing it right through and getting Ss to list the errors at the end.
- Ask Ss if they are surprised by any of the points in the recording.

> Customer needs are changing because of developments in three key areas: <u>environmental issues</u> [*no: social environment*], technology, and time.
> The change in social environment concerns the type of households that we live in. The classic family unit – mother, father and <u>family pets</u> [*no: mum, dad and some kids*] – only constitutes about <u>50%</u> [*no: 25%*] of the UK population, and is being replaced by a variety of other forms. These include single-person households, single-parent households, and households where <u>children</u> [*no: adults*] share a house – but live as individuals rather than as a single family.
> The changes caused by technological developments are being driven in particular by the rapid expansion in <u>the use of e-mail</u> [*no: everyone now has a telephone*] and <u>the growing importance of household appliances</u>. [*no: the web*
> Finally, as our lives become <u>less busy</u> [*no: more busy*], customers are starting to expect 'value for time' when making a purchase. This can mean *saving* customers' time, for example through Internet shopping; or, on the other hand, creating an environment where shopping is treated <u>as a business transaction</u> [*no: as a leisure activity*] that customers actually want to *spend* time on and enjoy.

(B)

- Ask Ss to discuss the three questions in pairs or as a whole-class activity.

> 1 It tracks what it calls 'time availability'. (This is part of its wider work on consumer trends. The Henley Centre has an attractive website at www.henleycentre.com)
> 2 Amazon.com save you time (and money) by allowing you to order books on the Internet, while Waterstones are trying to create a rich leisure experience.
> 3 Ask Ss if they actually enjoy shopping as a way of developing this point.

Vocabulary 1: Expressions about time

Ss study expressions used to talk about the future and the probability that particular things will happen.

A

◉ Do as a quick-fire activity with the whole class.

> 1 up-to-date
> 2 a thing of the past
> 3 at the forefront
> 4 old-fashioned
> 5 state-of-the-art
> 6 the way forward
> 7 out of date
> 8 up to the minute
> 9 at the leading edge
> 10 behind the times

B

◉ Go round the class for some quick-fire off-the-cuff predictions.

Reading: Products and services of the future

Ss read some predictions for the decades ahead, and the effect they will have on business.

A

◉ Discuss Question 1 with the whole class.

> This is very important, obviously. See the Business brief on page 123 for some ideas here.
> **Scenario planning** and the **Delphi method** are available only to governments and large organisations with massive resources, of course. Many companies use **market research**, and this can tell them quite a lot about the current situation, but even short-term market forecasts can be unreliable, especially when based on asking people if they would buy a new product if it was available: it costs nothing to say *yes*, and many new products have failed because the anticipated consumer behaviour did not happen.
> A lot of information about trends is available free or to buy from government and other sources, but the danger here is of extrapolating the future from the past: thinking that current trends will continue. A related problem is taking trends in one place and imagining that they will happen in another in the same way. There are similarities of course, but for all the talk of globalisation, there are still major differences even between superficially similar countries such as those in the English-speaking world, or the fast-growing economies in Asia.

◉ Ask Ss to discuss Question 2 in pairs. Circulate, monitor and assist.

◉ Ask the pairs to report back to the whole class. Invite comments and encourage discussion.

B

◉ Read the first five paragraphs with the whole class, explaining any difficulties. (You may want to leave *cutting edge of fashion* (line 34) and *mass marketing is becoming obsolete* (lines 50–51) for the moment, as there are questions about them in Exercise D below.)

◉ Ask Ss to list the first predictions made.

> The letters after each item refer to the categories in Question 2 of Exercise A2.
> – dog and cat retirement homes – b)
> – snacks to combat depression – e)
> – massage clothing – a)
> – dream-inducing machines
> – computerised-fit jeans – a)
> – personalised storybooks and videos for children – f)

◉ Ask Ss to read the rest of the article in pairs, continuing to list the predictions, not just in specific products but also the social trends behind them. Circulate and assist if necessary, explaining any difficulties.

◉ Ask the whole class for the remaining predictions.

◉ Write on the board the headings in bold in the box below, and ask Ss to organise the predictions using these headings.

> **Ageing population**
> – financial products
> – packaging that is easy to open
> – demand for top-end cars
> – the most elderly to live in homes with children and pets – a)
> **Children**
> – children's food to increase intelligence and health (This could also come under 'food' below.) – e)
> – anti-bacterial toys – f)
> – educational products – f)
> – organic cotton clothes – a)
> – services that 'child-proof' hi-tech homes
> – *personalised story books and videos – f)*
> **Food**
> – food with added health benefits – e)
> – mood-changing and memory-improving snacks – e)
> – intelligent fridges that transmit shopping lists to delivery services – c)
> – 'smart' cookers that know personal tastes – e)
> – meal trucks to provide full meals to homes – e)
> **Other consumer trends**
> – parks, beaches, and theme parks for members only
> – personal shoppers
> – *dog and cat retirement homes – b)*
> – *massage clothing – a)*
> – *dream-inducing machines*
> – *computerised-fit jeans – a)*
> **The main danger**
> – technological haves and emerging class of have-nots

◉ With the whole class, ask the Ss to shout out the predictions and write them on the board. Then add the predictions from the first part of article (in italics in the box above: *snacks to combat depression* are already there, because reference to them is also made in the second part of the article).

Ⓒ

◉ With the whole class, ask if the statements are true or false. Ask Ss to cite the places in the article that relate to these statements.

1	true
2	false
3	true
4	true
5	true
6	false

Ⓓ

◉ With the whole class, ask for the answers.

1 b	2 a

Ⓔ

◉ Ask Ss to discuss the predictions on the board in pairs or threes. Circulate and assist if necessary.
◉ Ask the groups for their conclusions. Invite comments and encourage discussion.
◉ Go round the class for some quick-fire off-the-cuff predictions.

Vocabulary 2: Describing the future

Ⓐ–Ⓑ

◉ Ask your Ss to work on these words in pairs and then use them to write down some predictions.

very bad	bad	good	very good
bleak	depressing	bright	brilliant
dire	doubtful	promising	great
dreadful	uncertain	prosperous	magnificent
terrible	worrying	rosy	marvellous

◉ With the whole class, go through the words and ask the pairs for their predictions.

Language review: The language of prediction

Ss look at verb tenses such as *will*, *going to*, *might* and *may* used to talk about the future and put them into action to make their own forecasts.

◉ Go through the points in the Language review box with the whole class.
◉ Ask Ss for the rule about *going to* and *will*.

> We use *going to* when there is present external evidence for a future event and *will* when we state our own intuitions.

◉ Go through the other ways of making predictions. For b), explain that the future can be indicated lexically, i.e. with words, rather than by using particular verb tenses, as in *Tomorrow's fashions are almost upon us*.

Ⓐ

◉ Get individual Ss to match sentences 1–7 to a)–g) in the Language review box.

1 g	2 d	3 b	4 f	5 c	6 a	7 e

Ⓑ–Ⓒ

◉ Ask Ss to work on Exercises B and C in pairs, and then ask them to report back to the whole class.

> B
> 1 Correct
> 2 Correct
> 3 By the end of this century electric cars will have become common.
> 4 By the end of next year we will have been in business for 25 years.
> 5 Correct
> 6 By this time next year we will have paid off this loan.
> 7 Correct
> 8 Correct

◉ Invite comments and encourage whole-class discussion about the predictions made by the pairs.

Skills: Getting the right information

Ss listen to situations where there are breakdowns of communication, look at language that can remedy these, and apply it to role play situations.

(A) 🎧 14.2

- Tell your Ss that they are going to hear a number of telephone conversations where people have trouble getting the right information.
- Play the first dialogue and, with the whole class, ask the Ss what the problem is.

> 1 Carla wants to get more information about a range of hairdryers sold by a company. She wants to speak to Li Wang, presumably in the sales department, but gets put through to Ken Tang in accounts, who transfers her back to the switchboard. The switchboard puts her through to Li Wang's extension but a colleague of his, Dan Chen, says that he is out of the office and asks if he can help.

- Play the other dialogues and ask Ss to give descriptions of the situations in order to answer the questions relating to each dialogue.

> 2 Michael Bishop is angry because some cash machines he ordered are now two weeks overdue. He gets through to someone who asks him to give details of the order, including the date, model number and order number. The supplier promises to look into the problem and call back as soon as possible.
>
> 3 A supplier and a customer are discussing an order. There is confusion over the reference number, but this is cleared up when the customer reads back the details to the supplier. There is also a mistake in the delivery date on record. The customer corrects this and the supplier confirms the new delivery date is feasible.
>
> 4 The customer is calling about an invoice that they have received for 50 CD players. The customer is surprised because they only inquired about prices and availability and did not actually place an order. The customer explains that they have obtained the CD players elsewhere and the supplier cancels the order. The customer apologises for any inconvenience caused and the supplier says they will tell the sales assistant to be careful in the future.

- Make sure that Ss use expressions such as *put someone through* and *transfer someone back* correctly.
- Go through the expressions in the Useful language box and ask individual Ss to read them with feeling.
- Play the dialogues again and ask your Ss to tick the expressions as they hear them.

> The numbers refer to the dialogues on recording 14.2.
> **Making contact**
> Could you put me through to Mr Li Wang please? – 1
> You seem to have got the wrong extension. – 1
> **Asking for information**
> Could you give me a few details? – 2
> **Asking for repetition**
> I'm sorry, I didn't catch that. – 3
> What did you say the reference number was? – 3
> **Checking information**
> Fine. Shall I just read that back to you? – 3
> **Clarifying**
> I'm sorry, I don't follow you. – 4
> Are you saying that ...? – 4
> **Confirming understanding**
> Fine – 3 / OK – 1, 2, 3, 4 / Right – 2 (and, as a question, 3)
> **Confirming action**
> I'll check it out right away. – 2
> I'll call you back as soon as I can. – 2

- Check the answers with the whole class.

(B)

- Tell the Ss that they will now have a chance to use these expressions in role play situations.
- Divide the class into pairs. Some pairs can do role play 1 and others role play 2.
- Allocate the roles and get the Ss to absorb the information. Circulate and assist if necessary.
- When the Ss are ready they can do the role plays. If you have telephone equipment, you can use it. Otherwise, ask Ss in each pair to sit back to back.
- Circulate and monitor. Note language points for praise and correction, especially in relation to the expressions in the Useful language box.
- When Ss have finished, praise good language points from the discussion and work on three or four points that need improvement, getting individual Ss to say the correct forms.
- Ask one or two individual pairs to do a performance of their situation for the whole class.

> **1 to 1**
>
> These role plays can be done 1 to 1. Don't forget to note language points for praise and correction afterwards. Highlight some of the language you chose to use as well.

Case study

Yedo Department Stores

A chain of Japanese department stores is in trouble, in the face of social changes and foreign competition. Ss suggest some solutions.

Stage 1: Background

◎ Ask the Ss to read the background information about Yedo. Meanwhile, write the points in the first column of the table on the board.

◎ With the whole class, elicit the information to complete the table.

Activity of company	Department stores: six in Japan, one each in London and New York
Image	Prestigious, high quality
Strategy	Wide range of products, personalised service
Problems	Falling profits, similar situation elsewhere

Stage 2: Market research

◎ Divide the class into three groups, A, B and C.

◎ Each group will specialise in studying the information in one part of the market report commissioned by Yedo. Members of each group can work collaboratively in pairs or threes, but tell the Ss that one member of each group, chosen later at random, will give an overview of the information for the whole class.

◎ The three groups can start working separately. Go to each group and give them the specific instructions for that group.

◎ Ss in Group A work on the Yedo Department Stores fact file, commenting on its contents. Tell them that the person talking about it for the whole class will have to make a coherent presentation including comments, beginning something like this:

> Yedo was founded more than 100 years ago, in 1895. It employs about 3,200 people, mostly full-time, around the world and one of the first impressions that people get when they go into the stores is the number of assistants available to serve customers.
> Opening hours are 10 till 6, with late opening on Fridays till 7, allowing people to do some shopping after they leave work. Many of the stores are situated near main railway stations, which is very convenient for commuters, of whom of course there are large numbers, especially in Tokyo, New York and London.

◎ Ss in Group B look at Yedo's competition, as detailed in part 3 of the report. The person making the presentation will speak as if they are a member of TWCB, the marketing agency, talking to senior managers at Yedo. The speaker will expand on the notes in the market report, adding comments to back it up, like this:

> We've identified four potential sources of competition for Yedo. First, there are convenience stores. We used to think of these as being rather downmarket, for students and young people, but I'm sure you've all noticed how more and more different types of people are using stores like this. You can get a wide range of goods and services from them. (You can even pay your phone bill there!) What they offer changes very quickly in response to customer demand. And of course, they're open 24 hours a day, which is one of the reasons they're called convenience stores.

◎ Ss in Group C study the general trends in part 4 of the report. The person making the presentation will speak as if they are a member of TWCB, the marketing agency, talking to senior managers at Yedo. The speaker will expand on the notes in the market report, adding comments and examples to back it up, like this:

> As people in Japan grow older, there will be new opportunities for sales growth. One of the results of this is that there will be increased demand for clothes for older people but that make people feel young, for new health products, and for new financial products. I mention these just to give an idea of how widespread the effects of this change in the population will be.

◎ Choose one person at random from each group to come to the front of the class and give their presentation.

◎ Invite comments and encourage brief discussion after each presentation, but don't pre-empt the issues that will be discussed during the discussion task below.

Stage 3: Discussion task

◎ Divide the class into groups of five or six. The Ss are TWCB agency personnel. They should concentrate on giving specific answers to the seven key questions posed by Yedo's CEO.

◎ Appoint a chair for the meeting. This person should control the meeting, using the seven questions as an agenda.

◎ Appoint one of the participants to be a notetaker who should take coherent and legible notes that can later form the basis for a writing task.

◎ Circulate and monitor, but do not intervene unless necessary. Note language points for later praise and correction.

◎ When the meeting(s) end(s), praise good language points from the discussion and work on three or four points that need improvement, getting individual Ss to say the correct forms.

◎ Discuss the meeting(s) with the whole class, getting each group to explain what happened.

1 to 1

This case study can be done 1 to 1, with the student analysing the information and then discussing recommendations. Don't forget to note language points for praise and correction afterwards. Highlight some of the language you chose to use as well.

Writing

◉ Ask the Ss to base their writing on the notes taken by the member of their team during the simulated meeting.

◉ The writing can be done collaboratively in class or as homework.

◉ If your Ss are doing the writing task for homework, you may want to photocopy the notes made by the notetaker in each group so that each student has a record of what was said and decided in their group.

 Writing file pages 144–145

Revision

This unit revises and reinforces some of the key language points from Units 8–14, and links with those units are clearly shown. You can point out these links to Ss if you think that would be useful.

This revision unit, like Revision Unit A, concentrates on reading and writing activities. Some of the exercise types are similar to those in the Reading and Writing section of levels 2 and 3 of the Business English Certificate examination organised by the University of Cambridge Local Examinations Syndicate.

For more speaking practice, see the Resource bank section of this book beginning on page 196. The exercises in this unit can be done in class individually or collaboratively, or for homework.

8 Team building

Fixed pairs

(A)–(B)

◉ These exercises revisit the fixed pairs in the Reading section, Exercise C, on page 71 and introduce some new ones.

> A
> 1 b   2 e   3 c   4 a   5 d   6 f   7 g
>
> B
> 1 wax and wane
> 2 loud and clear
> 3 hard and fast
> 4 nuts and bolts
> 5 boom and bust
> 6 touch and go
> 7 pros and cons

Modal perfect

◉ The modal perfect, from the Language review section on page 72, is tested in a different form.

> 1 had: have
> 2 must: might
> 3 would: should
> 4 working: worked
> 5 succeed: succeeded
> 6 be: been
> 7 had: have
> 8 use: used

9 Raising finance

Negotiating expressions

◉ Ask your Ss to look again at the negotiating expressions in the Useful language box on page 81 to remind themselves about the different categories.

> Pre-negotiation small talk – 3   Softening phrases – 1, 7
> Open questions – 4   Signalling phrases – 5
> Closed questions – 6   Summarising – 2
>
> 1 d   2 c   3 b   4 e   5 g   6 a   7 f

Reading

◉ This exercise extends the ideas in the Skills section, Exercise A on page 81.

1 d	2 c	3 b	4 a	5 c	6 b	7 d

10 Customer service

Idioms

◉ This exercise revises some of the idioms in Vocabulary, Exercise B, on page 87 and introduces some new ones. Point out that it's important to get idioms word-perfect, otherwise they can sound comic!

1 The ball is in their court.
2 the last straw
3 slipped my mind
4 light at the end of the tunnel
5 pass the buck
6 straight to the point
7 get to the bottom

Reading

◉ This activity relates to the general theme of the unit, and includes some gerunds (see the Language review section on page 88).

1 c	2 d	3 b	4 b	5 c	6 b	7 c	8 a

11 Crisis management

Comparisons

◉ Ss look again at the language of similarity and difference, as in the Language review section on page 96.

1 g	2 e	3 d	4 f	5 a	6 c	7 b

Writing

◉ This exercise relates to the article *Handling a disaster*, in the Reading section, on page 94.

◉ The 'model' answer here is designed only to give an idea of what Ss should produce, not the actual ideas, which should be their own, of course.

Model answer

> If there is an incident similar to the one that happened recently to one of Serene Cruises' liners, I recommend using specialised crisis management consultants, who are experienced in handling such emergencies. In close collaboration with Carefree's management team, they would issue press statements and generally co-ordinate the communications effort.
> I recommend that the families of all passengers should be contacted and reassured by phone, using a professional call centre, as making more than 1,000 phone calls is something that can only be handled in this way.
> Carefree should give each passenger $10,000 cash in compensation for distress, inconvenience and immediate expenses, and also offer a free cruise to be taken any time up to five years after the incident.
> Carefree would not want to suffer the same sort of negative publicity that has recently affected Serene's reputation and image. I cannot emphasise how important it is to have a contingency plan in the unlikely event of a similar incident with one of Carefree's ships.

12 Management styles

Opposites

◉ These activities look again at the compound adjectives in the Vocabulary section on page 101, and add some new ones.

Exercise A
1 unfair, unfairness
2 informal, informality
3 illegal, illegality
4 disobedient, disobedience
5 impatient, impatience
6 irresponsible, irresponsibility
Exercise B
1 disobedience
2 illegalities
3 impatience
4 informality
5 irresponsibility
6 unfairness

Text reference

◉ Ss work further on the text reference ideas introduced in the Language review section, page 104.

1 b   2 c   3 e   4 a

13 Takeovers and mergers

Reading

◉ This exercise looks at the general theme of the unit, and asks Ss to think about logical sentence construction.

1 over
2 off
3 ✓
4 to
5 up

Presentation language

◉ Ask Ss to look again at the expressions in the Useful language box in the Skills section on page 113 before doing this activity.

1 h   2 f   3 g   4 e   5 a   6 d   7 b   8 c

14 The future of business

Reading

◉ Ss look at some texts about the general topic of the unit.

1 b   2 a   3 c   4 a   5 c   6 b   7 d

Writing

● Ss write a short report about their ideas about the future. The 'model' answer here is designed only to give an idea of what Ss should produce, not the actual ideas, which should be their own, of course.

Model answer

Housing and work

By 2050, most people will be working from home, connected by high-capacity wireless data and video links. House construction will have changed, with special additional office rooms with space for business equipment. But there will be a demand for 'traditional' materials such as bricks and wood, and houses will look very similar to those of today.

With the trend towards homeworking, sometime in the next 20 years many large companies will start to leave the central business districts of cities. However, urban living will again be the lifestyle of choice. Many office towers will be transformed into flats.

Leisure and transport

People will want to socialise with others after working all day at home. The workaholism of the late 20th century will have been forgotten, and a six-hour day, four-day week working pattern will be normal. Big sports and music events will be very popular. Getting to them will be easy, with clean, efficient electrically-powered public transport.

Food production

The countryside will be used much less for agriculture than it is today, as food will be produced on intensive, organic farms, many of them in climates where crops are easier to grow. If politics allow, Africa will be the main source of food for Europe. The European countryside will consist mainly of theme parks showing how people used to live in the countryside a century or two earlier, along with vast sports facilities, long-distance paths for walkers, and so on.

Quality of life

A lot of present-day frustrations will have disappeared. People will only travel for leisure and social purposes, so rush hours will be a thing of the past. A new post-nuclear energy source will have been found, for fuelling cars and providing electricity. There will be a new emphasis on quality of life. For those with money, the future in 2050 looks bright.

Text bank

Teacher's notes

Introduction

The text bank contains articles relating to the units in the *Market Leader Upper Intermediate* Course Book. These articles extend and develop the themes in those units. You can choose the articles that are of most interest to your students. They can be done in class or as homework. You have permission to make photocopies of these articles for your students.

Before you read

Before each article there is a discussion point, a warmer that allows students to focus on the subject of the article and prepares them for it. This can be done as a whole class discussion, or in pairs or small groups, with each group then reporting its ideas to the whole class.

Reading

If using the articles in class, it's a good idea to treat different sections in different ways, for example reading the first paragraph with the whole class, and then getting students to work in pairs on the following paragraphs.

The first comprehension question for each article is often designed to help Ss get an overview of the whole article. If you're short of time, get different pairs to read different sections of the article simultaneously. You can circulate, monitor and give help where necessary. Ss then report back to the whole group with a succinct summary and/or their answers to the questions for that section.

A full answer key follows the articles.

Discussion

In the Over to you sections following each article, there are discussion points. Again, these can be dealt with by the whole class, or the class can be divided, with different groups discussing different points. During discussion, circulate, monitor and give help where necessary. Ss then report back to the whole class. Praise good language production and work on areas for improvement in the usual way.

Writing

The discussion points can also form the basis for short pieces of written work. Ss will find this easier if they have already discussed the points in class, but you can ask Ss to read the article and write about the discussion points as homework.

UNIT 1   Communication

Communication with employees

Level of difficulty: ● ● ○

Before you read

In your organisation or school, do you have a system for
making suggestions for improvements in the way it is run?

Reading

Read this article from the *Financial Times* and answer the
questions.

Beyond the suggestion box

Nikki Tait

Three years ago, American Freightways, an Arkansas haulage
company, had a little wooden
"suggestions box". Its 13,300 staff
dropped in about one offering a
month. But things have changed.
It now has a contract with an out-
sourced, telephone-based employee feedback service – and receives
200 calls a month from its workforce. Suggestions have ranged
from how to maintain equipment
to the best way to bid for work on
certain routes. "All people have to
do is pick up a phone – it has been
very beneficial," says Mr John
Sherman, vice-president for "people management". The person
behind In Touch is Peter
Lilienthal, a Minneapolis busi-
nessman. The concept is simplici-
ty itself, yet clients as varied
as Pillsbury, Chase Manhattan,
Arthur Andersen Consulting and
Coca-Cola have nothing but
praise.

In Touch provides a freecall
number, which the client's employees can dial at any time.
Messages are then transcribed
verbatim and forwarded to the
company's executives within one
working day. For companies with
5,000 employees or more, In Touch
will provide a monthly breakdown
of calls, highlighting areas of concern, and so on. It can also provide
some foreign-language services –
Spanish, for example. It is successful, says Mr Lilienthal, partly
because the service is independent and, unlike typical in-house
communication systems, callers
can remain anonymous.

Having watched tens of companies implement the system, Mr
Lilienthal says it is almost impossible to predict what the response
will be. But he notes that there is
often a quiet interval at the outset, while employees wait to see
whether messages will be taken
seriously. That is followed by a
period when minor, bottled-up

grievances emerge. Finally, once
the system is established, the
number of calls typically falls
away, and their value increases.
This, too, is confirmed by clients.
Pillsbury, which began using the
service in the early 1990s, shortly
after it was acquired by Britain's
Grand Metropolitan, says it still
receives about 50 calls a month.

Mr Lilienthal has a couple of
tips for anyone introducing the
system. First, make sure the service is relatively unrestricted, and
not advertised as a "complaint"
line. Second, convince workers
that calls will be taken seriously.
American Freightways, for example, promises to get back to all
employees who leave their name
within ten days. Executives to
whom the messages are forwarded
are given five days to respond.
Pillsbury makes a point of pub-
licising the most relevant messages, together with responses, via
its in-house newspaper or internal
e-mail system.

From the *Financial Times*

UNIT 1   Communication

1 Look through the whole article and put these paragraph headings into the correct order.

   a) Typical response patterns after the system is introduced
   b) How the system works
   c) Hints on how to introduce the system
   d) A new system for employee suggestions

2 True or false (lines 1–26)?

   a) American Freightways is based in Arkansas.
   b) Before, the suggestions scheme received no suggestions at all.
   c) The new suggestions scheme is run in-house.
   d) Employees make suggestions by e-mail.
   e) The system is hard to use.
   f) American Freightways' vice-president for people management thinks that the system has been very useful.
   g) On the whole, other clients for the system have been satisfied, but they have made some criticisms.

3 Find expressions in lines 27–44 that mean the same as those in italics.

   a) In Touch *gives a number that people can call without paying*.
   b) What the callers say is then *written down word for word*.
   c) They are *sent* to the company's managers.
   d) In Touch will *give details of the numbers of different calls*.
   e) In Touch will *give details of the things that a company's employees are particularly worried about or interested in*.
   f) Callers *do not have to give their names*.

4 Put these phases for the system into the order they may typically occur, as described in lines 45–64.

   a) a phase with a moderate number of calls
   b) a phase with a high number of calls
   c) a phase with a low number of calls

5 Now match each phase in Question 4 to typical employee reactions for those phases.

   a) The system settles down, and people call less often, but what they have to say is more useful to the company.
   b) Employees hesitate to use the system because they don't know if it will work.
   c) Employees call more frequently, often to complain about things that have annoyed them for a long time.

6 Which of these hints to managers for making the system successful is *not* mentioned in lines 65–82?

   a) Don't say that the system is mainly for making complaints.
   b) Make the system relatively open for anyone to use.
   c) You should promise not to try to find the people who call without giving their names.
   d) You should respond to messages within a particular time.

   e) Publicise the most important messages and their responses.
   f) Where relevant, you should get the appropriate manager to respond to messages.

Over to you 1

Imagine you put three suggestions into your organisation's suggestions box. What would they be?

Over to you 2

Now imagine that you are phoning a service like In Touch with one of your suggestions. Enact or write down the conversation.

Text bank

UNIT 1   Communication

Communication with the world at large

Level of difficulty: ●●●

Before you read

Find a copy of your company's annual report, or the report of a company that you admire. What sections does it consist of? What types of information does it provide?

(There is a range of reports from companies around the world, not just in the UK, available at Company Annual Reports Online: www.carol.co.uk.)

Reading

Read this article from the *Financial Times* and answer the questions.

The bad news as well as the good

Peter Knight

While society magazines such as *Hello!* and *People* sell millions, company publications telling of charity work are ignored as cor-
5 porate trash. Why? The answer is spin – the way facts are rearranged to present a story in the best possible light. Readers love the positive spin put on the
10 stories of minor royals and fading celebrities as they "talk openly" of their wonderful marriages and "graciously open the doors" of their palatial homes. Readers
15 know it is a load of nonsense, but it is a bit like eating chocolate – great fun and nobody gets hurt.

The same readers, though, are highly suspicious of the slant put
20 on corporate stories about the good work companies do in the community. Readers heavily dis-count anything a company says on the issue. They realise they are
25 getting only one side of the story, and want to hear the bad news as well as the good. There are good reasons for this. We are losing our respect for traditional authorities
30 and social structures. Large companies are being called on to act as moral entities, to uphold codes of conduct and to take on social responsibilities in return for the
35 freedoms they enjoy.

But consumers know, too, that companies, like priests and government ministers, are never perfect. They face dilemmas and
40 often act in error. By far the biggest mistake companies can make is to wear a halo; yet judging by the quality of corporate publications, many do just this. But
45 some leading companies have begun to modify the way they communicate, especially about their social responsibilities. They have shaken off the halo and
50 reduced the spin.

Take the Shell Report. It was well received mainly because it confronted the difficult issues: human rights, bribery and corrup-
55 tion. Publishing this information – including the number of people fired for taking bribes – is embarrassing but honesty gains good marks from the public. The Shell
60 Report is the first of its kind from such a big, mainstream multinational. It marks the beginning of not only a new form of non-financial reporting, but – more
65 important – a decline in the amount of corporate spin in company communications.

From the *Financial Times*

UNIT 1   Communication

1 Look through the whole article and put these paragraph headings into the correct order.

a) The Shell Report is a model of a new kind of company reporting.
b) People like society magazines.
c) Some companies have started to communicate in a new way.
d) People are suspicious of company reports.

2 What definition of 'spin' is given in lines 6–8?

3 Which two-word expressions in lines 1–17 mean

a) work done by volunteers with a social purpose?
b) unimportant members of royal families?
c) people who were famous but are now less famous?
d) very expensive houses?
e) the way that a story is told so that it will have the best effect?

4 In lines 18–35, which verbs are used to link these nouns? (In e, f and g, find the verbs used to talk about what companies should be doing.)

a) readers/what companies say about their charity work
b) readers/one side of the story
c) readers/bad news and good
d) people in general/respect for authority
e) companies/moral entities
f) companies/codes of conduct
g) companies/social responsibilities

5 Look at the references to 'halo' in lines 40–50.

a) Who normally wears a halo?
b) Why is it a mistake for organisations to try to wear a halo?
c) If an organisation shakes off its halo, what happens?

6 Why is the Shell Report important (lines 51–67)?

Over to you 1

What sort of things count as 'bad news' in company reports? Would you buy shares in a company that had bad news in its report?

Over to you 2

You work for a company that believes in honest reporting of its activities. Write a press release about one of the following events, following the 'philosophy' given in the last paragraph of the article above.

- One of the company's products has caused people to become ill.
- The company's activities have caused environmental pollution.
- A senior manager has been fired for corruption.
- Workers have been falsifying records about product quality.

Towards a global brand

Level of difficulty: ● ● ○

Before you read

Which is the most global brand you can think of? Is it marketed in the same way all over the world?

Reading

Read this article from the *Financial Times* by Jean-Noël Kapferer and answer the questions.

Making brands work around the world

No one contests the economic necessity of geographically extending a product – it is a source of economies of scale, of amort-
5 isation of rising research-and-development costs and of competitive advantage in local markets. But how far do we push the global idea? For example, the Mars brand
10 is not absolutely global. The Mars chocolate bar is sold as an all-round nutritious snack in the UK and as an energiser in Europe (two different concepts and positioning
15 for the same physical product). Nestlé adapts the taste of its worldwide brands to local consumer expectations. The Nescafé formulas vary worldwide.
20 Global marketing implies the wish to extend a single marketing mix to a particular region (for example Europe or Asia) or even to the world. It also denotes a situ-
25 ation in which a firm's competitive position in one country can be significantly affected by its position in other countries. The global approach sees the role of indi-
30 vidual countries as only part of a wider competitive strategy.

The aim of marketing globalisation is not to maximise sales but to increase profitability. In the
35 first place, it cuts out duplicated tasks. For example, instead of bringing out different TV advertising for each country, a firm can use a single film for one region.
40 The McCann-Erickson agency is proud of the fact that it has saved Coca-Cola $90 million in production costs over the past 20 years by producing films with global
45 appeal.

Globalisation allows a firm to exploit good ideas, wherever they come from. Timotei shampoo was developed in Finland and spread
50 to other European countries. The beverage Malibu, which is sold worldwide, was created in South Africa.

In drinking Coca-Cola, we drink
55 the American myth – fresh, open, bubbling, young, dynamic, all-American images. Young people in search of identity form a particular target. In an effort to stand
60 out from others, they draw their sources of identity from cultural models provided by the media. Levi's are linked with a mythical image of breaking away down the
65 lonely open road – an image part James Dean, part Jack Kerouac, tinted with a glimpse of a North American eldorado. Nike tells young people to surpass them-
70 selves, to transcend the national confines of race and culture.

From the *Financial Times*

UNIT 2   International marketing

1 List all the brands mentioned in the article, and the products they relate to. Which two products have different positionings in different markets?

2 A Match the expressions 1–5 with their meanings a–e (lines 1–34).

1   amortisation of rising R&D costs
2   competitive advantage in local markets
3   economies of scale
4   maximisation of sales
5   increased profitability

a) the idea that the larger amount you produce, the lower the cost of each unit
b) spreading the cost of research and development over a higher level of sales
c) being able to successfully compete in a particular place
d) making more profit
e) selling as much as possible

B In the article as a whole, which of these reasons is *not* given as one of the real reasons for extending a brand geographically?

3 True or false (lines 20–45)? Global marketing means …

a) using the same combination of marketing activities in a particular region or the whole world.
b) that a company's position in one country will not be affected by its position in other countries.
c) that companies can always use the same advertising campaign all over the world.
d) that individual countries are part of a wider global strategy.
e) that companies do not have to do certain tasks more than once.

4 Match the verbs with the nouns they go with in the article (lines 32–55).

1   maximise   a)   profitability
2   increase   b)   sales
3   bring out   c)   films
4   produce   d)   tasks
5   drink   e)   advertising
6   duplicate   f)   the American myth

5 Choose the correct alternatives to explain the words in italics from lines 57–71 relating to young people.

a) Young people in search of identity *form a particular target*. This means that they are
   i) a market that can easily be identified.
   ii) a market that should be treated like any other.
   iii) a special market that should be approached in a special way.

b) … *an effort to stand out from others* means that young people want to be considered
   i) the same as other people.
   ii) differently from other people.
   iii) the same as other people, but also different.

c) They draw their sources of identity *from cultural models provided by the media* means that they establish their identity
   i) by basing it on people and ideas they see in films, on TV, etc.
   ii) by rejecting what they see in films, on TV, etc.
   iii) by wanting to change what they see in films, on TV, etc.

d) *North American eldorado* gives the idea that, for young people, North America is
   i) a bad place.
   ii) a perfect place.
   iii) an ordinary place.

e) If young people *surpass themselves*, they
   i) do worse than they thought they were capable of.
   ii) do the same as they thought they were capable of.
   iii) do better than they thought they were capable of.

f) If young people *transcend the national confines of race and culture*, they
   i) go beyond what is expected of people from their race and culture.
   ii) do the same as what is expected.
   iii) do less than what is expected.

Over to you 1

Go back to your list of all the brands mentioned in the article. Which of them do you know? How are they positioned and marketed in your country?

Over to you 2

What or who are the models for young people in your country? Where do they draw their identity from? What is the role of international media such as films and television series?

Text bank

Cultural problems in international marketing

Level of difficulty: ●●○

Before you read

Which of these retailers are present in your country? What do they sell? What is their image? Do you associate them with their home country, or do you think of them as international?

- Benetton
- Borders
- C&A
- Carrefour
- Marks and Spencer
- Wal-Mart

Reading

Read this article from the *Financial Times* by Bertrand Benoît and answer the questions.

Wal-Mart finds German failures hard to swallow

Wal-Mart, the world's largest retailer, is losing up to $300 million a year in its German venture after misjudging both corporate culture and the market. When German shoppers gathered in Mannheim for the opening of the renovated Wal-Mart Supercenter, they were treated to a novel experience. There was space to walk around, freshly-baked bagels, free carrier bags and, according to Alfred Brandstetter, the store manager, "probably the biggest fish counter in Baden-Wurttemberg". Yet behind the smiles of its uniformed attendants, the world's largest retailer is increasingly worried about the challenges faced by its German venture.

Bolted together from two acquisitions in 1997 and 1998, Wal-Mart Germany is the country's fourth largest hypermarket chain with ten per cent of the market. Although a drop in the ocean for the worldwide group – it generates less than two per cent of Wal-Mart's sales – its poor performance has been a stain on the group's record.

Making a mark on Europe's largest and most competitive food retail markets was never going to be easy. But some of Wal-Mart's early mistakes may be impossible to redress. The most glaring one, says an insider, was to disregard the structure of distribution in German food retailing. Drawing on the US model, Wal-Mart decided it wanted to control distribution to stores rather than leave it to suppliers. The result was chaos because suppliers could not adapt to Wal-Mart's centralised demands. With many deliveries failing to arrive in time, out-of-stock rates were sometimes up to 20 per cent, compared to a seven per cent average for the industry, although there have been marked improvements recently.

Then the group fuelled discontent at Wertkauf, its first acquisition, by filling top positions with US expatriates, a move perceived as arrogant. The ensuing exodus of German managers, which accelerated after the closure of the Wertkauf headquarters in 1999, deprived the group of local expertise.

Facing renovation costs up to five times those in the US, and struggling to navigate Germany's Byzantine planning and social regulations, the group has only refurbished a quarter of its 95 stores, and many sites remain unattractive, too small, cramped or poorly located.

Lack of scale has also worked against the group, by preventing it from dictating to suppliers and distributors. Although sizeable in the hypermarket segment, Wal-Mart Germany is a midget in the food retail industry as a whole, with less than two per cent of the market. With a joint market share of 30 per cent, Edeka and Rewe, Germany's two leaders, have far greater purchasing muscle.

"The problem is that Germany is beginning to raise questions about the group's entire international strategy," says Andrew Fowler, food retail analyst at Morgan Stanley Dean Witter.

From the *Financial Times*

UNIT 2   International marketing

1 Put these paragraph summaries into the correct order.

a) Another mistake was to employ US managers. German managers were offended by this and left the company in large numbers.

b) Renovating its stores is expensive, and many of them are unattractive or in the wrong place.

c) They knew that succeeding in Germany would be difficult. One of their biggest mistakes was to use a distribution system unlike the usual German one.

d) Wal-Mart Germany has relatively low bargaining power with suppliers because of its small size.

e) Wal-Mart Germany was formed through two companies it bought. German sales form a very small part of Wal-Mart's sales worldwide, but the problems with its German operations have not been good for its image.

f) Wal-Mart has opened another store in Germany, but its German operations are losing money.

g) Wal-Mart's problems in Germany are causing analysts to wonder about its international strategy in general.

2 Match the two parts of these phrases from lines 1–21.

1	German	a)	attendants
2	largest	b)	counter
3	novel	c)	culture
4	uniformed	d)	experience
5	corporate	e)	manager
6	store	f)	retailer
7	fish	g)	shoppers
8	German	h)	venture

3 Choose the correct alternative to define these expressions from lines 22–32.

a) Wal-Mart Germany was *bolted together from two acquisitions* means that it was formed from two acquisitions,

   i) but the two companies may not work very well together.

   ii) and the two companies work extremely well together.

   iii) and the two companies have remained completely separate.

b) The German market is *a drop in the ocean* for the worldwide group means that sales from this market

   i) are of no importance at all.

   ii) form a very small part of Wal-Mart's overall sales.

   iii) form a large part of Wal-Mart's overall sales.

c) Wal-Mart's *poor performance has been a stain on the group's record* means that its performance in Germany

   i) has damaged its reputation.

   ii) doesn't matter.

   iii) is relatively unimportant.

4 True or false (lines 33–54)?

a) Succeeding in the German retail market is difficult.

b) It will certainly be possible to correct some of Wal-Mart's early mistakes there.

c) Using the wrong distribution methods was its least serious mistake.

d) Suppliers were not used to sending orders when instructed by the head offices of retailers.

e) A lot of shops were out of stock of many products, and the situation is getting worse.

5 Find adjectives in lines 55–73 that describe

a) what German managers thought of putting people from the US into senior jobs (8 letters).

b) the departure of German managers that followed this (7).

c) the knowledge that German managers had about German retailing (5).

d) costs related to repainting and modernising stores (10).

e) Germany's planning regulations (9).

f) many of Wal-Mart's sites in Germany (12).

g) many of Wal-Mart's sites in Germany (3, 5).

h) many of Wal-Mart's sites in Germany (7).

i) many of Wal-Mart's sites in Germany (6, 7).

6 Match the two parts of these statements about lines 74–91.

1 The fact that Wal-Mart is small means that

2 Although it has a lot of very big supermarkets,

3 The two leading retailers have a lot more bargaining power with suppliers

4 Wal-Mart's problems in Germany are causing analysts

a) to wonder about its international strategy in general.

b) it does not have bargaining power with suppliers.

c) it is small in food retailing as a whole.

d) because they have much bigger market share.

Over to you

You are a consultant advising an international supermarket group that wants to set up in your country by building a completely new chain of stores. What advice would you give about the following?

- The strengths and weaknesses of existing competitors.
- Whether to employ expatriate managers or local managers at their head office in your country.
- Planning regulations: are they Byzantine or straightforward?
- How big its new stores should be.
- Where to put its stores.
- What to sell in its stores.
- Local tastes in food and other products.
- Cultural issues about which it should be sensitive.

Employer–employee relationships

Level of difficulty: ●●○

Text bank

Before you read

Should companies have a responsibility to employ people for life? Think about past and present employment patterns.

Reading

Read this article from the *Financial Times* by Lucy Kellaway and answer the questions.

Managing separation after that perfect relationship

At some point this month, I will be called in by my team leader for a career chat. This is an annual date in the diary, and tends to take a
5 predictable form. They say their bit and you say yours, and no one is left much the wiser. The minutes are subsequently written up, signed by both parties and filed
10 away, nice and tidy.

Compare this to how they do things at Motorola. That progressive US company doesn't have career chats. It has Individual
15 Dignity Entitlement Programs, which take place four times a year. Every quarter, all employees are asked such questions as "Do you have a personal career plan, and is
20 it exciting, achievable and being acted upon?" and "Do you receive candid positive or negative feedback at least every 30 days that is helpful in improving or achieving
25 your career plan?"

The Individual Dignity Entitlement Program is mentioned in the current issue of *Strategy & Business*, the magazine of Booz-
30 Allen & Hamilton, as a shining example of something the magazine calls "New People Partnerships". This is the perfect relationship that is supposed to exist
35 between employer and employee in an age when there are no longer jobs for life.

The general idea is that employees "own" their own careers, and
40 that employers support them in realizing their full potential, whether that involves staying with the company or moving on. In this brave new world, quitting a
45 job or being fired become things of the past. Instead, what happens is that the partners "separate". Companies, the magazine warns, must learn to manage separation
50 as something perfectly normal, but must also be firm about "separating those who consistently underperform".

Companies can set up New
55 People Partnerships. They can help employees "own" their careers and design appraisal systems – sorry, dignity entitlement systems – to that end. But when it
60 comes down to it, nothing much has changed. The ones who do not perform get chucked out, same as before. You can call it separating and pretend that it is natural. But
65 when it happens to you, you will know: you've been fired.

From the Financial Times

UNIT 3   Building relationships

1 Choose the heading that best suits each paragraph. (Two of the headings are not used.)

   a) Individual Dignity Entitlement Programs at Motorola
   b) If you don't perform, you're fired, whatever the system is called
   c) Jobs for life no longer exist, and people must be willing to change companies
   d) Employers and employees in partnership
   e) Career chats for journalists at the *Financial Times*
   f) Company profits increase with job flexibility
   g) Jobs for life make a comeback

2 Match the expressions 1–7 to their meanings a–g (lines 1–10).

1	I will be called in by my team leader for a career chat.	a)	Someone makes a report of the meeting.
2	This is an annual date in the diary.	b)	Everyone knows what's going to happen at the meeting.
3	The meeting tends to take a predictable form.	c)	Each person says something, but there is no real exchange of ideas or opinions.
4	They say their bit and you say yours.	d)	No one knows much more afterwards than before.
5	No one is left much the wiser.	e)	This happens once a year.
6	The minutes are written up.	f)	The minutes are put in a drawer, but probably no one looks at them again.
7	They are filed away, nice and tidy.	g)	My manager will ask me to come and see him / her so that we can talk 'informally' about my work.

3 Look at lines 11–25 and complete the statements by choosing the correct alternative.

   a) A progressive organisation is
      i) forward-looking.
      ii) fast-moving.
      iii) politically on the left.
   b) An achievable aim is
      i) unrealistic.
      ii) realistic.
      iii) irrelevant.
   c) If you act on something, you
      i) ignore it.
      ii) like it.
      iii) do something about it.
   d) Candid feedback is
      i) honest.
      ii) dishonest.
      iii) neither honest nor dishonest.

4 'New People Partnerships' are an example of the 'perfect relationship that is supposed to exist between employer and employee' (lines 32–37). Does the author think this relationship really exists? How can you tell what her view is?

5 Find four different expressions in lines 38–66 to talk about leaving a company. (For example, 'separate' and 'separation' count as one expression.)

6 According to the writer, if you are 'separated', is it any different from being fired?

Over to you 1

Do you have a regular appraisal system in your organisation? How does it work?

Over to you 2

List the arguments in favour of:
- lifetime employment;
- 'employability': the idea that people should be trained and willing to move at any time from company to company.

Text bank

Relationships between companies: strategic alliances

Level of difficulty: ● ● ●

Before you read

Does your organisation communicate with its competitors?
Does it sometimes work together with them?

Reading

Strategic alliances are key to the survival of technology companies and they greatly benefit other business sectors.

Read this article from the *Financial Times* and answer the questions.

The trend is ally or die

Charles Wang

Of all the trends sweeping across the business landscape, few will have more of an impact on companies than strategic partnerships. We have all seen the power of 'partnering' in almost every industry. The revival of the US automotive industry, which was partly the result of co-operative agreements with Japanese car makers, is a good example. We have also witnessed the disastrous effects of 'going it alone' – the US steel industry almost collapsed because it failed to ally itself with strategic players. The information technology (IT) industry is no exception. Not only does it encourage business relationships, it also develops tools, such as Electronic Data Interchange (EDI) technology, that facilitate business partnerships in other markets.

Strategic partnerships also promote the development of technologies that would not, or could not, be developed by manufacturers working independently. Strategic alliances will create new playing fields for enterprises. Those companies involved in strategic alliances will benefit greatly from the standards and economies of scale that result. On the other hand, industries that insist on keeping a 'hands-off' relationship between suppliers, customers and competitors will be left behind.

Why is all this good for the client? Because strategic alliances enable user organisations to develop critical standards, create new markets, jointly fund large efforts in their common interests, quickly respond to new opportunities, and share information. Customers today are not well served by vendors operating in a vacuum, and increased competition has made users much more demanding.

Consider the IT industry: from the early 1960s through the 1980s, account control was the name of the game. Clients were locked into a particular supplier's systems. Their choices were limited, and they had little, if any, control over price increases. Eventually, computer users rebelled. The world of open systems, in which customers became empowered to exercise much wider freedom in selecting hardware and software vendors, killed the practice of account control forever.

But open systems were a two-edged sword. On the upside, freedom of choice presented great opportunities for large-scale savings. On the downside, clients had to become in-house systems integration experts as they tried to cope with multiple IT providers who rarely, if ever, talked to one another.

Over time, users began insisting that vendors co-operate among themselves to guarantee that computer systems, networks, applications and databases could be managed together. They needed to be certain that the hardware and software they licensed operated together flawlessly.

In the end, systems integration became such a daunting task that many customers began relying on a few, loyal, hand-picked vendors. In return, the best hardware and software suppliers transformed their relationships with clients into much more than buying/selling agreements. They formed complex, strategic partnerships with their fellow suppliers.

From the *Financial Times*

UNIT 3   Building relationships

1 Complete these expressions with words from lines 1–18, and related words.

  a) If you decide to work closely with someone, you a_ _ _ yourself with them.
  b) Someone you work with is an a_ _ _ or p_ _ _ _ _ _ .
  c) Another name for an alliance is a _ _ _ _ _ _ _ship.
  d) The adjective related to 'co-operation' is
      co-_ _ _ _ _ _ _ _ _ .
  e) If you don't co-operate with anyone, you go
      _ _ _ _ _ _ _ .

2 Which three industries are mentioned specifically in lines 1–23? Which present good examples of strategic alliances at work?

3 What are the two advantages for companies belonging to an alliance? What is the disadvantage of not belonging? (lines 24–39)

4 What are the five advantages for customers who work with companies that are part of alliances? What effect has this had on customers? (lines 43–52)

5 True or false (lines 53–77)?

  a) From the 1960s to the 1980s, most companies had only one computer supplier.
  b) Companies at that time could easily change suppliers.
  c) Most companies still have the same relationship with their computer system supplier.
  d) Customers are now much freer to choose the systems they want.
  e) This has its advantages and disadvantages.
  f) At first, when a company had several systems suppliers, these suppliers often communicated with each other.

6 Find words in lines 78–97 that mean

  a) sellers of computers (7 letters).
  b) systems of computers working together (8 letters).
  c) jobs that computers are used for (12 letters).
  d) large amounts of information held on computer (9 letters).

7 Which of these things are *not* mentioned in lines 78–97? Computer systems users

  a) insisted that systems suppliers work together.
  b) insisted that their systems work perfectly.
  c) started to buy equipment instead of licensing it.
  d) found that systems integration was easy.
  e) were willing to pay more for systems that worked perfectly.
  f) were a factor in encouraging systems suppliers to form alliances.

Over to you 1

Who provides and maintains the computer system in your organisation? Do you have just one supplier or several? Make a list of the factors that make for a good supplier of maintenance.

Over to you 2

What are some of the disadvantages of working together with competitors? Think of any examples you know or could imagine.

Text bank

Corporate Training (S) P
nt Road
4
3868 Fax: (65) 324

UNIT 4   Success

What makes product innovations successful?   Level of difficulty: ●●●

Before you read

Why do some products succeed and others fail? Think of one big success and one big failure, and list the factors that were important in each case.

Reading

Read this article from the *Financial Times* by Gabriele Marcotti and answer the questions.

Stay tuned to consumer taste

Eight out of ten new products are commercial failures. Why do so many companies get it wrong?

Today we are told we live in a rapidly changing, technology-driven world, hungry for better, more powerful products. More money than ever is spent on research, development and invention. Yet it is generally accepted that eight out of ten new products fail. Worryingly, the ratio has remained constant over the past 30 years. Two conclusions can be drawn: either consumers are not as interested in innovation as we think or they are not being offered the right products.

Art Fry knows a thing or two about innovation: he invented the Post-It note on behalf of 3M. "People hate change, and many companies still don't really understand that," explains Mr Fry. "People follow their own established patterns. They figure that even if a new product is better, perhaps all the work involved in learning how to use it and getting accustomed to it simply isn't worth it."

Not necessarily, maintains Vijay Jolly, professor of strategy and technology management at the Institute for Management Development in Lausanne, Switzerland. He has identified a number of elements crucial to success: "The first is what I call the use paradigm: what is the product going to be used for and how. Take multimedia functions, for example. Some contend that they are part of the personal computer paradigm, that people will access and use them as they do with PCs. Others believe it's a television paradigm, it's a passive process rather than an interactive one. Either way, you need to be very clear about what your product is for.

"Another factor to keep in mind is that more often than not, class association is more important than added value," he adds. "That is, in class association, when designing a product, avoid making it unique. People will accept a substitute for an existing product much more easily if they can relate it to the existing product. Of course, it has to be a better substitute as well. The only exception to this is when the relative added value of the new product, from the consumer's point of view, is immensely greater, but that is extremely rare."

Bearing this in mind, consumers will reject, say, a pyramid-shaped television, even if it is ten per cent "better" than existing ones, because it will not have the required class association. According to Professor Jolly, a conventional-looking television that is just two per cent better has more chances of success than the pyramid TV...

From the *Financial Times*

UNIT 4   Success

1 Read the whole article and find the most appropriate summary for each paragraph. (Some of the summaries are not used.)

a) Why a pyramid-shaped television would fail.

b) How the product is going to be used is more important than the value it will add for consumers.

c) Products fail partly because people don't like change.

d) Professor Jolly discusses multimedia technology.

e) One success factor is how the product is going to be used, with an example about computers.

f) Art Fry describes how the Post-It note was developed.

g) A lot of money is spent on R&D, but most new products fail.

2 Find the meanings of these items from lines 16–28, as they are used there.

a) 'Art Fry knows a thing or two about innovation' (lines 16–17) means that he knows
  i) one thing.
  ii) two things.
  iii) a lot.

b) 'People follow their own established patterns' (lines 22–23) means that they
  i) tend to behave in ways in which they have always behaved.
  ii) prefer particular designs rather than others.
  iii) always buy things from the same shops.

c) If people 'figure' that a new product is better (lines 23–24), they .... that it will be better.
  i) doubt
  ii) certify
  iii) think

d) If you get 'accustomed' to something (lines 29–49), you
  i) get fed up with it.
  ii) get used to it.
  iii) get on with it.

e) If you think that something 'isn't worth it' (lines 27–28), you think that, in relation to the benefits it may bring,
  i) too much time and effort are involved.
  ii) too much money is involved.
  iii) too much emotion is involved.

3 True or false (lines 24–43)?

a) Professor Jolly entirely agrees with Art Fry.

b) Professor Jolly has identified only one thing that is very important for the success of new products.

c) The 'use paradigm' is concerned with how and why the product is going to be used.

d) Some people think that multimedia will be accessible through PCs.

e) Some people think that multimedia will be accessible through TV.

f) Professor Jolly thinks that multimedia will definitely only be accessible through PCs.

4 Find words in lines 50–77 to complete these statements.

a) If something is unlike anything else, it is ....

b) If one product replaces another, it is a .... for it.

c) If a new product is worth more to a consumer than an existing product, the consumer thinks that there is .... in the new product.

d) If something does not happen very often, it is extremely ....

e) If a product looks like existing products, it is ....-............ .

f) If consumers do not like a new product and do not buy it, they .... it.

Over to you 1

Why have these things been so successful? If possible, relate their success to the ideas in the article.

- personal stereos
- café chains like Starbucks
- video games

And why do you think each of these things failed, or became much less successful than before? Is it to do with any of the reasons in the article?

- 3-D cinema (viewing films with special glasses to get a three-dimensional effect)
- motor scooters
- trams

Over to you 2

Think of a company in trouble. You are a company 'doctor', and the company has hired you to turn it round and get it out of trouble. What remedies would you suggest?

Text bank

UNIT 4 Success

What makes countries successful?

Level of difficulty: ●●●

Before you read

Which countries in the world are currently models for others to follow economically? Which particular features of each country are the ones to imitate?

Reading

Read this article from the *Financial Times* by Michael Porter and answer the questions.

Successful Japanese companies are the ones with a strategy

Ten years ago, the threat of competition from Japan was the worst nightmare of every chief executive and head of state. Today, however, as one remedy after another fails to revitalise the world's second-largest economy, it is clear Japan's problems are not merely a question of getting consumers to spend more, recapitalising the banking system, or abolishing lifetime employment. The malaise goes beyond any single practice. It is rooted in how Japan competes.

Japan's share of world exports peaked in 1986, well before the bubble burst, and the profitability of Japanese companies has been chronically low. Japan's style of competing on total quality and continuous improvement – on doing the same thing as rivals but doing it better – did lead to success in the 1970s and the first part of the 1980s. But in today's global economy, best practices spread rapidly. By the mid to late-1980s, western companies began to close the productivity gap by adopting Japanese practices. Then they surged ahead, capitalising on Japanese weaknesses in white collar productivity and information technology.

The missing link in Japanese management is strategy. Strategy requires establishing a unique position by creating a different mix of value than competitors. In Japan's personal computer industry, for example, imitation is rampant and no company has registered attractive financial returns. Contrast that with the success of Dell and Apple, the US computer makers, each with a distinctive strategy. Advantages that come from best practice alone can be imitated away. Advantages that come from strategy are far more sustainable. That is as true in Japan as it is in the rest of the world.

Sifting through the performance of hundreds of Japanese companies bears this out. Having a strategy is the exception in Japan rather than the rule. Where Japanese companies stake out unique positions, they achieve sustained profitability. Japan's video-game makers are one example, as are companies such as Nidec in disk-drive micro-motors, Rohm in the silicon-chip sector, and Shimano, the bicycle-components maker. In vehicle manufacture, the most profitable company is Honda. Honda makes no trucks; it aims to build higher performance vehicles with innovative engines, embodying its own distinctive styling philosophy.

Can Japan compete? Many of its practices have become weaknesses, and deeply ingrained cultural norms and attitudes towards competition seem inconsistent with innovation, entrepreneurship and risk-taking. Yet Japan has done well where it has embraced competition.

From the *Financial Times*

UNIT 4   Success

1 In lines 1–14, find nouns that mean
   a) bad dream
   b) danger
   c) solution
   d) bad situation
   e) way of doing things

2 Which of these things are mentioned among Japan's problems in lines 1–14?
   a) increasing manufacturing productivity
   b) increasing personal spending
   c) limiting the power of the construction industry
   d) refusing government help to bankrupt companies
   e) making the banking system solvent again
   f) stopping the custom of giving people jobs for life

3 Are the problems mentioned in lines 1–14 the main reasons for Japan's difficult situation? Which two sentences indicate this?

4 Read lines 15–34 and complete the statements using the correct alternative.
   a) 'Japan's share of world exports peaked in 1986' means that, in that year, its share
      i) increased.
      ii) was at its highest point.
      iii) fell.
   b) If the bubble bursts, the economic situation, which had been looking good,
      i) improves even more.
      ii) stays the same.
      iii) suddenly becomes bad.
   c) If companies close the productivity gap with others, the difference between what they produce and what the others produce
      i) becomes less.
      ii) increases.
      iii) stays the same.
   d) If something surges ahead, it makes progress
      i) slowly.
      ii) at average speed.
      iii) quickly.
   e) If you capitalise on an advantage, you
      i) exploit it in order to get an even bigger advantage.
      ii) lose it.
      iii) maintain it.

5 Which three management 'philosophies' are mentioned in lines 15–34?

6 Find adjectives that describe these things in lines 35–53.
   a) the link in Japanese management needed for success
   b) a strategic position different from those of all other competitors
   c) imitation between companies that all have the same position
   d) levels of profitability that are good for investors
   e) competitive advantages that can be maintained in the long run
   f) the statement that what is the case in the rest of the world is also the case in Japan

7 In lines 54–73, a number of companies with distinctive strategies are mentioned. In which industries are they?
   a) video games
   b) bicycle components
   c) hi-fi equipment
   d) cars
   e) disk drives
   f) silicon chips
   g) trucks

8 Find expressions in lines 74–82 to replace the underlined expressions below.
   a) Japan has performed well where it has behaved in competitive ways.
   b) There are things that are widely accepted in the culture that do not encourage new ideas.
   c) Some of Japan's way of doing things have become disadvantages.

Over to you 1

Look back at the 'Before you read' section before the article. Which countries did you mention? Which countries do you consider to be models in the following areas?
- education
- health care
- Internet use
- national transport system
- scientific research
- social policy: welfare, pensions, etc.

Over to you 2

How would you rate your country's performance in the areas mentioned above?

UNIT 5 — Job satisfaction

Job sharing

Level of difficulty: ●●○

Before you read

Could you imagine sharing your job with someone else?

Reading

Read this article from the *Financial Times* and answer the questions.

Flexible employment: job shares can work for everyone

Employers are finding that unconventional working patterns can be good for them as well as their staff, writes **Dido Sandler**.

Flexible working, often through a job share, is pushing its way up corporate agendas as a way to attract and retain staff in the unceasing 'war for talent'. More than 90 per cent of job sharers are women, and most of them have childcare responsibilities. The industries keenest on job shares include banking and finance, IT and public services. A recent report from Incomes Data Services says the number of workers in job shares has doubled to about 200,000 in ten years. Management jobs are now being shared, whereas formerly only occupations such as nursing and secretarial work featured.

Angela Baron, adviser (employee resources) at the Chartered Institute of Personnel and Development, believes all jobs can be shared, up to the highest level. She says: "After all, hospital nurses and doctors make life-affecting decisions based on handed-over information. What is more important than that?"

Most employers who allow job shares like them. Staff are more motivated because they can work the hours that suit them. There is less absenteeism, staff working half-weeks are often fresher, and two workers on the same job can be more creative. Ms Baron says: "When there's a tricky problem, you actually have two brains instead of one." One disadvantage for employers is potential difficulty finding a replacement if a job-share partner leaves. Extra training and equipment may also be necessary.

Workers like job sharing because it allows them to keep a firmer footing on the job ladder, when, for example, returning from maternity leave. There is, however, no blanket legal obligation on an employer to offer a job share or part-time working. If management opposes the creation of a job share, there may be no easy way to secure it. It is often easier in areas with a history of job sharing. They are far more prevalent in the public sector, for example. If your company has a flexible working culture, you are more likely to achieve a job share. Most shares operate on a 50/50 basis, with one partner working from Monday to Wednesday and the other from Wednesday to Friday.

The key to a successful job share is a compatible and trusting relationship with your partner, underpinned by a satisfactory contract. If you hoard and play power games with information, this sort of arrangement is unsuitable. Individuals need to be organised and good communicators. Sue Monk, chief executive of flexible workers' charity Families at Work, and a job sharer herself, says: "You've got to be prepared to put in extra effort to make it work. For example, if you're busy, you may need to put in a phone call in the evening. You have to be very responsible. It's easy to leave things for someone else to do."

From the Financial Times

UNIT 5   Job satisfaction

1   Read the whole article and match these headings to the
    paragraphs they relate to. (Two of the headings are not
    used.)
    a) Advantages and disadvantages of job sharing.
    b) Employers recount their bad experiences with job
        sharing.
    c) If nurses and doctors can job-share, why not others too?
    d) Job sharing in the engineering industry.
    e) The increasing popularity of job sharing.
    f) The secret of successful job sharing.
    g) Why people like job sharing, and the role of employers.

2   True or false (lines 1–19)?

    Job sharing is
    a) more common among men than women.
    b) a form of flexible working.
    c) not often found in the public sector.
    d) only found in hospitals.
    e) a way for companies to recruit and keep staff.

3   Choose the correct alternative to explain these expressions
    from lines 20–45.
    a) *Nurses and doctors make life-affecting decisions based
        on handed-over information* means that they make
        decisions based on information that
        i) they get from somewhere else.
        ii) they get from each other.
        iii) is out of date.
    b) When Angela Baron says, 'What is more important than
        that?' she means that
        i) doctors and nurses handing information to each
            other shows how this can work in the most
            important situation you can imagine.
        ii) nothing is more important to nurses than
            job-sharing, as many studies have shown.
        iii) they should only hand over life-affecting information
             but not other sorts of information.
    c) *Staff working half-weeks are often fresher* means that
        the employees who only work half-weeks
        i) have only just started in the company.
        ii) are more enthusiastic.
        iii) are less tired.
    d) *When there's a tricky problem you actually have two
        brains instead of one* means that
        i) it's easier for two people to solve problems than
            one.
        ii) tricky problems can only be solved by two intelligent
            people.
        iii) when someone has a tricky problem, they use twice
             their normal intelligence to solve it.

    e) *One disadvantage for employers is potential difficulty
        finding a replacement if a job-share partner leaves*
        means that if one of the two job sharers leaves,
        i) it is always difficult to find someone to replace them.
        ii) it is sometimes difficult to find someone to replace
            them.
        iii) replacing job sharers who leave is the only
             disadvantage of the system.

4   Find the verbs in lines 46–67 that connect these things.
    a) Employees and their footing on the jobs ladder.
    b) Mothers and going back to work after they have had
        maternity leave.
    c) Management and job sharing, if they do not like it.
    d) Employees and job sharing, if they try to obtain it
        (two verbs).
    e) Job shares and the way they work.

5   Find adjectives in lines 67–85 to match these definitions.
    a) able to get on with someone
    b) good enough in a particular situation
    c) involving something that works and produces results
    d) can be trusted to do what needs to be done
    e) ready to do something
    f) relying on someone and believing what they say
    g) working in a way that is not confused or inefficient

Over to you 1

Has the article changed your view of sharing your job with
someone else? What would the advantages and
disadvantages be?

Over to you 2

Put these jobs in an order of suitability for job sharing, and
explain your reasoning.

- company head
- engineering project head
- librarian
- local government clerk
- local government head of department
- newspaper editor
- shop assistant
- waiter

Text bank

Job loyalty

Level of difficulty: ●●○

Before you read

Should employees feel loyal to the organisation that they work for, or should they feel free to change jobs as often as they like? Why?

Reading

Read this article from the *Guardian* by Dolly Dhingra and answer the questions.

What price a job change?

Bosses think workers are slackers, and employees think too much is asked of them. Whatever happened to loyalty?

It used to be simple. Employees were loyal to their bosses, and in return, a job was for life. Things have certainly changed, and two recent studies, one 5 from Malpas HR Services and the other from the Chartered Institute of Personnel and Development, have concluded that there now exists a considerable discrepancy in expect- 10 ations between worker and boss.

Malpas, the UK's largest provider of personnel training, interviewed 180 general managers and personnel practitioners, and the results are 15 intriguing. For instance, more than half of employers felt that their staff performed little more than was required of them, whereas in fact 80% of employees were working well 20 beyond what their employment contract dictated. Staff also underestimated how solidly they were required to perform during working hours: 66% of employers thought it 25 fair that staff should work solidly for between 75% and 95% of their total hours, but only 46% of employees considered this to be a fair expectation.

30 'The survey reveals considerable discrepancies between what each side believes the other is contributing to the psychological contract, the unspoken assumption between an 35 employer and an employee relating to issues of job satisfaction, fair and honest treatment, job security and loyalty to a job. In a competitive recruitment market, it is vital that HR 40 people and employers develop a full understanding of employees' expectations and aspirations,' says director of Malpas, Margaret Malpas.

So are employers being plain 45 greedy or are workers a bunch of slackers? 'It seems that employees have higher expectations than they used to,' says Malpas. 'We have the media giving us lots of examples of 50 what it means to have a nice lifestyle, we've got things like the National Lottery making us believe we can be instant winners. It all leads to great expectations of want- 55 ing rather a lot and wanting it now.

'Because people want a tremendous amount, they are prepared to push themselves harder to get it.

Currently it's an employees' market, 60 and the workforce is far more mobile than it has ever been. They are prepared to move to get what they want from the right employer,' she adds.

So does this mean that a job for life 65 is a thing of the past? 'I don't think it has to be, but it won't be viable in the way that it used to be for a large mass of the population. A lot of people have given up on that and 70 they now want more flexibility over security,' argues Malpas.

Tricia Phillips, regional manager of recruitment consultancy Adecco, agrees. 'Good, skilled people can 75 always call the shots, especially when unemployment is low, but candidates should be careful when jumping from one job to another. Employers do look at staff for com- 80 mitment, and in a buoyant market, employees may be tempted to move for a rise in salary. But beware when there is a change in the market, employers will look at their staff to 85 see which of them have demonstrated loyalty in their career history.'

From the *Guardian*

UNIT 5   Job satisfaction

1 How many specialist recruitment firms are referred to in the article?

2 What do these words refer to? Choose the correct alternative.

  a) *It* (line 1)
     i) relationships between employees
     ii) relationships between employers and employees
     iii) relationships between employers

  b) *Things* (line 3)
     i) general social conditions
     ii) conditions around the world
     iii) conditions in the workplace

  c) *one* (line 4)
     i) the study by Malpas HR Services
     ii) the study by the Chartered Institute of Personnel and Development
     iii) one of the conditions in the workplace

  d) *the other* (lines 5–6)
     i) the study by Malpas HR Services
     ii) the study by the Chartered Institute of Personnel and Development
     iii) one of the conditions in the workplace

3 What was the first finding of the two studies mentioned in the article?

  a) There is a big difference between what employees expect from work and what employers expect from them.
  b) Employees have the same view of work as their employers.
  c) Employers want employees to work harder.

4 Put the questions in the same order as the information in lines 11–29 based on the answers that were obtained from them.

  a) How much of the day should your employees be working 'solidly'?
  b) As an employee, how much of the day is it reasonable for you to be working 'solidly'?
  c) Do you think your employees are doing more than the minimum that they should do?
  d) As an employee, do you think you do more than the minimum?

5 **A** Match the two parts of these expressions from lines 30–43. One of the words on the right occurs twice.

     1   unspoken   a)   understanding
     2   psychological   b)   treatment
     3   honest   c)   discrepancies
     4   full   d)   contract
     5   fair   e)   assumption
     6   considerable   f)   treatment

B Now match the expressions in **5A** to their meanings **a–e**.

  a) when people are dealt with in a just way (2 expressions)
  b) something that no one says out loud but that everyone thinks
  c) big differences
  d) an agreement between two people that may not be written down
  e) when you know all about a situation

6 Find expressions in lines 44–63 to complete these statements.

  a) If you don't work hard, people may accuse you of being a ………. .
  b) The way that you live, how you spend your money, etc. is your ………. .
  c) If you put a lot of effort into work, you ………. yourself ………. .
  d) All the people who work in a particular company, industry, country, etc. are its ………. .
  e) If people are willing to change jobs often, they are ………. .

7 True or false (lines 64–86)?

  a) Jobs for life no longer exist for anyone at all.
  b) Jobs for life still exist for some people.
  c) People are more interested in having a job that is guaranteed than in being able to change jobs easily.
  d) If you call the shots, other people tell you what to do.
  e) When the employment market is buoyant and employers are looking for workers, employees tend to change jobs in order to get a higher salary.
  f) When the employment market is less buoyant, employers become interested in employees who have shown loyalty to their organisations.

Over to you 1

Design a short questionnaire about job loyalty like the one referred to in the article. Which ten questions would it contain?

Over to you 2

In your country, is there a tradition of jobs for life and/or being loyal to the organisation that you work for?

Do these things depend on the type of organisation you work for? In what ways? Is this changing?

Text bank

UNIT 6   Risk

Computer crime

Before you read

Are the risks associated with the Internet, for example with hackers and viruses, so great that they will limit its growth?

Reading

Read this article from the *Financial Times* by Peter Spiegel and answer the questions.

US cybercops face challenge

The FBI finds many nations still lack the technology, and law, to fight growing computer crime.

When the FBI began investigating a computer break-in at New York-based Bloomberg News earlier this year, they came upon a troubling realisation: the hackers were based in Kazakhstan, a country more known for its occasionally shady oil dealings than international law enforcement co-operation. But when US lawmen contacted Kazakh government officials, they were in for another, more pleasant surprise: "The co-operation we received from the Kazakh authorities was very good," said the Federal Bureau of Investigation's Ron Dick. With the help of the Kazakhs, the two culprits were lured to London and arrested by UK police.

Such is the nature of investigating and stopping cybercrime, a scourge that by one estimate costs global businesses $1.5 billion annually. Although almost all crimes – from bank robberies to aeroplane hijackings – potentially have international links, computer-based crimes have become almost exclusively global in nature, whether because of off-shore "hop sites" used by criminals to confuse investigators or because computer security can be more lax in developing countries such as Kazakhstan.

"It's the nature of the crime," said Mr Dick, head of computer investigations at the FBI's National Infrastructure Protection Centre (NIPC), and thus America's top cybercop. "There are only a handful of cases where we're not addressing things from an international standpoint." But the global nature of cybercrime has raised some unique and troublesome problems for the FBI and its law enforcement partners in industrial countries. At the most basic level, for instance, some developing nations do not have laws making cybercrime illegal.

When the FBI tracked down the man responsible for the infamous "Love Bug" virus, they were hampered by the lack of computer crime laws on the books in the Philippines, where the hacker was based. "The Philippine government was embarrassed," said Mr Dick. "Here you have a country that wants to be part of the global economy and e-commerce and are training their people on these skills, and yet they don't have laws to deal with that."

The Philippines has since passed new computer crime statutes, but having laws on the books is only a first step. Mr Dick says very few countries around the world have the technological expertise to deal with the mounting problem. The FBI has tried to help. Overseas lawmen visit the NIPC on a weekly basis, and the FBI regularly sends its agents to train other law-enforcement agencies at international police academies in Budapest and Bangkok – but it is an uphill road to travel.

From the Financial Times

UNIT 6   Risk

1 Look through the whole article and put these paragraph headings into the correct order.

   a) The FBI has been helping police forces around the world to deal with computer crime, and overseas officials visit the FBI regularly to discuss it.
   b) The country where one recent computer virus was started did not have the laws to deal with the offender.
   c) Computer hackers in a recent case were based in Kazakhstan.
   d) Computer crime is international, but not every country is equipped to fight it.
   e) Computer crime is by its nature international, and most cases that the FBI is investigating involve more than one country.

2 A Look at lines 1–21 and find the verb phrases that connect these expressions.

   a) US lawmen/Kazakh officials
   b) two culprits/UK police
   c) the FBI/troubling realisation
   d) the FBI/a computer break-in at Bloomberg
   e) co-operation/Kazakh authorities
   f) two culprits/London

   B Now match the verbs that you found with other verbs a–e that could replace them.

   1 examining
   2 detained and charged by
   3 got in touch with
   4 had
   5 tricked into coming to
   6 obtained from

3 Are these statements about words used in lines 23–36 true or false?

   a) Cybercrime is crime using computers.
   b) A scourge is something pleasant.
   c) An aeroplane hijacking is when someone illegally takes control of a plane.
   d) If computer crimes have become almost exclusively global in nature, most of them involve people in just one country.
   e) If computer criminals use a hop site, it's not easy to see where they are based.
   f) Lax computer security is not strict.

4 Complete these words from lines 39–54 and then match them to make the expressions that they occur in.

   1 c_mp_t_r   a) standpoint
   2 t_p   b) problems
   3 _n__rn_t__n_l   c) nature
   4 tr__bl_s_m_   d) nations
   5 _n_q__   e) investigations
   6 gl_b_l   f) countries
   7 d_v_l_p_ng   g) cybercop
   8 _nd_str__l   h) problems

5 Choose the correct alternative to complete these statements (lines 55–62).

   a) The FBI tracked down the hacker means that they
      i) found him.
      ii) didn't find him.
      iii) arrested him.

   b) The infamous love bug virus means that
      i) no one has heard of it.
      ii) it was famous for good reasons.
      iii) it was famous for bad reasons.

   c) The FBI were hampered in their investigations means that they were
      i) slowed down.
      ii) speeded up.
      iii) helped.

   d) A lack of crime laws on the country's books means that
      i) there are no technical books about computer crime there.
      ii) the country's government has not passed laws against computer crime.
      iii) there are no law books about computer crime there.

   e) The government was embarrassed about the event means that they felt
      i) good about it.
      ii) bad about it.
      iii) indifferent about it.

6 Find words in lines 69–83 that mean
   a) laws (8 letters)
   b) know-how (9)
   c) increasing (8)
   d) policemen and other related officials (6)
   e) organisations that try to stop crime (3, 11, 8)
   f) schools for police personnel (6, 9)
   g) a difficult process (6, 4)

Over to you 1

Have you / your organisation ever been affected by a computer virus? What effects did it have?

What have you / your organisation done to protect against viruses?

Someone who creates a computer virus can cause billions of dollars of damage around the world. What do you think is an appropriate punishment for them?

Over to you 2

Which of these things is the biggest risk for the world in the next 50 years? Say why.

- global warming
- prolonged economic recession
- organised international crime, including computer crime

UNIT 6   Risk

Fraud and corruption

Level of difficulty: ● ● ○

Before you read

On a global level, what are the relative risks for someone doing business abroad? Put these risks on a scale from most likely to least likely. Being

- kidnapped;
- asked for a bribe;
- on a plane that is hijacked;
- involved in criminal activity without realising it.

Reading

Read this article from *The Economist* and answer the questions.

Fraud and developing countries

A survey of 121 European and American firms last year by Control Risks Group (CRG), a security consultancy, found that two-fifths had recently held back from an otherwise attractive foreign investment because of the
5 country's reputation for corruption. Western firms are tempting targets for local crooks, who may feel it is less morally reprehensible to steal from foreigners. Besides the risk of robbery, there is the risk of embarrassment from (sometimes unwitting) association with mobsters,
10 as when the Bank of New York was apparently used to launder Russian Mafia money. According to John Bray of CRG, fraud is the biggest risk of doing business in emerging markets, but most firms have no training programme to prevent it.
15 Before investing, firms should investigate prospective local partners to make sure that they are not crooks. In many poor countries, investors will be asked for bribes in return for a swift issue of necessary permits. Until recently, such expenses were tax-deductible for firms
20 from many European countries. Now, however, an OECD (Organisation for Economic Co-operation and Development) anti-bribery convention has come into force for all rich countries. These days, bribery can lead to bad publicity and even to prosecution at home, so
25 firms increasingly refuse to grease the palms held out to them.

Even if top managers are clean, locally hired middle managers may not be. Such reputable American banks as Citibank and American Express have discovered that
30 they had local managers with links to mobsters. And, faced with American-style sales targets, the temptation to clinch deals through bribes may be irresistible.

Local managers are also more vulnerable to threats; they cannot fly home to France or Canada. So firms should
35 teach them how to refuse demands for bribes without getting hurt. Techniques include insisting that somebody else is responsible for the decision in question and never going alone to meetings with people who may demand bribes. Most important, firms should make
40 sure that all accounts are scrupulously transparent. Fortunately, accountants are exceptionally mobile. All it takes for a big accounting firm to set up an office in Brazzaville or Vladivostok is for a partner to move there, so one can find a competent bookkeeper almost any-
45 where.

From *The Economist*

UNIT 6   Risk

1 Look through the whole article and find all the
   organisations mentioned by name. Put them into groups
   according to their activity.

2 Find words in lines 1–26, and other related words, to
   complete these definitions.

   a) Illegal payments, for example to officials for permission
      to do something are b _ _ _ _ _ and the activity of doing
      this is b _ _ _ _ _ _ . People who accept these payments
      are _ _ r _ _ _ _ and this is part of the wider picture of
      _ _ _ _ u _ _ _ _ _ .
   b) _ _ _ u _ is when people obtain money by criminal
      means, for example by tricking others.
      _ _ _ e _ _ l _ _ _ _ _ is when someone working for a
      company steals money from it.
   c) If criminals put money through the banking system in a
      way that disguises its criminal origins, they _ _ u _ _ _ _
      it.

3 True or false (lines 1–14)?

   a) If you hold back from making an investment, you go
      ahead with it.
   b) If a country has a reputation for corruption, it's a place
      where people think that a lot of bribes are offered.
   c) Actions that are morally reprehensible are good and
      deserve praise.
   d) If someone is a tempting target for criminals, the
      criminals avoid them.
   e) If you feel embarrassment about something you have
      done, you are happy about it.
   f) If you have unwitting association with criminals, you do
      not know you are dealing with criminals.

4 Rearrange these ideas in lines 15–26 into the order in which
   they appear there.

   a) Now there is an international agreement to fight bribery.
   b) In a lot of poor places, it is normal for officials to ask for
      bribes before they issue permits.
   c) Bribery can give a firm a bad name and even lead to it
      being taken to court in its own country.
   d) Before they put their money into a project somewhere,
      companies should check that the people they are going
      to work with are not criminals.
   e) Paying bribes was until recently considered normal by
      European companies.

5 Match these adjectives from lines 27–45 to their meanings
   a–g.

   1 clean   a) impossible to say 'no' to
   2 irresistible   b) not corrupt
   3 vulnerable   c) injured
   4 hurt   d) in a weak position
   5 transparent   e) able to move quickly
   6 mobile   f) efficient and knowledgeable
   7 competent   g) clear and honest

Over to you 1

Will it ever be possible to eliminate bribery and corruption?
Do you think laws against corruption have enough effect?
Why / Why not?

Over to you 2

Some say that corruption can be 'good' in a developing
economy, as it allows things to happen faster, deals to go
more smoothly and so on. Do you think that corruption can
have at least some positive effects?

UNIT 7   e-commerce

Difficulties of distribution 1

Level of difficulty: ●●●

Before you read

Have you bought any of these over the Internet? Was it a positive experience?

- cars
- PCs
- books
- CDs
- videos
- groceries
- pizza
- ice cream

Were you surprised by anything in this list? If so, why?

What is the image of couriers (delivery companies of letters and small packages other than the post office)? Do they have a good reputation?

Reading

Read this article from the *Financial Times* by Tim Jackson and answer the questions.

IT retailers face "last mile"

A San Francisco company may have the solution for online vendors struggling to make their delivery services
5 viable. The biggest business opportunity left in online retailing is the "last mile" – getting products to customers within an hour or two, from a warehouse that is
10 only a few miles away.

Yet the two companies attacking this market space most aggressively are facing problems. WebVan has a billion-dollar net-
15 work of automated distribution centres with hub-and-spoke dispatch, but a grocery business that is too small to fill them. Kozmo.com in New York has gen-
20 erated great enthusiasm and hype by selling ice cream and videos over the Web, but runs on negative gross margins because the costs of free delivery sometimes exceed
25 the value of the item.

A San Francisco company called dNet, which launches a commercial service next month, thinks it has found a better way to make
30 money from last-mile deliveries. Instead of being a merchant or a dispatch company, dNet has built a network allowing stores to buy delivery services from couriers.

35 DNet is run by Chris Moore, 35. Mr Moore says same-day dispatch is a large but highly fragmented market in the US; some 4,000 companies share total sales of $15 bil-
40 lion a year. Same-day service is not at the core of the businesses of FedEx, UPS and the US Postal Service.

For last-mile immediate deliv-
45 ery to make sense, Mr Moore believes each merchant needs to guarantee quality and cost by using multiple dispatch companies. Equally, each dispatch
50 company needs to serve multiple merchants in order to increase the number of drops a courier makes

in each mile of travel.

The company is recruiting dis-
55 patch companies in the top 15 US metro markets and is looking for merchants with a website and experience in providing local delivery. Pilot testing has started,
60 and dNet has signed up eight merchants. The company believes the most promising segments for instant urban deliveries are likely to be office supplies, auto parts,
65 prescription drugs, corporate gifts, tickets and alcohol.

When a customer buys something from a website, dNet checks the database and forwards the
70 request to a local courier company with spare capacity. If the courier company fails to respond within five minutes, the website beeps its computer; after another five min-
75 utes, the job is offered to a competitor. Once a dispatch company has accepted the job, its courier picks up the package.

From the Financial Times

UNIT 7   e-commerce

1 Match the companies mentioned in the article to what they do and where they are based. Three of the companies do the same thing, and the bases of four of the companies are not mentioned.

1	dNet	a) supplies of ice	i) New York
2	FedEx	cream and videos	ii) San Francisco
3	Kozmo.com	b) grocery supplies	
4	UPS	c) next-day deliveries	
5	US Postal	d) a network for	
	Service	same-day courier	
6	WebVan	companies	

2 Complete the diagram using words from the text to show the relationship between dNet and companies like WebVan and Kozmo.

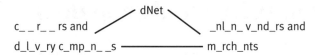

c_ _ r_ _ rs and   _nl_n_ v_nd_rs and
d_l_v_ry c_mp_n_ _s ——————— m_rch_nts

3 True or false (lines 1–34)?

a) There are few business opportunities left on the Internet.

b) The big problem in distribution is the last stage of the product's journey.

c) Most delivery services are profitable and viable.

d) WebVan's grocery delivery services are profitable.

e) There is a lot of excitement about and interest in Kozmo.com.

f) Kozmo does not make a profit.

g) DNet is a distributor.

4 Find the nouns that these adjectives describe (lines 35–66).

a) same-day
b) urban
c) instant
d) promising
e) metro
f) fragmented
g) local
h) immediate
i) pilot

5 Match the complete expressions (adjective plus noun) from Question 4 to their definitions i–v.

i) three expressions for when goods are sent very quickly

ii) three expressions to talk about where these take place

iii) one expression to talk about an experiment to see if something works

iv) one expression to say that there are lots of different companies all doing the same thing

v) one expression for particular parts of a market that look as though they will be profitable

6 DNet 'believes the most promising segments for instant urban deliveries are likely to be office supplies, auto parts, prescription drugs, corporate gifts, tickets and alcohol' (lines 61–66). Why do you think this is? Can you think of any other products for which there is demand for instant delivery?

7 In which tense is the underlined verb in each sentence being used (lines 54–77)? Match each underlined verb to one of the explanations a–d.

1 The company <u>is recruiting</u> dispatch companies in the top 15 US metro markets and <u>is looking for</u> merchants with a website and experience in providing local delivery (lines 54–59).

2 Pilot testing <u>has started</u>, and dNet <u>has signed up</u> eight merchants (lines 59–61).

3 The company <u>believes</u> the most promising segments for instant urban deliveries are likely to be office supplies, auto parts, prescription drugs, corporate gifts, tickets and alcohol (lines 61–66).

4 When a customer <u>buys</u> something from a website, dNet <u>checks</u> the database and forwards the request to a local courier company with spare capacity (lines 67–71).

a) present perfect: recent past, no specific time mentioned

b) present continuous: activity going on now

c) present simple: repeated actions

d) present simple: this verb is not normally used in continuous tenses

Over to you 1

In your city or area, what are the main obstacles to home delivery? Put these factors in order of importance and add any others you can think of.

- heavy traffic
- long distances
- lack of building doorkeepers to take in deliveries
- most people are out working during the day
- people like shopping in traditional shops

Over to you 2

Look again at the list of things in 'Before you read' and the goods mentioned in the article itself. Which items do you think would be of interest to these people for home delivery?

- a couple with two small children
- young men watching football on television
- a self-employed person working from home
- a car enthusiast rebuilding an old classic car

Text bank

Difficulties of distribution 2

Level of difficulty: ●●●

Before you read

What are the key factors in running an online business successfully?

Reading

Read this article from the *Financial Times* and answer the questions.

Europeans must get a foot in the virtual shop door

Patrick Forth and Neil Monnery

How often in business do you find a market growing at more than 200 per cent a year, where few of the participants have any form of
5 dominance? This is exactly the scenario in western Europe's online retail market. With online sales accounting for only two-tenths of a per cent of the entire
10 retail market, the field is wide open – but it will not be for long. Many established European retailers and Internet start-ups are already laying claim to this valu-
15 able online territory.

Already, US groups have some 20 per cent of the European online market. Europe's battle for the online consumer will be fought
20 quickly and won decisively by a few big online retailers. European retailers have more than a fighting chance to be among them but will have to move swiftly and
25 strategically on several fronts.

First, retailers must move quickly to secure space on the online consumer's virtual shelf. Consumers are becoming familiar
30 with online retail brands and are concentrating their spending on sites they recognise and trust.

Second, retailers need to exploit the interactivity of the Internet to
35 understand and cater for customers. European online retailers know surprisingly little about their customers. More than half do not track the number of unique
40 visitors to their sites, and only one-third know the number of repeat buyers.

Third, European retailers need to build international scale while
45 preserving local touch. The challenge for European online retailers is to scale their businesses to international levels while continuing to cater to diverse local mar-
50 kets. Their ability to do this will give European retailers a clear advantage over US competitors,

whose formidable online retailing experience has been tested only in
55 the relatively homogenous North American market. European companies have the home advantage of being more familiar with local consumer profiles, preferences,
60 cultures and languages.

Finally, retailers must strive for flawless fulfilment and customer service. European online retailers are still struggling to get
65 this right. As online consumers become more demanding and less tolerant of online purchase failures, the big winners in the battle for online market share in Europe
70 will be those businesses that successfully and consistently deliver a satisfying, end-to-end purchase experience. The losers will be those that promise a better online
75 purchase experience than they can deliver.

From the *Financial Times*

UNIT 7   e-commerce

1   Find a good title for each paragraph in the article. Two of the titles are not used.

   a) The importance of understanding customer needs and behaviour
   b) Think Europe-wide, act local
   c) The potential of online retailing in Europe
   d) Internet technology suppliers
   e) The need for perfect service
   f) The battle between European and US online retailers
   g) Establishing a presence
   h) Food and non-food retailing

2   Find sentences in lines 1–25 containing language that relates to

   a) war (two sentences).   **b)** colonisation.   **c)** racing.

3   In lines 1–42, what do these figures relate to?

   a) $>^1/_2$ **b)** $^1/_3$ **c)** $^1/_5$ **d)** 0.2%   **e)** >200%

4   Look at lines 26–63 and complete these statements with the correct alternative.

   a) '... retailers must move quickly to secure space on the online consumer's virtual shelf' means that retailers must
      i) act fast in order to establish their names so that consumers will recognise them.
      ii) also be present on supermarket shelves.
      iii) increase the capacity of their computer systems.

   b) 'More than half [of retailers] do not track the number of unique visitors to their sites' means that they do not count
      i) the total number of visits to their sites.
      ii) the number of different visitors to their sites.
      iii) the number of visitors with unusual needs.

   c) 'European retailers need to build international scale while preserving local touch' means that they should
      i) concentrate on one country.
      ii) apply the same approach in all countries.
      iii) apply different approaches in different countries.

   d) '... the relatively homogenous North American market' means that it
      i) is exactly the same everywhere.
      ii) is more or less the same everywhere.
      iii) is totally different in each region.

   e) '... retailers must strive for flawless fulfilment and customer service' means that
      i) they should aim not to exceed a particular number of errors in delivery.
      ii) it's OK to have a few mistakes in the order as long as it's delivered on time.
      iii) everything should be perfect.

Over to you 1

'European companies have the home advantage of being more familiar with local consumer profiles, preferences, cultures and languages.' How far do you think this is true of Internet retailers based in these countries?

- Belgium
- Denmark
- France
- Germany
- Switzerland
- UK

Over to you 2

The writers of the article refer to what they call the 'end-to-end purchase experience'. What are all the steps that make up this experience?

Team-building techniques 1

Level of difficulty: ● ● ●

Before you read

Do you think that activities like talking about your inner feelings have a place in management training?

Reading

Read this article from the *Financial Times* and answer the questions.

Learn to listen and let go

Vanessa Houlder

What would make an entire team of computer support staff lie on the floor and listen to the silence? For BZW, the investment bank, [5] this unlikely behaviour was prompted by some unpleasant feedback from users of its Information Technology support and service division. A survey [10] throughout the organisation found that only a third of users were favourably impressed by the department's performance. And the department's own opinion of [15] its performance was not much better: senior managers saw each other as rivals rather than colleagues.

Bryan Hotson, Managing Dir- [20] ector of the Information Technology Support and Service division, was convinced that it urgently needed to develop a less antagonistic culture. 'What prevents [25] technology from delivering is the people factor, not the technology,' he observes. But trying to build a sense of team spirit among the senior managers proved difficult. [30] They tried outdoor training, but found it hard to apply the lessons back in the office.

Hotson then contacted Harley Young, a Henley-based manage- [35] ment communications specialist run by a former actor and his wife, a psychotherapist. Communications training is becoming more popular at a time [40] when companies are trying to replace hierarchies with team work. But courses are often viewed with trepidation by managers, either because of a reputa- [45] tion for heavy-handed exercises in giving and receiving criticism, or because they encourage colleagues to bare their soul in public in a way they later regret.

[50] Harley Young tried to overcome the fears and scepticism by discussing the participants' personal goals on a one-to-one basis before the course began. Every exercise [55] was optional, and the organisers tried to build the course up gently so that participants became more confident about exposing their feelings. Nonetheless, the course [60] took the BZW team – all hard-driving, down-to-earth individuals – into unfamiliar territory, including the lying-on-the-floor-and-listening-to-the-silence exercise. At [65] another point, they were asked to write a poem describing their first five minutes at BZW. At times, the sessions were embarrassing, according to Hotson.

[70] Was the course successful? Probably not, in the sense of making a measurable difference to the organisation. Hotson's hopes of making a far-reaching change to [75] the culture and perception of the division ended when he moved jobs. But for the individuals, the course was outstandingly successful, he says. 'At the end of the ses- [80] sion we understood ourselves better. We were in a position to be more tolerant. Everybody would admit they were different as a result of it.'

From the *Financial Times*

UNIT 8   Team building

1 Look through the whole article and match each paragraph to one of the summaries a–e.

  a) The IT boss wanted to try communications training, but some managers are nervous about this.

  b) The course did not change the way the organisation worked, but it changed the participants.

  c) The communications training course contained activities that were unfamiliar to the participants, but the trainers had a careful approach.

  d) One of the IT bosses wanted to change the way managers behaved, and they tried teamwork training through physical activities, but it did not work.

  e) An investment bank finds that its IT department is badly thought of by people in the other departments.

2 Find all the people in the article (individuals and groups) in the order they are first mentioned. (The first two have been done for you.)

1) The computer support staff at BZW,

2) Users of computer support services ...

3 Find words and expressions in the article to complete the statements a–g. (Change their grammatical form if necessary.)

  a) If you ask people what they think of what you do and they say things that are not nice to hear, this is ....
.... You can also say that they are not ....
.... by what you do. (lines 6–7 and 12)

  b) An environment where there is a lot of conflict: ....
.... (lines 23–24)

  c) The feeling that people have when they are working together well as a group: .... (line 28)

  d) If you are very nervous about doing something, you do it with .... (line 43)

  e) Activities that do not take into account people's feelings are .... (line 45)

  f) People with a lot of energy and who are realistic are .... and ....
(lines 60–61)

  g) If you say exactly what you think and feel about something, you .... and ....
.... (lines 48 and 58–59)

4 Look at lines 1–32 and choose the correct alternative.

  a) The IT support staff lay on the floor
    i) because they were tired.
    ii) as part of a communications course.
    iii) to check the IT system.

  b) People in the other departments
    i) did not, on the whole, have a good opinion of the IT support team.
    ii) thought the IT support team was very good.
    iii) had not formed an opinion of the IT support team.

  c) The people in the IT support department
    i) thought their department was very good.

    ii) did not think it was good.
    iii) had not formed an opinion about it.

  d) Members of the IT support department did not work well together because
    i) their technical knowledge was not good.
    ii) they had old equipment.
    iii) its managers did not co-operate.

  e) Bryan Hotson organised training because
    i) there was conflict in the department.
    ii) the IT system was crashing regularly.
    iii) his boss told him to.

  f) The outdoor training did not work because
    i) people did not like going away at the weekend.
    ii) employees were not physically fit.
    iii) the lessons were hard to apply in the office.

5 Match the parts of the statements 1–6 and a–f relating to lines 33–84.

1 Hotson contacted Harley Young because	a) they are worried that they will have to show their real thoughts and feelings.
2 Communications training is becoming more popular because	b) they were asked to do things they had never done before.
3 Communications courses are viewed nervously by managers because	c) he wanted to try communications training.
4 The course took participants into unfamiliar territory because	d) companies want their people to work together in teams.
5 The course was successful for individual participants because	e) it made no real difference to how the IT division worked.
6 The course was not successful from BZW's point of view because	f) it made them more tolerant.

Over to you 1

BZW's head of IT says 'What prevents technology from delivering is the people factor, not the technology.' Do you think this is true of technology in companies in general?

Over to you 2

BZW tried outdoor training, but found it hard to apply the lessons back in the office. Do you think that activities like mountain climbing and sailing are a good form of team building for businesses?

Over to you 3

If you were offered training in team building, and you had the choice between outdoor activities and the types of activities mentioned here, like writing poetry and listening to the silence, which would you prefer and why?

Team-building techniques 2

Level of difficulty: ●●○

Before you read

Have you ever done voluntary work, working without pay to do something of benefit to other people? What sort of organisations exist in your country for this?

Reading

Read this article from the *Guardian* and answer the questions.

Building new skills in Brazil

Roger Cowe and Colin Walkey

The fad for team-building exercises which put managers into tough, even life-threatening situations, in an attempt to see what they are real-ly made of and to build a common bond, is fading. There are still com-panies which look for their future leaders on the side of a mountain or on a sailing ship in the middle of the ocean, but many now feel that the business-school classroom, the facto-ry floor and the executive suite are more appropriate venues for leader-ship development and selection.

There is no doubt, however, that young managers gain from being put into difficult and unfamiliar situ-ations which test their resourceful-ness and their ability to work with their peers. This notion led to one group of executives finding them-selves in São Paulo, Brazil, recently, faced with the task of building a bak-ery for an orphanage.

The lucky seven came from GKN, the British-based engineering group whose main business is supplying the car industry with parts. They were participants in the 25-strong leadership programme of the group's Automotive Driveline Division, designed to develop the unit's future bosses.

The idea came from one of the participants, Anna Koster, who had heard of the orphanage's plight and felt the challenge fitted the course aims of testing the group's courage, innovation and motivation. It also tested their technical skills, since they knew very little about building – especially working with bricks and concrete in the pouring rain.

Dave Millman, one of the Bir-mingham-based managers, says, "We found ourselves in a completely different environment and atmos-phere from our normal work". He feels that the experience cemented much closer bonds than had been formed during the formal part of the course.

"In the space of a week, we became like a team of brothers and sisters. The target and the objective became of paramount importance. I don't think we talked about work once – everything was so focused on building the bakery."

He is convinced the experience will carry over into his work, to the advantage of GKN. He says, "I am more confident in my own abilities and judgements and in working with other people now. We all felt we would be going back to a culture where sometimes you were told things were not possible, or couldn't be done in a certain way, or that there were political considerations. But the project has shown us we can exercise our will and make a differ-ence. If we apply that to tasks back in the company and be single-minded, we can overcome any hurdles that might be there."

From the *Guardian*

UNIT 8   Team building

1 Read the whole article and find which of these team-building activities are mentioned. Which one is the article mainly about?

a) climbing
b) battle simulations on computer
c) cooking a meal together
d) yachting
e) building a place to bake bread for children who have lost their parents
f) business school classes

2 Sometimes short words can be surprisingly difficult. Match the words 1–6 to their definitions a–f.

1	fad (line 1)	a)	determination
2	bond (line 6)	b)	obstacle
3	peer (line 20)	c)	difficult situation
4	plight (line 36)	d)	fashion
5	will (line 72)	e)	equal
6	hurdle (line 75)	f)	relationship

3 Now find which of the words in 1–6 above are being referred to in these statements. In the article, they are used with the verbs in italics. (The answer is in the singular in a and b, and in the plural in c to f.)

a) You *exercise* and *apply* this.
b) If you *hear about* this, you may want to do something about it.
c) These *fade*.
d) You *build* or *cement* these.
e) You *overcome* these.
f) You *work with* these.

4 True or false, according to the writer (lines 1–33)?

a) Physical, outdoor team-building activities are becoming more popular.
b) More companies think that business-school classes and actual work experience are good ways of developing teamwork and leadership skills.
c) It benefits young managers for them to be put in unusual situations.
d) The main voluntary activity described in the article required the managers to use exactly the skills and knowledge they use in their normal work.
e) Twenty-five people went to work on this activity.
f) The Automotive Driveline Division is one of the production divisions of GKN.

5 Look for nouns and adjectives in lines 14–76 used to talk about the qualities developed by working in a team related to the words a–f.

a) resource (noun)
b) courageous (noun)
c) innovate (noun)
d) motivate (noun)
e) confidence (adjective)
f) mind (adjective)

6 Look at lines 34–76 and choose the correct alternative to complete each of these statements.

a) The idea for the voluntary activity came from
 i) GKN top management.
 ii) one of the participants.
 iii) a national newspaper.

b) The technical skills required on the project were ones that the participants
 i) already possessed.
 ii) taught to local people.
 iii) had to learn.

c) When Millman says that the experience allowed the participants 'to cement closer bonds', he means that it permitted them to
 i) work together more closely.
 ii) improve their bricklaying techniques.
 iii) improve their financial knowledge.

d) When he says that they 'became like a team of brothers and sisters', he means that
 i) they quarrelled more than before.
 ii) someone took the role of big brother.
 iii) they understood each other better than before.

e) Millman thinks that the lessons from the project
 i) will have no effect on his normal work.
 ii) have changed the way he will work.
 iii) will be impossible to apply because of company politics and culture.

Over to you 1

Which of these activities would work best for team building among the staff of your organisation or your fellow students? Which would you personally most enjoy?

- cooking a meal together
- deep-sea sailing
- rock climbing
- paintball (a game where participants are in the countryside and have to 'shoot' each other with special guns that shoot paint, not bullets)
- go-kart racing (racing in small, open cars on a special circuit)
- a voluntary activity with benefits for other people

Over to you 2

Which of these activities would be of most benefit a) to volunteers, b) to the people for whom they are intended? Which would you personally most enjoy?

- Going into schools to teach pupils about personal finance.
- Helping young people develop CVs and interview skills.
- Building houses in poor areas.
- Countryside conservation: clearing paths, doing work on trees, improving gardens, etc.
- Voluntary Service Overseas: going to a developing country for a time to teach, work on agricultural projects, etc.

UNIT 9   Raising finance

Business incubators

Level of difficulty: ●●○

Before you read

A business incubator is an organisation that helps new, small companies to develop. What sort of help do you think they might provide?

Reading

Read this article from the *Financial Times* by James Buxton and answer the questions.

Pioneering venture takes fledglings a step further

Adaptive Venture Managers has already scored one success and is intent on extending its reach

A new type of business incubator is soon to spread across northern Britain. It is pioneered by Adaptive Venture Managers, a company based near Edinburgh that specialises in setting up
5 and running businesses for people who create new products centred on established technology. Most business incubators – there are now about 100 in the UK – select fledgling companies and give them a place to operate, help them gain specialist advice and in
10 some cases supply them with investment capital. Adaptive Venture Managers goes a step further: in addition to providing its three client companies with office space in its premises at Livingston, it also manages them, for which they pay £10,000 a month.
15   AVM this month joined the Alternative Investment Market in a £1.4 million placing and is seeking up to £1.1 million from private client stockbrokers and individuals. The proceeds will enable it to invest in more companies (usually about £300,000 each over two
20 years) and create up to three more centres. It hopes to have an office in every principal regional centre in the UK. AVM intends to sell off or float its client companies within about five years, to the benefit of itself, the client company's founders and the business
25 angels it has brought in as co-investors.

The company was formed in 1995 by Richard Muir-Simpson, managing director, a specialist in development capital; Walter Jacobs, an electronic engineer; and Jeremy Scuse, a marketing specialist. In assess-
30 ing companies, Mr Jacobs examines a potential client's technology and whether the product can be made cheaply and in large quantities. Mr Scuse studies its potential market with major customers, while Mr Muir-Simpson determines whether the pro-
35 ject can be financed and how best to do it.
   AVM's most successful client is Hearing Enhancement. It produces a mini-loop system that was invented by a retired sound engineer and is used by retailers such as Marks & Spencer to improve the quality of
40 sound received by customers wearing hearing aids. Turnover in the first half of this year was £360,000, double that for the previous year. Its shares on Ofex, a London stock market for new companies, have nearly trebled this year.
45   Its other two companies, both at earlier stages of development, are Safedip, which has developed safe and environmentally friendly biocides for human and animal conditions, and D.C. Heat, which is developing markets for portable heating systems based on a new
50 type of plastic.

From the *Financial Times*

UNIT 9   Raising finance

1 Look through the whole article and put the people and organisations a–i into three groups:

   A a business incubator and the people who work for it
   B the companies that the incubator is developing
   C stock markets for new small companies

   a) Walter Jacobs
   b) Safedip
   c) D.C. Heat
   d) Richard Muir-Simpson
   e) Ofex
   f) Jeremy Scuse
   g) Hearing Enhancement
   h) Alternative Investment Market
   i) Adaptive Venture Managers

2 Which of these things is *not* mentioned in lines 1–14 as something that AVM provides for small companies?

   a) office space
   b) specialist advice
   c) staff recruitment services
   d) tax advice
   e) investment capital

3 If AVM uses all the capital it has raised and plans to raise, about how many typical start-up companies could it finance for two years at typical cost levels (lines 15–25)?

4 Which of these things would most typically be done by each AVM executive mentioned in lines 26–35?

   a) meet AIM officials to discuss raising further capital
   b) meet the founder of a start-up to see if its technology works
   c) have lunch with a potential client for one of the start-up's products
   d) discuss with a start-up's founder how a new product could be manufactured
   e) commission research into the market potential for one of the start-up's products
   f) contact private investors to see if they are interested in contributing capital

5 True or false (lines 36–50)?

   a) AVM is currently developing four companies.
   b) D.C. Heat is the furthest advanced of the companies that AVM is developing.
   c) Hearing Enhancement's product was developed by someone with good technical knowledge of sound systems.
   d) Hearing Enhancement's profits were £360,000 in the first half of this year.
   e) If Hearing Enhancement's sales continue at the same rate, it will sell four times as much this year as last year.
   f) Safedip's products might have agricultural applications.
   g) D.C. Heat's product is based on existing materials.

Over to you 1

Using the information in the article, tell the founder of a start-up what sort of services a business incubator could provide.

Over to you 2

What sort of help is given to start-ups in your country? Who provides it? What else could be done?

UNIT 9   Raising finance

Venture capital in Europe

Level of difficulty: ● ● ○

Before you read

Should governments be involved in developing new technologies and industries, or should it be left to the private sector?

Reading

Read this article from the *Financial Times* by David Ibison and answer the questions.

A low regard for high-tech

The capital is there, but an aversion to risk and bureaucracy is preventing it being channelled to Europe's entrepreneurs

The vision of European Union countries being at the forefront of the Internet revolution is exactly that – a vision. In fact, high-tech entrepreneurs are being left unfinanced, ideas are going begging and talent is going overseas. That, at least, was the message that made listeners sit up at a seminar in a dreary conference room in Monte Carlo. They paid even more attention when the figures backing the message up were brought out.

Jacques Michel, vice-president of the European Patent Office, said the amount of early stage capital available in the US and the EU was broadly similar – about $9.4 billion last year in the US and $8.5 billion in the EU. "In the US, 50 per cent of this is allocated to the information technology sector. In the EU, it is seven per cent. The difference in allocation is startling. The US has a head start, and in this business it is first come, first served," he said. Mr Michel was speaking at this month's European Inventions Competition, an annual event designed to celebrate Europe's ability to generate ideas, finance them and take them to market.

But this year, a disturbing message emerged. The life blood of the Internet economy – small, start-up, innovative, high-tech companies at the leading edge of the industry – are being stillborn through lack of capital. Participants at the seminar all told the same story – Europe is risk-averse; there are barriers to investment; the seed capital market is immature, research is left unfunded, and the EU's place in the new economy is being undermined.

In a report, the commission offers ambitious targets and promises to overhaul the way seed capital finds its way to entrepreneurs. It says it will "propose innovative forms of capital raising, including public-private partnerships coupled with refocusing some Community spending". The commission's plans have fuelled the long-running debate about its role in the European risk-capital field.

James Dobree, chief executive of Zygon, an Internet software company based in London, and also an adviser to the commission, said the commission was going about things completely the wrong way. Using public money or re-allocating EU spending were ideas that smacked of bureaucracy and centralised control, he said. "The fact that they think public money will help indicates how behind the times they are. No Internet entrepreneur is going to try and access public money – it comes with too much baggage."

Instead, Mr Dobree restated growing calls to empower the private sector by reducing the tax it pays on capital gains. In the US, capital gains tax is 20 per cent, much lower than any of the varying rates across Europe. In the UK, the tax is 40 per cent. "In Europe, this money gets creamed off by the government. Instead, it should be kept in the hands of the people who can make things happen," he said.

From the *Financial Times*

UNIT 9   Raising finance

1 Put these paragraph headings into the correct order.

   a) Europeans do not like risk and Europe's place in the new economy is being weakened because of this.

   b) James Dobree says that public money should not be used for financing start-ups.

   c) Mr Dobree thinks corporation tax should be reduced in Europe.

   d) The amount of capital available for start-ups is about the same in the US as Europe, but much more of it is spent on IT by companies in the US than in Europe, says Jacques Michel.

   e) The European Community is looking at new ways of financing start-ups.

   f) The vision of a hi-tech future cannot be realised in Europe because of lack of finance.

2 Use correct forms of expressions in lines 1–14 to complete the statements.

   a) An idea for the future that may or may not come true is a ....

   b) If an idea cannot get backers, it ....

   c) People in a particular place who have a particular skill can be referred to collectively as ....

   d) If someone says something that makes you listen, you ....

   e) If information supports a particular idea, it .... it ....

   f) If you are one of the first people to do something, you are at the .... of this movement.

3 Find expressions from lines 15–34 by combining elements from the three columns. There are four expressions with two elements each and three expressions with three elements each.

	1	2	3
a)	European	president	sector
b)	vice	patent	allocation
c)	information	start	office
d)	head	technology	
e)	first come	event	
f)	annual	in	
g)	difference	first served	

4 Find words in lines 35–49 that describe these things.

   a) companies that do not have enough finance to develop (9 letters)

   b) companies developing new technologies (4-4)

   c) new companies with new ideas (10)

   d) people and organisations that do not like risk (4-6)

   e) research for which there is no money (8)

   f) the development of the new economy (10)

   g) the idea that EU countries are not investing enough in IT-related projects (10)

5 Which verbs link the European Commission and its plans, and these ideas in lines 50–62?

   a) new ways of raising capital

   b) objectives for the amount of capital for entrepreneurs

   c) the discussion about the role it should play in this area

   d) the system for getting money to entrepreneurs

   e) the way the community spends money in this area

6 Use expressions from lines 63–91 to replace the expressions in italics.

   a) We should reduce *the tax on profit from investment*.

   b) We should *give more power to commercial organisations*.

   c) They are *not modern in their thinking*.

   d) The commission *was approaching things badly*.

   e) Taxpayers' money comes with *too many conditions attached*.

   f) *Someone founding a start-up* is not going to try to *obtain taxpayers' money*.

   g) In the EU, money that could be invested in start-ups is *taken by* the government.

   h) In the EU, money should *remain with* the people who know what to do with it.

   i) *Changing* EU spending so it is spent on something else *seemed bureaucratic*.

Over to you 1

Go back to the 'Before you read' section. Do governments have a role to play in providing finance for business development, or should it be left to the private sector? Have your opinions changed now that you have read the article?

Over to you 2

Should investors concentrate on firms developing Information Technology? What other areas should they be investing in? Put start-ups in these industries in your order of priority for investment.

- pharmaceuticals and biotechnology
- new methods of food production
- new sources of energy
- new materials for industry, e.g. very strong and light materials for use in manufacturing
- new power sources for vehicles

Text bank

UNIT 10   Customer service

Earning customer loyalty

Level of difficulty: ● ● ○

Before you read

How do companies normally collect information about their customers? Would you mind if companies of which you are a customer knew more about you so that they could offer you better service?

Reading

Read this article from the *Financial Times* by Penelope Ody and answer the questions.

Tying in an asset

Organisations with successful customer-responsive strategies are alike in a number of ways. There is a willingness to serve customers differently, with the best customers getting the best treatment. The airline
5 industry, for example, has created multi-level frequent-flyer programmes, with dedicated reservation lines, priority upgrades, rapid check-in privileges and so on to recognise the best customers.

Decisions are based on detailed information about
10 customers. Databases pull key data from internal operating systems (such as a retailer's transaction system) and merge it with information from external sources. This enables database marketing and "micro-marketing" campaigns.

15 A "have it your way" attitude prevails. This can range from tailoring messages to micro-segments – such as *Parents* magazine in the US, which is customised according to the age of the buyer's children – to Nordstrom's department store allowing its clerks to
20 go through the entire store to put together clothing ensembles for their customers.

A customer-responsive strategy is likely to gain an advantage if it:
• delivers superior customer value by personalising
25   the interaction;
• demonstrates trustworthiness;
• tightens connections with customers.

Too often, these are only traditional mass-marketing efforts that overwhelm consumers with too many
30 products, messages and appeals for personal information. Often they are badly designed, as when a bank's "privileged" customers were sent offers of special

35 credit-card rates that were normally available only to new customers. A lot of money has been wasted on short-term rewards through gifts or one-time reductions for loyal customers. These are nice to receive but do nothing to strengthen the relationship.

40 There was a time when there were no loyalty schemes in the UK grocery market (with the exception of Co-op's stamp scheme), but once Tesco started its scheme, all the others were forced to do the same. No doubt Tesco benefited because it was first, but for
45 the rest, the frequency rewards became a costly burden. Once everyone has a programme, most customers are able to obtain points with whichever shop they use and loyalty patterns remain unchanged.

The difference between repeat behaviour and
50 loyalty is that the former is for sale while the other is earned. This sums up why gifts and other one-time rewards have little lasting impact – they demonstrate neither more benefits nor lower costs than the competition.

55 Guarantees, by contrast, build trust by symbolising a company's commitment to fair play with its customers. They also maintain the pressure on the entire organisation to continue to improve performance in order to avoid the costs and conflicts created by
60 frequent payouts and replacements. Guarantees can also put intolerable pressure on competitors if they cannot match the terms. Xerox gained 4.5 percentage points of the office copier market when it introduced a "no questions asked" guarantee whereby customers
65 could decide they wanted the copier replaced.

From the *Financial Times*

UNIT 10   Customer service

1 Which of these industries are mentioned in the article, and in which order?

a) pharmaceuticals
b) supermarkets
c) airlines
d) photocopiers
e) chemicals
f) banking
g) publishing
h) department stores

2 Match the companies in the industries you found in Question 1 with the things they offer to develop loyalty. Which of these things are given as good examples and which as bad examples?

a) different versions of a magazine for different readers
b) schemes for people who often travel by plane
c) offering to replace equipment even if there is nothing wrong with it
d) salespeople going through the whole store to choose items for customers
e) special credit card rates

3 Complete these definitions relating to expressions from lines 1–27.

a) An advantage that some customers have that others do not is a p_ _ _ _ _ _ _ _ .
b) If you want to buy one level of service but are offered a better one, you get an u _ _ _ _ _ _ .
c) M_ _ _ _ -marketing is when marketing activities are aimed at very small groups of consumers.
d) A telephone line for communication with a particular group of customers is a d_ _ _ _ _ _ _ _ line.
e) If you can choose exactly what version of a product or service you get, you can 'h_ _ _ i _ y_ _ _ w_ _ '.
f) Something designed for a particular customer is t_ _ _ _ _ _ _ or c_ _ _ _ _ _ _ _ for that customer.
g) When a company deals with a customer in a special way, it p_ _ _ _ _ _ _ _ _ _ its communication with that customer.

4 True or false (lines 28–46)?

a) Traditional mass marketing is an example of building customer relationships.
b) Rewards and gifts are often a waste of money from the point of view of the company offering them.
c) Customers see absolutely no benefit in receiving rewards or gifts.
d) There was absolutely no form of loyalty scheme in UK supermarkets before 1995.
e) When all store chains have loyalty schemes, the schemes have no effect on where people do their shopping.
f) Loyalty schemes and rewards can help offer benefits that are not available from competitors.

5 Which verbs are used with these nouns in lines 53–63?

a) pressure (two verbs)
b) commitment
c) costs
d) guarantee
e) performance
f) trust

Over to you 1

Do you have a loyalty card for a supermarket? Do you belong to a frequent-flier programme? Do these schemes influence your buying behaviour? Can you think of other schemes which would influence you?

Over to you 2

You are a manager in a company in one of these activities. Find schemes for each activity that will develop customer relationships in ways that go beyond loyalty cards.

- dry cleaners
- bookshop
- concert hall
- travel agency
- hairdresser
- hotel

Text bank

Difficult customers

Level of difficulty: ●●○

Before you read

Have you ever taken something back to a shop because you weren't satisfied with it? What happened?

Reading

Read this article from the *Financial Times* by Lucy Kellaway and answer the questions.

Can't get no satisfaction

Instead of making extravagant claims in their guarantees, companies should concentrate on giving customers excellent service.

A man I know recently bought a large, green sponge bag* from the US retailer L.L. Bean. He took the bag with him on a business trip, and hung it on a light fitting in a hotel. The strap of the bag was made of plastic and it did what plastic does when you put it near a source of heat: it melted.

What is the moral of the story? Don't hang your sponge bag – or anything else for that matter – on a light. But this man didn't see it like that. As one of the City of London's top corporate lawyers, he wasn't going to be defeated by a melted strap on a sponge bag. So he composed an e-mail to L.L. Bean, quoting the company's guarantee, "Our products are guaranteed to give 100 per cent satisfaction in every way". He suggested they replaced the bag.

L.L.Bean replied to the effect that the guarantee was only meant to cover "defects in the appearance and performance of our products during normal use". And so the e-mails, getting more angry now, flowed backwards and forwards. The lawyer pointed out that the company promised "satisfaction *in every way*".

The guarantee was not qualified, and certainly did not specify that the customer had to be reasonable, he said. There was no warning that the bag should not have been hung on a light. He was NOT SATISFIED, and therefore he was due another sponge bag.

In the end, he got his free bag. "We value you as a customer, Mr X, and all of us at L.L.Bean welcome the opportunity to serve you," alleged the final e-mail from the company. So what is the moral of the story now? In the world of small print, the lawyer was quite right, as lawyers so often are. The company had promised satisfaction, he was not satisfied: the case was cut and dried.

Back in the real world, I am more inclined to side with L.L.Bean. One wonders about high-powered lawyers who spend their precious free time on missions to get a free sponge bag – when the opportunity cost of all that time would have secured a lorry full of the said items.

Companies should discriminate between reasonable and unreasonable customers. The customer should be king, but only if he behaves himself. The real moral is that the cult of customer service is in a mess. The balance of power between customers and companies has swung too far towards the customer.

From the *Financial Times*

* A sponge bag is a small bag to carry the things that you wash with.

UNIT 10   Customer service

1 Which of these is the best summary of the overall sense of the article?

   a) When customers complain, the company should always do whatever it takes to make the customer happy.

   b) In dealing with customers who complain, companies should make a refund or replace a product if the complaint is reasonable or not.

   c) Customers should not make complaints if the time it takes is worth more to them than the value of the product they are complaining about.

2 Complete these statements about customer service using expressions from the article, as well as other related expressions. Use a dictionary if necessary.

   a) If you complain about a product, the shop or manufacturer may make a r _ _ _ _ _ and give you your money back, or r _ _ _ _ _ _ the product, giving you another one instead.

   b) If a customer is pleased with what they have bought, or pleased with the way a complaint has been dealt with, they are s _ _ _ _ _ _ _ _ . The corresponding noun is s _ _ _ _ _ _ _ _ _ _ .

   c) A promise by a manufacturer to replace a product if it does not work is a g _ _ _ _ _ _ _ _ or w _ _ _ _ _ _ _ . A product covered in this way is g _ _ _ _ _ _ _ _ _ .

   d) A promise like this may contain a lot of conditions, perhaps presented in a way that is not clear. This is the s _ _ _ _ p _ _ _ _ .

3 Why is the word 'alleged' used in line 47?

4 Why, from the lawyer's point of view, was the case 'cut and dried' (line 54)?

5 What is the opportunity cost of a particular activity (line 61)?

6 True or false (lines 55–73)?

   a) The writer thought the lawyer was in the right.

   b) In the time he lost complaining, the lawyer could have earned enough money to buy hundreds of sponge bags.

   c) When the writer refers to customer service as a cult, she is being negative about it.

   d) When she says that customer service is in a mess, she means that it is badly organised from a practical point of view in many companies.

   e) She thinks that customer service now works too much in favour of customers.

Over to you 1

- In a fast-food restaurant, a woman spilt hot coffee over herself and sued the restaurant chain because the coffee was too hot.
- Someone put their poodle (a type of small dog) into a microwave oven to dry after taking it for a walk in the rain. The poodle died, of course, so the dog owner sued the makers of the microwave because there was no instruction on the oven saying 'Do not dry wet poodles in this microwave'.

Do you know other 'absurd' customer service stories like this?

Over to you 2

Do you agree with the writer of the article when she says that 'The balance of power between customers and companies has swung too far towards the customer'? Can you think of some examples, perhaps things that have happened to you, that prove or disprove her point?

Over to you 3

You have bought one of these things. What might typically go wrong and give you cause to complain?

- car
- personal computer
- clothes
- holiday
- mobile phone
- brand-new house

Text bank

UNIT 11   Crisis management

Crisis of confidence

Level of difficulty: ●●●

Before you read

What is the most recent business crisis covered by the media?
How was it handled by the company involved?

Reading

Read this article from the *Financial Times* and answer the
questions.

Caught in media crossfire: business education crisis management

Kathy Harvey is a freelance journalist. This month, she joined other journalists at Cranfield University School of Management to put executive MBA students through a crisis management learning curve as part of their media training programme.

'It is a journalist's dream and every chief executive's nightmare. In the face of a breaking crisis, the entire board of the company has
5 agreed to go before the assembled business press in a desperate bid to defend their share price and their reputation. OK, so it is only a training session, but this is my
10 chance to put all those questions I never got to ask last time I covered a big story like this.

Enter Mel Briggs, the head of Pharaoh Tours, a company with a
15 reputation for offering City traders the kind of thrills they no longer get on the dealing room floor. Unfortunately for Mr Briggs, his company has sent these
20 unlucky City types into a war zone without an English-speaking guide or a single mobile phone. Three of them have just been killed by terrorists.
25 My first question is relatively tame: "Could the company's Tours Director confirm that it and its customers are adequately insured for this kind of terrible tragedy?"
30 The body language says it all. Before he can formulate an answer, the hapless Tours Director is backing away from the microphone, his hands clutching
35 the press conference table in an effort to maintain some sort of balance. "We always encourage our customers to take out insurance," he mumbles into his notes.
40 The interviewee is now opening and closing his mouth like a fish gasping for air, and things are about to get worse.

The Finance Director assures us
45 the company has a clear plan to solve the "potential" crisis it faces. With three dead and many injured, his is the kind of understatement designed to send his
50 public relations team into a cold sweat. "How about the survivors?" we ask. Doesn't Pharaoh Tours want to make a statement apologising to them for this catas-
55 trophe? Apparently not. "Being sorry is not my priority," intones the MBA student playing Mr Briggs, the company chairman. "Our priority at this point in time
60 is to reassure relatives that we are doing all we can to solve this potential crisis and will try to rectify the situation."

How the company is going to
65 rectify death among its customers is a mystery, but apparently the crisis plan drawn up before the conference prioritised giving relatives a sense that something was
70 being done. This meant the first rule in a crisis situation – say sorry to those affected – was ignored.'

From the Financial Times

UNIT 11   Crisis management

1 Choose the heading that best suits each paragraph. (Two of the headings are not used.)

a) The importance of saying sorry
b) Good for journalists, not so comfortable for business students
c) Journalist praised for intelligent questions
d) Simulated travel company in crisis: the background
e) Techniques for coping with any crisis
f) Travel company finance director 'not sorry'
g) Travel company head thrown off balance

2 True or false (lines 1–24)?

a) Kathy Harvey is an employee of a news organisation.
b) She enjoys the training session.
c) This press conference situation is for real.
d) The travel company referred to is not a real one.
e) Only a few members of Pharaoh's board are present.
f) Pharaoh Tours only offers beach holidays.
g) City traders have thrilling jobs and go on holiday for a quiet time.

3 Complete these statements about lines 25–43 with the correct alternative.

a) Harvey's first question is, in her opinion,
   i) not too aggressive.
   ii) very aggressive.
   iii) not understood.
b) The tour company director's reaction is
   i) confident.
   ii) aggressive.
   iii) not self-assured.
c) His reaction can be seen
   i) only in what he says.
   ii) in his body language and in what he says, but not in how he says it.
   iii) in his body language, in what he says, and how he says it.
d) He speaks
   i) clearly.
   ii) unclearly.
   iii) totally incomprehensibly.

4 Use correct forms of words and expressions in lines 44–73 to complete the statements.

a) The Finance Director doesn't think there is a crisis, only a .... one.
b) He is guilty of .... , not saying how bad things really are.
c) If someone is extremely nervous about something, they may go into a ....
d) If you say sorry to someone for something, you .... to them for it.
e) A disastrous situation is a ....

f) When you have a number of things you can do, the most important thing is the .... ; you .... it.
g) If you correct a problematic situation, you .... it.
h) If you prepare a plan, you .... it ....

5 Match the two people mentioned in lines 44–73 to the things that they say or don't say.
1 The Finance Director
2 The Company Chairman

a) does not apologise because it was not part of the plan.
b) makes things worse by not wanting to apologise to survivors.
c) says exactly the wrong thing by saying that the crisis is 'potential'.
d) says that the most important thing is to reassure relatives.

Over to you 1

If you had been a journalist at this simulated press conference, what questions would you have asked?

Over to you 2

What questions might be asked at press conferences with company managers in these crisis situations?

- An oil company. One of its tankers has been wrecked off the coast and caused an environmental catastrophe by leaking oil, with hundreds of miles of coastline affected.
- A soft drinks company. Pieces of glass have been found in bottles of lemonade.
- A cosmetics company. It has been found that suppliers to the company have been testing cosmetics on animals, when the company says that this does not happen, and bases a lot of its advertising around this.

Crisis management

Internal crises

Before you read

Counselling is when experts called counsellors listen to people and support them in their problems. People sometimes get counselling after a trauma, a very unpleasant and unsettling experience.

Reading

Read this article from the *Independent on Sunday* by Kate Hilpern and answer the questions.

After the crisis at work, enter the counsellors

The words "workplace" and "trauma" appear to be unrelated. But employers are starting to believe that trauma is a risk for all staff in all environments and are hiring "trauma counsellors" to help them. A destructive fad or an example of caring company ethics?

Andrea Walsh, an accounts manager in the City, wholeheartedly believes the latter. She walked into the office one morning to dis-
5 cover that her closest colleague – aged just 26 – had died from an asthma attack on the bus. "A professional was sent in immediately to help our department discuss
10 our grief, with the option of one-to-one counselling afterwards," she says. "We were all unprepared for how upset we'd be, so it really helped. I then began to suffer from
15 severe panic attacks and think I'd have resigned if it wasn't for the help on offer."

Bank cashier Nicky Andrews did just that. Held at knifepoint by
20 an enraged customer, she was left unwounded but severely traumatised. "With nothing but a bunch of flowers from my employers, I started suffering from dreadful
25 headaches and lack of concentration. Quite simply, I couldn't work."

Typical reactions to violent or distressing incidents also include
30 tremors, flashbacks, stomach upsets and feeling dazed. "These responses are quite normal and very often disappear within a few days," says trauma counsellor
35 Thelma Williams. "But when sufferers can't acknowledge their emotions about the event, these symptoms may be heightened or prolonged. That's where 'critical
40 incident debriefing' by a trained counsellor can help. Just one session with everyone affected by the incident provides them with a caring framework in which they can
45 make sense of their feelings."

Margaret Jarvie, who has provided an after-raid service to a bank for ten years, believes many counsellors rush in too quickly.
50 "No one should intervene professionally for several days because before that, people are too shocked to deal with their feelings. Employees themselves may

55 also be put off the idea of trauma counselling."

According to the Health and Safety Executive, there has been a fast rise in the number of
60 violent attacks in the workplace. Teachers and librarians, for instance, work in higher-risk environments than ever before. More market researchers and social
65 workers have to cope with being threatened with dogs, being punched or spat at, while staff from council housing departments have the odd kitchen sink
70 thrown at them. All the more reason, say occupational health experts, that while the nature of counselling on offer is likely to continue fuelling debate, it's a ser-
75 vice that must become the norm. As Thelma Williams says, "It's not the incident itself that's the crisis, but the reaction to it."

From the *Independent on Sunday*

UNIT 11   Crisis management

1 Which of these statements best summarises each paragraph? (Two of the summaries are not used.)

  a) Counselling following the death of a colleague helps department members through a difficult time.

  b) Employers are beginning to take counselling at work seriously. Is this a passing fashion or something that will last?

  c) Ignoring trauma is the best solution. If people don't discuss a traumatic event, they soon forget about it.

  d) Lack of counselling following a violent attack leads to an employee's resignation.

  e) There are typical symptoms following traumatic events, but the underlying causes can be dealt with through counselling.

  f) Training trauma counsellors is essential if they are to be effective.

  g) Trauma counsellors should not rush in immediately after a traumatic incident.

  h) Workplaces are becoming more violent, and trauma counselling is here to stay.

2 Which of these people are counsellors and which are trauma victims?

  a) Andrea Walsh

  b) Thelma Williams

  c) Margaret Jarvie

  d) Nicky Andrews

3 Which of these jobs are mentioned in the article and in what order? What jobs did the victims in Question 2 above have?

  a) librarian

  b) social worker

  c) train driver

  d) teacher

  e) market researcher

  f) ambulance driver

  g) accounts manager

  h) bank clerk

4 Which of these incidents is mentioned in the article and in what order? What happened to the victims mentioned in Question 2 above?

  a) being punched and spat at

  b) being threatened with dogs

  c) being present at a road accident

  d) being violently threatened by a customer

  e) experiencing an armed robbery

  f) having objects thrown at you

  g) hearing a friend has died

5 Look at lines 3–31 and match these symptoms to their definitions. Use a dictionary if necessary.

1	feeling traumatised	a)	pain in the stomach
2	panic attacks	b)	feeling extremely upset and unsettled
3	lack of concentration		
4	headaches	c)	pain in the head
5	tremors	d)	feeling confused
6	flashbacks	e)	not being able to focus on something
7	stomach upsets		
8	feeling dazed	f)	having sudden memories of a traumatic incident
		g)	shaking of arms or legs
		h)	having the feeling, without a logical reason, that something terrible is going to happen

6 Find words and expressions in lines 46–78 to complete these definitions. If you

  a) offer a service, you .... it.

  b) offer help and advice in a particular situation, you .... in it.

  c) hear something that makes you dislike an idea, you .... the idea.

  d) think about your feelings so that they do not upset you, you .... them.

  e) manage to survive a threatening situation, you .... it.

  f) contribute ideas to a discussion, you .... the debate.

Over to you 1

Some people say that the best way to deal with a traumatic incident is not to talk about it and to try to forget about it. What do you think?

Over to you 2

What sort of advice, help or support should an employer give in each of these situations?

- An employee is being verbally abused and bullied by their manager.
- An employee has been involved in a factory accident in which a colleague has been severely injured.
- An employee complains that they are suffering from stress through severe overwork.
- An employee has been assaulted (physically attacked) by a colleague for no apparent reason.
- There is a state of shock in a small company that has just been taken over without warning, and people are worried about their jobs.

Text bank

UNIT 12   Management styles

Styles of corporate leadership

Level of difficulty: ● ● ●

Text bank

Before you read

Does the management style of a company's boss have an
effect on the organisation as a whole? In what ways?

Notes

In the UK, the chair of a company is the most senior manager,
and chairs the meetings of the board of directors. (The
equivalent title in the US is usually 'president'.) This job may
be combined with the job of Chief Executive Officer (CEO),
actually running the company on a day-to-day basis. The jobs
of chair and CEO are often combined. A company's most senior
executives sit on its board, as well as non-executive directors
from elsewhere. Non-executive directors bring their experience
of other companies and industries to boardroom discussions.

Reading

Read this article from the *Financial Times* by Diane Summers
and answer the questions.

Four styles of corporate leadership

What does it take to be a good
chairman? CCG, the London-
based headhunters, has attempted
to find out. It interviewed 48
5 chairs – 28 of whom were from the
100 biggest UK companies listed
on the London Stock Exchange –
and 12 chief executives. It then
sent questionnaires to more than
10 400 main board members of 151
large Stock Exchange-listed UK
companies and analysed replies
from 117 individuals, including 36
of those interviewed.

15   Four distinct, preferred styles of
corporate leadership emerged:

   Facilitators are hands-off, working with and through a chief executive. They have warm and open
20 personal relationships with all
board members. Their style is
trusting, supportive, sensitive,
aware and purposeful. There is a
balance between head and heart,
25 between deliberately standing
back to see the wider perspective
and involvement with people,
issues and vision. This style was

the most popular, favoured by 32
30 per cent of respondents.

   Thinkers work through a chief
executive but have no doubt about
their own power and are likely to
get their own way on the big
35 issues. They can be a formidable
combination with a chief executive, provided both agree on fundamentals. Although they are
trusted, relationships will be more
40 distant and based on respect, with
a recognition of private agendas.
Penetrating understanding of the
issues and the people is likely to
be accompanied by strongly held
45 (but not always disclosed) views.
Favoured by 25 per cent.

   Drivers are likely to dominate
by force of personality. There is
variety in the importance, close-
50 ness and style of their relationships, which are not always consistent but are not difficult to
read. There is less emphasis on
sophisticated analysis, or on the
55 communication of a vision, and
more on strategy, action and

results. They require total loyalty
and commitment, both to themselves and the company. They are
60 unquestionably the boss; anyone
carrying the title of chief executive will be at best a number two
or a chief operating officer.
Favoured by 23 per cent of respon-
65 dents, though not much liked by
chief executives.

   Integrators are talented at winning both hearts and minds, and
intellectually brilliant, with a flair
70 for communication and relationships. Their style is open, trusting,
empathic and empowering. They
have strong strategic and analytical skills, and are able to see the
75 big picture. They are immersed in
the business. They are more interested in strategy than operations
and would work best sharing
leadership with a chief executive
80 who complements their qualities.
Preferred by 20 per cent of respondents, but most popular among
non-executive directors.

From the *Financial Times*

UNIT 12   Management styles

1 Each of the statements a–d was made by someone with one of the four management styles in the article. Match each statement with the management style of the person who said it.

a) I believe in delegating responsibility as much as possible. I try to be open and trusting towards the people I work with. I leave detail to my managers and focus on longer-term strategy, rather than day-to-day operations. I get on really well with non-executive directors.

b) I'm really interested in what motivates people and I try to balance emotional issues with intellectual ones. I think it's really important to get on with other people and understand their concerns. I try and support the people I work with as much as possible.

c) I work very closely with the CEO and we make a great team. I have very clear and strong views about what needs to be done, but I don't always tell people what they are! I have respect for the people I work with, and I expect them to respect me.

d) I need people who think about the company 25 hours a day. I'm the boss round here. All this stuff about the chair and the CEO being equals is nonsense! I believe in having a clear strategy and carrying it through. Once a strategy is decided, continual analysis of what we're doing is not helpful.

2 True or false (lines 1–14)?

a) CCG has its headquarters in London.

b) All the board members to whom a questionnaire was sent replied.

c) All the people who were interviewed completed a questionnaire.

d) The board members all come from companies whose shares are listed on the London stock market.

e) More chief executives than chairs were interviewed.

3 Make nouns from the adjectives that are used to describe Facilitators (lines 17–30).

a) aware_ _ _ _
b) open_ _ _ _
c) purposeful_ _ _ _
d) sensitiv_ _ _
e) supportive_ _ _ _
f) tr_ _ _

4 Match the expressions 1–6 with their meanings a–f, relating to Thinkers (lines 31–46).

1 They are likely to get their way on the big issues.
2 They can be a formidable combination with a chief executive, provided both agree on fundamentals.
3 Relationships will be more distant and based on respect.
4 penetrating understanding of the issues
5 strongly held (but not always disclosed) views
6 a recognition of private agendas

a) very good knowledge of the subjects
b) The chair and chief executive will work very well together, as long as they agree about basic policy.
c) Directors will understand each other's worth, without necessarily liking each other.
d) On important questions, what he wants to happen will happen.
e) opinions you really believe in, but don't always discuss with other people
f) an understanding that other people have their own priorities

5 Find expressions in lines 47–83 that mean

a) when you support your organisation and do nothing to harm it (7 letters)
b) when you spend a lot of time understanding figures, facts, etc. (13, 8)
c) when you put all your energy into the company you work for (10)
d) when you have a clear idea of what the future will be like (6)
e) the way you relate to different people (13)
f) strength of character (5, 2, 11)

6 Complete these nouns and then find adjectives in lines 67–83 that relate to them.

a) t_l_nt
b) _mp_thy
c) str_t_gy
d) _n_lys_s
e) _mm_rs_ _n
f) _nt_r_st

Over to you

**Put these characteristics into your order of importance for
a) a department manager;
b) a company CEO.**

- has the trust of colleagues
- awareness of what is going on at every level of the company
- intellectual brilliance
- strategic sense
- talented communicator
- strong analytical skills – good with figures
- good with people

Give reasons for the order you choose.

Text bank

Corporate culture and management styles

Level of difficulty: ●●○

Before you read

Which is more important, the job you have to do or the type of organisation you work for? Is it possible to work for an organisation whose values you don't share? Why / Why not?

Reading

Read this article from the *Financial Times* by Beth Taylor and answer the questions.

A well-appointed position: employees moving to new positions could benefit from a company culture checklist

Finding the right cultural "fit" is vital to a successful career move. If you join a company with a corporate culture that you find uncomfortable, you could find yourself demotivated and dissatisfied. The trouble is that organisational culture is hard to assess – especially from only a brief job interview. You would do much better to adopt a more structured approach. One such approach was developed by McKinsey, the consulting group. This established a "7 Sigma" model for analysing organisations based on their "shared values" which influence the other "6 Sigma": strategy, structure, systems, style, staff and skills.

First comes strategy: ask to see the company's mission statement or vision. It can be illuminating, setting out the long-term vision of the organisation. It may mention underpinning beliefs and values. However, mission statements are often written by senior management and are frequently aspirational. The reality may be quite different. Ask to what extent the organisation feels that it achieves its mission statement.

The size and structure of a company can also be informative. Large organisations with many divisions in different regions will have a number of sub-cultures, especially if they are global organisations. It is important to visit the department where the job will be based and to meet potential colleagues. An interview at head office may suggest a very different culture to the eventual place of work. Ask to see the organisation and departmental chart. A steep hierarchy or highly centralised structure is often bureaucratic and inflexible. People who value autonomy may be stifled.

Style is visible from such features as logos, physical layout, the way people dress (up or down) and management style. You can get a good feel for the place by walking around. Is the atmosphere informal, lively and active or calm, hushed, traditional? Try to discover the management style of the head of department or chief executive, as their style is likely to be mirrored by others. Most managers will lean towards either a concern for task or a concern for people. Which do you prefer? Staff are your best source of information about the corporate culture. If you have the opportunity to talk informally, ask what they most like or dislike about the company.

Skills can be tricky to assess. Often the company will over-sell itself, so probe the real strengths and weaknesses and discover what skills are most valued. Honest answers to these will be useful guides to the organisation's values and what behaviour is rewarded. You can then assess how well this matches your own skills and values.

Corporate cultures do not change overnight, so it is worth trying to find a culture that will suit you from the outset. If you join a company that encourages and rewards behaviour you do not personally value, it could be a career move you live to regret.

From the *Financial Times*

UNIT 12   Management styles

1 Find expressions in lines 1–12 to complete the statements.

a) The relationship between you and the organisation you work for, and how good this is, is the .... between you and the organisation.

b) The values that an organisation has, the way it works, etc. is its ....

c) If you work for an organisation whose values you don't like, you feel .... , ... and ....

d) The way an organisation works is difficult to understand and ....

e) If you decide to do something in a methodical way, you adopt a ....

2 The article discusses strategy, structure/size, style and skills in organisations. Read the whole article and match each aspect (1–4) to an expression that describes it (a–d).

1	strategy	a)	informative
2	structure/size	b)	visible
3	style	c)	illuminating
4	skills	d)	tricky to assess

3 Replace the word in italics with the correct alternative (lines 21–31).

a) The company's mission statement or vision can be *illuminating*.
   i) informative   ii) useless   iii) frightening

b) It may mention *underpinning* beliefs and values.
   i) undermining   ii) supporting   iii) overbearing

c) Mission statements are *aspirational* means that they
   i) say what the company would like to achieve, rather than what they are really doing.
   ii) are totally untrue.   iii) will never be achieved.

d) The reality may be *quite* different.
   i) a little   ii) partly   iii) completely

4 A Look at lines 34–51 and match the items 1–8 to the expressions they relate to a–f. (Two of the expressions a–f each occur twice.)

1	bureaucratic	a)	colleagues
2	global	b)	place of work
3	highly centralised	c)	people who value autonomy
4	potential	d)	structure
5	steep	e)	organisations
6	stifled	f)	hierarchy
7	inflexible		
8	eventual		

B Now match the complete expressions in A to their meaning. (Two of the expressions have the same meaning.)

a) somewhere you may work in the future
b) companies that have activities all over the world
c) a company where all important decisions are made at head office
d) people you may work with in the future
e) when there are many layers of management in an organisation
f) when all decisions have to follow strict procedures

g) those who like working independently and the feeling they have if they can't do this.

5 True or false (lines 52–71)?

a) A company's style is visible from the way its buildings are organised.
b) You can easily get an impression of a company's style by walking around.
c) The management style of the company boss will not be copied by other managers.
d) Most managers think either in terms of the work to be done or the people who do it.
e) Talking to employees is not a good way of finding out about a company's culture.
f) It's not good to ask employees directly what they think of the company they work for.

6 Complete these statements about lines 72–90 by choosing the correct alternative.

a) Evaluating the skills that a company's employees have is
   i) impossible.   ii) difficult.   iii) easy.

b) The company will often say that its employees' skills are
   i) better than they really are.
   ii) different from what they really are.
   iii) worse than they really are.

c) The writer suggests finding out which skills are
   i) most difficult to acquire.   ii) most common.
   iii) worth most.

d) Finding out what employees' skills are
   i) is of no help in evaluating your own skills.
   ii) is a good way of seeing how your own skills relate to other employees' skills.
   iii) is of no use in finding out about the values of the organisation.

e) Corporate cultures do not change
   i) ever.   ii) in the long run.   iii) immediately.

f) It's important to take the time to find a corporate culture that
   i) you can adapt to in the long run.
   ii) you can try to change.
   iii) suits you from the beginning.

g) If you join a company whose values you do not approve of,
   i) you can always ignore them.
   ii) you can always leave.   iii) you will be sorry.

Over to you 1

Describe your own organisation in terms of McKinsey's six-sigma model:

- strategy
- structure
- systems
- style
- staff
- skills

What are its shared values?

Over to you 2

Imagine you are applying for a job in another company. Think of two or three questions that you would ask about it under each of the six points above.

Photocopiable   © Pearson Education Limited 2001

UNIT 13   Takeovers and mergers

Takeovers across cultures 1

Level of difficulty: ●●○

Before you read

Do you know of foreign managers working in firms in your country? What are the secrets of their success?

Reading

Read this article from the *Financial Times* by Peter Marsh and answer the questions.

Volvo digs deep in Korea

MANAGEMENT: FOREIGN VENTURES   Under the astute leadership of Tony Helsham, the Swedish industrial group has made a success of its takeover of Samsung's building machinery business

It is rare for executives to use South Korea as a springboard for their rise to the top. But Tony Helsham, a straight-talking
5 Australian who last week was appointed president of the construction equipment operations of Volvo, the Swedish industrial group, has achieved just that. In
10 so doing, Mr Helsham has shown that the famously impenetrable culture of South Korean industry can be successfully united with that of a foreign multinational.
15 And that is a welcome lesson at a time when the country's chaebol, or family-controlled conglomerates, need to spin off some of their diverse activities.
20   Mr Helsham was sent to Seoul in 1998, when Volvo acquired the building machinery operations of Samsung Heavy Industries for $500 million. To the surprise of
25 many, Volvo transferred the head office of its heavy excavator operations to Seoul and closed its main excavator plant in Sweden. The Swedish company transferred pro-
30 duction to the former Samsung plant in Changwon, an hour's flight from Seoul.

   The takeover was viewed sceptically by those outside Volvo. Few
35 western companies had successfully assimilated existing businesses in the region, and many believed the Swedish company had paid over the odds for the
40 Samsung division. However, Volvo asserted that the takeover gave it a vital production and marketing base in south-east Asia. In spite of its recent economic problems, the
45 region looks certain to open up a vast market for construction and related equipment as economic development speeds up.

   Volvo quickly introduced a
50 series of tough measures at the company. The Swedish company cut employment at the plant plus ancillary offices from 2,300 to 1,700. It also introduced a range of
55 new factory procedures, including more rigorous quality checks and used "benchmarking" to compare its own operations with those in factories around the world. Mr
60 Helsham and a new 12-strong management group, of which half are Koreans, have transformed the earth-moving equipment division by introducing new production
65 methods based on teamwork. Productivity was boosted by giving more responsibility to employees so they could determine better machining and assembly tech-
70 niques.

   Another key step was to appoint Kurt Jonsson, a Swedish industrial relations expert, as the division's human resources manager.
75 Mr Jonsson has introduced a range of initiatives, including western-style scales of remuneration, that pay people according to their capabilities rather than how
80 long they have been at the company. Volvo has also recognised trade unions at the plant – something Samsung had previously avoided – as a way of putting rela-
85 tions between workers and managers on a more clearly defined basis.

From the Financial Times

UNIT 13   Takeovers and mergers

1 Put these paragraph headings into the correct order.

a) Reduction of the workforce and introduction of benchmarking.

b) Some criticised the takeover, but Volvo said it was necessary.

c) The introduction of new human resources techniques.

d) Tony Helsham succeeded in integrating a Korean firm into the Volvo group and has now been promoted.

e) Volvo bought the building machinery operations of Samsung Heavy Industries.

2 True or false, according to the article (lines 1–32)?

a) It's usual for managers to be promoted to the top of a multinational after a period in Korea.

b) Tony Helsham is Swedish.

c) Helsham says what he really thinks.

d) South Korean industrial groups are not easy to understand.

e) South Korean industrial groups need to sell off some of their activities.

f) Volvo kept its office for heavy excavators in Sweden and opened another head office in Seoul.

g) Volvo transferred production from Sweden to Changwon.

3 Find expressions in lines 35–48 that mean

a) a very large number of potential customers.

b) acquired and absorbed.

c) an essential centre for manufacturing and sales.

d) considered unwise.

e) growth quickens.

f) paid too much.

g) stated firmly.

4 Give the verbs that are used with these expressions in lines 50–70.

a) tough measures

b) employment

c) new factory procedures

d) benchmarking

e) the earth-moving equipment division

f) productivity

g) more responsibility to employees

5 Find expressions from lines 71–87 that mean

a) making things easier to understand.

b) a variety of innovations.

c) another important move.

d) pay systems as used in the west.

e) someone in charge of personnel.

f) someone who knows a lot about dealings between managers and employees.

Over to you

Give advice to the head of a foreign company taking over a firm in your country, for example in these areas:

- ways of introducing change;
- the extent of consultation with the people affected;
- organisation of work;
- pay scales;
- union recognition.

Takeovers across cultures 2

Level of difficulty: ●●○

Before you read

Do you know of a firm in your country that has been taken over by a foreign company? What happened? Was the takeover a success?

Reading

Read this article from the *Financial Times* by Tony Major and answer the questions.

Avoid merger most horrid

Sensitivity to language and culture is needed by Anglo-American companies attempting German takeovers

When a brash, aggressive US group bought a 180-year-old, family-owned *Mittelstand* company with a strong culture and well-known brand, it did not take long for the deal to turn sour. Within weeks, senior management at the German company had left, and the second-line managers were dashing for the exits. The Americans used first names with everybody, spoke English and closed the canteen in the belief that staff could eat sandwiches on the run. They did not. Germans like hot lunches. The last straw was a morning "cheerleader" session, when German staff were expected to take part in a rousing two-minute "we are the best" call to arms.

This is just one example of a recent merger involving a *Mittelstand* company that failed. "It was a cross-border catastrophe," says Valerie Lachman of M&A International, a consultancy that specialises in advising the *Mittelstand* – Germany's thousands of small and medium-sized companies. "The Americans were not aware of the big cultural differences and they didn't want to spend time trying to understand the German company and integrating it into their operations," says Ms Lachman. "The whole deal quickly unravelled. If buyers don't do their homework properly, there will be more failed mergers."

There were almost 2,000 acquisitions involving German companies last year. About 600 of them involved the sale of a German company to foreign buyers, the bulk of them US or British. But the gulf in understanding between a typical Anglo-American concern used to a highly competitive capitalist marketplace, and a *Mittelstand* company with 65 employees and a turnover of DM20 million (£6.2 million) is problematic for potential partners.

The Anglo-American buyer is financially oriented, looking to "get bigger" in Europe and has targeted Germany, the largest and most technically sophisticated market in Europe. It needs a high return on investment – probably close to 20 per cent – and the lowest possible purchase price. Above all, it wants figures from the target company. But *Mittelstand* owners find it hard to part with figures. "They have a strong desire for financial privacy," says Ms Lachman. "Very often it is because the owner does not really understand financial matters." These owner-managers, often engineers, usually have a detailed knowledge of the technical side of a business they may have built from scratch over 40 years. They are proud of their companies and probably control most aspects of the firm's running. But when it comes to the accounting, this has usually been in the hands of their tax advisers. "You have to understand that they usually don't want to be seen to be making too much money because it gets taxed heavily," Ms Lachman adds.

From the *Financial Times*

UNIT 13   Takeovers and mergers

1 Look through the whole article and find what these figures refer to.

a) 6.2 million		**e)** 65	
b) 20 million		**f)** 180	
c) 20		**g)** 600	
d) 40		**h)** 2,000	

2 A Match the two parts of these expressions from lines 1–21.

1	aggressive	a)	management
2	brash	b)	call to arms
3	last	c)	culture
4	rousing	d)	brand
5	senior	e)	group
6	strong	f)	straw
7	well-known	g)	group

B Now match the expressions to their definitions.

a) the last problem in a series of problems that finally makes you give up

b) a collection of companies that often buys other companies (two expressions)

c) a short ceremony designed to make employees more motivated in their work

d) top managers

e) famous name

f) a way of doing things that is very clearly defined

3 Choose the correct alternative to complete these statements about expressions from lines 1–40.

a) If a *deal turns sour* or *unravels*, it
  i) succeeds.
  ii) fails.
  iii) neither succeeds nor fails.

b) If managers *make a dash for the exits*, they want to
  i) have lunch.
  ii) leave the company.
  iii) get promotion.

c) Another word for *catastrophe* is
  i) disaster.
  ii) success.
  iii) event.

d) *Mittelstand* is German for
  i) middle stand.
  ii) large companies.
  iii) small and medium-sized companies.

e) If a group *integrates another company into its operations*, it
  i) closes the company.
  ii) finds ways of making the company work well with the other companies.
  iii) forces the company to do what all the other companies do.

f) If *you don't do your homework*, you don't
  i) prepare enough.
  ii) work hard enough.
  iii) spend enough time at home.

4 Find expressions in lines 41–55 to contradict these statements. The first one has been done for you.

a) Most of the foreign buyers of German firms last year were French.
No, the bulk of them were American or British.

b) American and British firms understand German companies.

c) The relationship between a German company and a British or US buyer is straightforward.

d) The typical German company mentioned here has sales of DM30 million.

5 True or false (lines 56–87)?

British and American buyers of German companies …
a) are interested in acquiring technical know-how.
b) require a high level of profit from their acquisitions.
c) are not willing to pay more than necessary for their acquisitions.
d) do not want to know the financial details of the company they are taking over.

The German owners of the target companies …
e) are keen to discuss their firms' finances.
f) don't always understand their firms' finances.
g) usually don't understand the technical side of their businesses.
h) present their accounts to show as much profit as possible.

Over to you 1

Using the information in the article, give advice to the owner of a German *Mittelstand* firm who is nearing retirement and would like to sell up to a US company.

Over to you 2

To prevent problems like the ones in the article, should countries be able to pass laws that prevent companies from being bought by foreigners? Why / Why not?

Text bank

Will services become more important than manufacturing?

Level of difficulty: ● ○ ○

Before you read

Could you imagine not owning a car and renting one when you need it?

Reading

Read this article from the *Independent* and answer the questions.

Steering an uncertain course to a future of services, not goods

Car maker Ford thinks the day will come when we don't own cars – all we will want is mobility.

Hamish McRae

Bill Ford, great-grandson of Henry Ford and chairman of the Ford Motor Company, was in London yesterday – suggesting
5 that Ford would get out of making cars. Well, not quite. What he said was: "The day will come when the whole notion of car ownership is antiquated. The whole notion of
10 you owning a car won't be appealing: you will own access to mobility."

You can see why the motor manufacturers want to rebalance their
15 activities towards the service game and away from manufacturing. One is going up, the other down. But the skills needed to run a service business are very differ-
20 ent from those needed to run a manufacturing one. You can always buy a service business: Ford owns the car-rental group Hertz. But making services is very
25 different from making goods.

A Ford Focus is pretty much the same wherever it is sold in the world. But mobility is different. We have different commuter pat-
30 terns; our cities are differently designed; we spend our weekends in different ways. To design a new car needs enormous resources: only a handful of companies in
35 the world have the necessary size to do that.

But in the new service industries, speed beats size. The giant companies of the new economy –
40 such as AOL, Vodafone or Microsoft – did not even exist 30 years ago. The giants of another 30 years' time don't exist now, except maybe in the minds of
45 some teenagers, listening to pop music in their bedrooms. The great technological breakthrough always comes from new companies, not the existing giants.
50 Besides, our notions of mobility will, I think, change. A generation ago the luxury was having access

to a car. Now the luxury is not having to drive when everyone
55 else is trying to do so. The luxury is a house or flat within walking distance of work, flexible working hours at an interesting occupation, or just to go for a country
60 walk when no one else is.

You can see what Ford is trying to do. This is to make moving about the world a nicer experience. But that is not what it is
65 good at; what it is good at is making vehicles. There is a moral here. Every large manufacturing company is going to become more of a service company in the
70 future. It is that or a slow death. But not all will succeed in making the transition. Sure, there will still be a Ford Motor Company in another 30 years' time. And it will
75 be selling a higher ratio of services to goods than it does at present. But in terms of power in the world, it will be less important.

From the *Independent*

UNIT 14   The future of business

1 Which of these statements best sums up the whole article?

a) Over the next 30 years, Ford will stop making cars altogether and become purely a service company.

b) Like all manufacturing companies, Ford may try to become more of a service company, but even if it does, it will be less important in 30 years' time.

c) As a company, Ford will remain unchanged over the next 30 years.

2 'The day will come when the whole <u>notion</u> of car ownership is <u>antiquated</u>. The whole *notion* of you owning a car won't be <u>appealing</u>: you will own <u>access to</u> mobility.'

Use these expressions to replace the underlined expressions above, leaving other expressions as they are and the overall sense unchanged. (One of the expressions is used twice.)

a) attractive

b) be able to obtain

c) idea

d) old-fashioned

e) the possibility of moving around

3 True or false (lines 13–49)?

a) It's hard to understand why manufacturers want to move away from making things, into services.

b) Managing a service company is very different from managing a manufacturing company.

c) Manufacturers can only develop service activities in-house.

d) The Ford Focus is nearly the same wherever it is sold.

e) The need for transport is the same everywhere in the world.

f) Even small companies have the capacity to design new cars that will be bought all over the world.

4 Find expressions in lines 13–36 to complete these statements:

a) When one thing is almost the same as another, it is ....

b) The regular way in which something happens is a ....

c) If only a small number of companies can do something, only a .... can do it.

d) A very large company is a ....

e) The equipment, knowledge, employees, etc. that you need to do something are your ....

f) A completely new idea, product, etc. is a ....

5 How many luxuries are named in lines 50–60? How many are luxuries of 30 years ago, and how many are luxuries now?

6 Look at lines 61–78. Match the underlined expressions in 1–4 with their meanings a–d.

1 <u>This</u> is to make moving about the world a nicer experience.

2 But <u>that</u> is not what it is good at; what it is good at is making vehicles.

3 There is a moral <u>here</u>.

4 It is <u>that</u> or a slow death.

a) the fact that it is better at making vehicles than providing services

b) providing services

c) the fact that manufacturing companies will in the future provide more services

d) Ford's objective

Over to you 1

Do you believe Bill Ford's prediction? How do you see car ownership changing in the next 30 years? For example, can you see private cars being banned altogether for reasons of pollution, congestion and so on?

Over to you 2

You don't buy a car, you buy mobility. You don't buy a washing machine, you buy clean clothes. What services do the products produced by the companies below provide? Can you imagine ways in which the companies that make them could become service providers, rather than just manufacturers? Would it be easy for them to make the change?

- cosmetics companies
- aircraft builders
- clothes manufacturers
- house builders
- frozen food producers
- publishers

UNIT 14   The future of business

Technological revolutions

Level of difficulty: ● ● ○

Before you read

Has there really been an information 'revolution' with the personal computer and the Internet? Or do you think their importance has been exaggerated? How have they affected you?

Reading

Read this article from the *Financial Times* and answer the questions.

The first and second information revolutions

Peter Drucker talks about sweeping technological changes

Tony Jackson

At a conference last week, an audience of chief executives and other VIPs was lectured on the information revolution and what
5 to do about it. One of its star speakers was the management guru Peter Drucker.

The starting point of the conference was familiar: that the
10 changes wrought by the personal computer are comparable to the industrial revolution. This has become such a cliché that it is tempting to challenge it. The
15 Industrial Revolution – the substitution of machinery for human and animal power – was a change so profound that parts of the world have yet to catch up with it.
20 Are personal computers really that fundamental? Drucker's response to that question was forthright. There is no real comparison with the Industrial Revolution, he
25 said. What is happening now is far more profound. His argument is that the comparison is mistaken. The real analogy is with what he terms 'the first information revo-
30 lution' – Gutenberg's invention of moveable type, and the advent of the printed book.

In Drucker's view, the first information revolution – like the sec-
35 ond – differed from the Industrial Revolution in two crucial respects. First, it spread much faster. Second, it immediately changed not just methods of production,
40 but what was produced. 'The Industrial Revolution,' he says, 'was mechanically very fast and socially very slow. It was not until the railways came in the 1840s
45 that ordinary people became aware of change at all. When I was born in 1909, the revolution had just started to affect the home. People still had oil lamps – electric
50 light had arrived only around 1900.'

And, he points out, it was not until after the end of the Napoleonic wars – 50 years after
55 the first introduction of textile machinery – that the revolution moved outside the UK. Contrast, he says, the first information revolution. 'Printing took just 50 years
60 to infiltrate the entire West. Gutenberg's invention was in 1455. By 1465, the number of printed books was six to ten times as great as the number of manuscripts. It
65 was that fast. By the end of the century, the handwritten manuscript was as obsolete as the adding machine on which I worked as a young banker in 1930.'
70 As for his second point: 'The Industrial Revolution did not replace a single commodity. It made existing commodities available and plentiful, and it made
75 them as like the hand-made version as possible. Factory-made shoes were so close to hand-made ones that only the expert could tell the difference.
80 'The steam ship was as like the sailing ship as possible: it followed the same routes. The first new product of the Industrial Revolution was the railroad.' Not so
85 with the information revolution: '50 years before it, literature meant the Bible and the Greek and Roman classics. Not long after, it meant Shakespeare and
90 Cervantes.' Or take the huge growth in printed maps. 'Without those, you could not have had the age of discovery.'

From the *Financial Times*

UNIT 14   The future of business

1   Put the summaries for each paragraph into the correct order.

    a) The first information revolution – the invention of moveable type for printing – was much more profound than the Industrial Revolution. The second information revolution – the personal computer – should be compared in its effects to the first information revolution, rather than to the Industrial Revolution, according to Drucker.

    b) The first really new product of the Industrial Revolution was the railway, but changes in book and map production due to the invention of printing were much more profound.

    c) The Industrial Revolution caused goods to be much cheaper, but there were no totally new goods.

    d) There are two key differences between the two information revolutions and the Industrial Revolution.

    e) There was a conference about the information revolution, and Peter Drucker was one of the main speakers.

    f) The Industrial Revolution was slow to spread, but the first information revolution was much faster.

2   List all the products and technologies mentioned in the article.

3   Complete these statements about the language of change used in lines 8–32.

    a) If one thing replaces another, there is a process of s........ .

    b) If two events are equally important, they are c........ .

    c) A very important change is p....... and f........ .

    d) Another way of saying that change is caused by something is to say that change is w....... by it.

    e) When you compare two different events, you make an a....... between them.

    f) Instead of talking about the invention or introduction of something, you can talk about the a....... of something.

4   Complete these statements about lines 33–51 by choosing the correct alternative. In Drucker's view,

    a) the differences between the first information revolution and the Industrial Revolution were
      i) not big or important.
      ii) quite big and important.
      iii) very big and important.

    b) compared with the Industrial Revolution, the first information revolution spread
      i) much more slowly.
      ii) at about the same speed.
      iii) much faster.

    c) the Industrial Revolution was
      i) slow in every way.
      ii) slow in one way but not another.
      iii) not slow at all.

    d) ordinary people only became aware of the Industrial Revolution when
      i) railways arrived.
      ii) textile machinery arrived.
      iii) gas lamps arrived.

    e) by 1900, the Industrial Revolution
      i) had only begun to be felt in the home.
      ii) had not been felt at all in the home.
      iii) had been felt in the home for a long time.

5   Find expressions in lines 52–69 that mean the same as those underlined.

    a) It took 50 years for printing to <u>reach and cover</u> the <u>whole of the western world</u> (2 expressions).

    b) The number of printed books was six to ten times as great as the number of <u>handwritten books</u>.

    c) Handwritten books, like <u>machines for making calculations</u>, reached a point were they were <u>no longer useful</u> (2 expressions).

6   True or false, according to Drucker (lines 70–93)?

    a) It was easy to tell factory-made shoes from hand-made ones.

    b) The Industrial Revolution did not produce any totally new goods.

    c) The steam ship was not that different from the sailing ship.

    d) The first truly new product of the Industrial Revolution was the steam ship.

    e) After the invention of printing, the literature that people read was not the same.

    f) The great discoveries could have been made without the invention of printing.

Over to you 1

In your view, which of these past inventions had the greatest effect, and why?

- the wheel
- printing
- personal computers
- steam ships
- railways
- telephones

Over to you 2

If they become generally available, which of these inventions might have the greatest effects on the way people live and work? In what ways?

- non-polluting car engines
- instant, automatic translating and interpreting of conversations and documents
- videophones
- a new generation of cheap, quiet supersonic jets to replace Concorde
- mobile phones with Internet access

Text bank answer key

Unit 1

Communication with employees

1 d, b, a, c

2 **a)** true **b)** false **c)** false **d)** false **e)** false **f)** true
   g) false

3 **a)** In Touch provides a freecall number.
   b) Messages are then transcribed verbatim.
   c) They are forwarded to the company's managers.
   d) In Touch will provide a monthly breakdown of calls.
   e) In Touch will highlight areas of concern.
   f) Callers can remain anonymous.

4 c, b, a

5 **a)** moderate number of calls **b)** low number of calls
   c) high number of calls

6 c

Communication with the world at large

1 b, d, c, a

2 'The way facts are rearranged to present a story in the best
   possible light.'

3 **a)** charity work **b)** minor royals **c)** fading celebrities
   d) palatial homes **e)** positive spin

4 **a)** discount **b)** are getting **c)** want to hear **d)** are losing
   e) act as **f)** uphold **g)** take on

5 **a)** A saint. **b)** Because it makes them look as if they want
   to be thought of as perfect, like saints. **c)** It stops
   behaving as if it wants to be thought of as perfect.

6 The Shell Report is important because it is the first time
   that a large company has tried to give an overall, balanced
   account of its activities, even if some of the news is
   negative.

Unit 2

Towards a global brand

1 Mars: chocolate bar; Nestlé: Nescafé coffee; Coca-Cola:
   soft drinks; Timotei: shampoo; Malibu: beverage; Levi's:
   jeans; Nike: trainers
   Mars and Nescafé have different positionings in different
   parts of the world.

2 **A** 1 b 2 c 3 a 4 e 5 d
   B Maximisation of sales.

3 **a)** true **b)** false **c)** false **d)** true **e)** true

4 1 b 2 a 3 e 4 c 5 f 6 d

5 **a)** iii **b)** ii **c)** i **d)** ii **e)** iii **f)** i

Cultural problems in international marketing

1 f, e, c, a, b, d, g

2 1 g/h 2 f 3 d 4 a 5 c 6 e 7 b 8 h/g

3 **a)** i **b)** ii **c)** i

4 **a)** true **b)** false **c)** false **d)** true **e)** false

5 **a)** arrogant **b)** ensuing **c)** local **d)** renovation
   e) Byzantine **f)** unattractive **g)** cramped **h)** too small
   i) poorly located

6 1 b 2 c 3 d 4 a

Unit 3

Employer–employee relationships

1 1 e 2 a 3 d 4 c 5 b

2 1 g 2 e 3 b 4 c 5 d 6 a 7 f

3 **a)** i **b)** ii **c)** iii **d)** i

4 The author does not think this relationship really exists
   because she says: 'But when it comes down to it, nothing
   much has changed. The ones who do not perform get
   chucked out, same as before.'

5 quitting, be fired, separate/separation/separating, get
   chucked out

6 No.

Relationships between companies: strategic alliances

1 **a)** ally **b)** ally; partner **c)** partnership **d)** co-operative
   e) go it alone

2 Cars, steel and information technology (IT). Cars and IT
   offer good examples of strategic alliances at work.

3 Advantages of belonging to strategic partnerships: they
   allow companies to develop technologies that they couldn't
   develop alone. Strategic alliances will 'create new playing
   fields' for companies: the rules of their industry will change
   to their benefit.
   Disadvantage of not belonging: companies that don't
   participate will be 'left behind'.

4 Critical standards, new markets, joint funding, rapid
   response and shared information. Customers benefit from
   increased competition.

5 **a)** true **b)** false **c)** false **d)** true **e)** true **f)** false

6 **a)** vendors **b)** networks **c)** applications **d)** databases

7 c, d, e

Unit 4

What makes product innovations successful?

1 1 g 2 c 3 e 4 b 5 a

2 **a)** iii **b)** i **c)** iii **d)** ii **e)** i

3 **a)** false **b)** false **c)** true **d)** true **e)** true **f)** false

4 **a)** unique **b)** substitute **c)** added value **d)** rare
   e) conventional-looking **f)** reject

What makes countries successful?

1 **a)** nightmare **b)** threat **c)** remedy **d)** malaise **e)** practice
2 b, e, f
3 No. 'The malaise goes beyond any single practice. It is rooted in how Japan competes.'
4 **a)** ii **b)** iii **c)** i **d)** iii **e)** i
5 total quality, continuous improvement, best practices
6 **a)** missing **b)** unique **c)** rampant **d)** attractive **e)** sustainable **f)** true
7 a, e, f, b, d
8 **a)** embraced competition **b)** deeply ingrained cultural norms; seem inconsistent with **c)** practices; weaknesses

Unit 5

Job sharing

1 e, c, a, g, f
2 **a)** false **b)** true **c)** false **d)** false **e)** true
3 **a)** ii **b)** i **c)** iii **d)** i **e)** ii
4 **a)** keep **b)** return **c)** oppose **d)** secure, achieve **e)** operate
5 **a)** compatible **b)** satisfactory **c)** successful **d)** responsible **e)** prepared **f)** trusting **g)** organised

Job loyalty

1 two
2 **a)** ii **b)** iii **c)** i **d)** ii
3 a
4 c, d, a, b
5 **A** 1 e 2 d 3 b/f 4 a 5 f/b 6 c
   B 1 b 2 d 3 a 4 e 5 a 6 c
6 **a)** slacker **b)** lifestyle **c)** push, hard **d)** workforce **e)** mobile
7 **a)** false **b)** true **c)** false **d)** false **e)** true **f)** true

Unit 6

Computer crime

1 c, e, d, b, a
2 **A** **a)** contacted **b)** were arrested by **c)** came upon **d)** began investigating **e)** received from **f)** were lured to
   B 1 d 2 b 3 a 4 c 5 f 6 e
3 **a)** true **b)** false **c)** true **d)** false **e)** true **f)** true
4 1 e computer investigations 2 g top cybercop
   3 a international standpoint 4 b/h troublesome problems
   5 h/b unique problems 6 c global nature
   7 d developing nations 8 f industrial countries
5 **a)** i **b)** iii **c)** i **d)** ii **e)** ii
6 **a)** statutes **b)** expertise **c)** mounting **d)** lawmen **e)** law-enforcement agencies **f)** police academies **g)** uphill road

Fraud and corruption

1 Control Risks Group (CRG): a security consultancy
   Bank of New York, Citibank and American Express: financial institutions
   Organisation of Economic Co-operation and Development (OECD): an international organisation of economically advanced countries
   Russian Mafia: a criminal organisation
2 **a)** bribes, bribery, corrupt, corruption
   b) Fraud, Embezzlement **c)** launder
3 **a)** false **b)** true **c)** false **d)** false **e)** false **f)** true
4 d, b, e, a, c
5 1 b 2 a 3 d 4 c 5 g 6 e 7 f

Unit 7

Difficulties of distribution 1

1 1 d ii 2 c 3 a i 4 c 5 c 6 b
2
    dNet
    couriers and delivery companies —— online vendors and merchants
3 **a)** true **b)** true **c)** false **d)** false **e)** true **f)** true **g)** false
4 **a)** dispatch **b)** deliveries **c)** deliveries **d)** segments **e)** markets **f)** market **g)** delivery **h)** delivery **i)** testing
5 **a)** i **b)** ii **c)** i **d)** v **e)** ii **f)** iv **g)** ii **h)** i **i)** iii
7 1 b 2 a 3 d 4 c

Difficulties of distribution 2

1 c, f, g, a, b, e
2 **a)** Europe's battle for the online consumer will be fought quickly and won decisively by a few big online retailers. European retailers have more than a fighting chance to be among them but will have to move swiftly and strategically on several fronts.
   b) Many established European retailers and Internet start-ups are already laying claim to this valuable online territory.
   c) With online sales accounting for only two-tenths of a per cent of the entire retail market, the field is wide open – but it will not be for long.
3 **a)** The number of European online retailers who do not know the number of unique visitors to their sites.
   b) The number of European online retailers who do not know the number of repeat buyers.
   c) The share of the European market held by US companies.
   d) The proportion of retail sales currently done over the Internet.
   e) The rate at which the European online retail market is growing.
4 **a)** i **b)** ii **c)** iii **d)** ii **e)** iii

Text bank

193

Unit 8

Team-building techniques 1

1 e, d, a, c, b
2 1 the computer support staff at BZW 2 users of computer support services 3 senior managers 4 Bryan Hotson 5 Harley Young (former actor and his psychotherapist wife) 6 managers in general 7 course participants 8 course organisers
3 a) unpleasant feedback; favourably impressed b) antagonistic culture c) team spirit d) trepidation e) heavy-handed f) hard-driving; down-to-earth g) bare your soul; expose your feelings
4 a) ii b) i c) ii d) iii e) i f) iii
5 1 c 2 d 3 a 4 b 5 f 6 e

Team building techniques 2

1 a, d, e, f (the article is mainly about e)
2 1 d 2 f 3 e 4 c 5 a 6 b
3 a) 5 b) 4 c) 1 d) 2 e) 6 f) 3
4 a) false b) true c) true d) false e) false f) false
5 a) resourcefulness b) courage c) innovation d) motivation e) confident f) single-minded
6 a) ii b) iii c) i d) iii e) ii

Unit 9

Business incubators

1 A a, d, f, i
  B b, c, g
  C e, h
2 c, d
3 About eight. (AVM has a total of £1.4 million plus £1.1 million = £2.5 million to invest. Each company costs about £300,000 over two years to incubate. Eight companies incubated in this way would cost £2.4 million.)
4 Muir-Simpson: a, f Jacobs: b, d Scuse: c, e
5 a) false b) false c) true d) false e) true f) true g) false

Venture capital in Europe

1 f, d, a, e, b, c
2 a) vision b) goes begging c) talent d) sit up e) backs it up f) forefront
3 a) European Patent Office b) vice-president c) information technology sector d) head start e) first come, first served f) annual event g) difference in allocation
4 a) stillborn b) high-tech c) innovative d) risk-averse e) unfunded f) undermined g) disturbing
5 a) propose b) offers c) have fuelled d) overhaul e) refocusing
6 a) capital gains tax b) empower the private sector c) behind the times d) going about things completely the wrong way e) too much baggage f) entrepreneur, access public money g) creamed off by h) be kept in the hands of i) re-allocating, smacked of bureaucracy

Unit 10

Earning customer loyalty

1 c, g, h, f, b, d
2 a) publishing: good example
  b) airlines: good example
  c) photocopiers: good example
  d) department stores: good example
  e) banking: bad example
3 a) privilege b) upgrade c) Micro d) dedicated e) have it your way f) tailored; customised g) personalises
4 a) false b) true c) false d) false e) true f) false
5 a) maintain; put b) symbolise c) avoid d) introduce e) improve f) build

Difficult customers

1 c
2 a) refund; replace b) satisfied; satisfaction c) guarantee; warranty; guaranteed d) small print
3 By this point, L.L.Bean was probably not sincere in saying, 'We value you as a customer …'
4 He thought there was no room for discussion about whether the bag should be replaced or not.
5 The cost to you because of the things you are not able to do instead.
6 a) false b) true c) true d) false e) true

Unit 11

Crisis of confidence

1 1 b 2 d 3 g 4 f 5 a
2 a) false b) true c) false d) true e) false f) false g) false
3 a) i b) iii c) iii d) ii
4 a) potential b) understatement c) cold sweat d) apologise e) crisis f) priority; prioritise g) rectify h) draw; up
5 1 c 2 a, b, d

Internal crises

1 1 b 2 a 3 d 4 e 5 g 6 h
2 Counsellors: b, c; victims: a, d
3 g, h, d, a, e, b
  Victims: g and h
4 g, d, e, b, a, f
  Victims: g and d
5 1 b 2 h 3 e 4 c 5 g 6 f 7 a 8 d
6 a) provide b) intervene c) are put off d) deal with e) cope with f) fuel

Unit 12

Styles of corporate leadership

1 a) Integrator b) Facilitator c) Thinker d) Driver
2 a) true b) false c) false d) true e) false
3 a) awareness b) openness c) purposefulness d) sensitivity e) supportiveness f) trust

4 1 d 2 b 3 c 4 a 5 e 6 f
5 a) loyalty **b)** sophisticated analysis **c)** commitment
d) vision **e)** relationships **f)** force of personality
6 a) talent/talented **b)** empathy/empathic
c) strategy/strategic **d)** analysis/analytical
e) immersion/immersed **f)** interest/interested

Corporate culture and management styles

1 a) cultural fit **b)** corporate culture **c)** uncomfortable,
demotivated, dissatisfied **d)** hard to assess
e) structured approach
2 1 c 2 a 3 b 4 d
3 a) i **b)** ii **c)** i **d)** iii
4 A 1 d 2 e 3 d 4 a 5 f 6 c 7 f 8 b
 B 1 f 2 b 3 c 4 d 5 e 6 g 7 f 8 a
5 a) true **b)** true **c)** false **d)** true **e)** false **f)** false
6 a) ii **b)** i **c)** iii **d)** ii **e)** iii **f)** iii **g)** iii

Unit 13

Takeovers across cultures 1

1 d, e, b, a, c
2 a) false **b)** false **c)** true **d)** true **e)** true **f)** false
 g) true
3 a) a vast market **b)** assimilated **c)** a vital production and
marketing base **d)** viewed sceptically **e)** economic
development speeds up **f)** paid over the odds
 g) asserted
4 a) introduced **b)** cut **c)** introduced **d)** used **e)** have
transformed **f)** was boosted **g)** giving
5 a) a more clearly defined basis **b)** range of initiatives
c) Another key step **d)** western-style scales of
remuneration **e)** human resources manager **f)** industrial
relations expert

Takeovers across cultures 2

1 a) the turnover in pounds of a 'typical' German company
 b) the turnover in Deutschmarks of a 'typical' German
 company
 c) the percentage return on investment required by a
 typical American acquirer
 d) the time in years that the 'typical' German company has
 existed
 e) the number of employees of the 'typical' German
 company
 f) the age in years of the German company bought by an
 American group
 g) the number of German firms sold to foreign buyers last
 year
 h) the number of German firms sold last year
2 A 1 e/g 2 g/e 3 f 4 b 5 a 6 c 7 d
 B a) 3 **b)** 1, 2 **c)** 4 **d)** 5 **e)** 7 **f)** 6
3 a) ii **b)** ii **c)** i **d)** iii **e)** ii **f)** i
4 b) No, there's a gulf in understanding between them.
 c) No, it's problematic.
 d) No, it has turnover of DM20 million.
5 a) false **b)** true **c)** true **d)** false **e)** false **f)** true
 g) false **h)** false

Unit 14

Will services become more important than manufacturing?

1 b
2 The day will come when the whole <u>idea</u> of car ownership is
<u>old-fashioned</u>. The whole <u>idea</u> of you owning a car won't be
<u>attractive</u>: you will <u>be able to obtain</u> the possibility of
<u>moving around</u>.
3 a) false **b)** true **c)** false **d)** true **e)** false **f)** false
4 a) pretty much the same **b)** pattern **c)** handful **d)** giant
 e) resources **f)** breakthrough
5 five (having access to a car, not having to drive when
everyone else is, a house / flat within walking distance of
work, flexible working hours at an interesting occupation,
going for a country walk when no one else is)
one (having access to a car)
four (not having to drive when everyone else is, a
house / flat within walking distance of work, flexible working hours at an interesting occupation, going for a country
walk when no one else is)
6 1 d 2 b 3 a 4 c

Technological revolutions

1 e, a, d, f, c, b
2 personal computer, moveable type, printed books,
railways, oil lamps, electric light, textile machinery,
handwritten manuscripts, adding machine, factory-made
shoes, hand-made shoes, steam ships, sailing ships, the
Bible and the Greek and Roman classic books, books by
Shakespeare and Cervantes, printed maps
3 a) substitution **b)** comparable **c)** profound, fundamental
 d) wrought **e)** analogy **f)** advent
4 a) iii **b)** iii **c)** ii **d)** i **e)** i
5 a) infiltrate, entire West **b)** manuscripts
 c) adding machines, obsolete
6 a) false **b)** true **c)** true **d)** false **e)** true **f)** false

Resource bank

Teacher's notes

Introduction

These Resource bank activities are designed to extend and develop the Skills sections in the main Course Book. Each Resource bank unit begins with a language exercise that takes up and takes further the language points from the Course Book unit, and then applies this language in one or more role play activities.

What to give the learners

You have permission to photocopy the Resource bank pages in this book. In some units, you will give each student a copy of the whole page. In others, there are role cards which need to be cut out and given to participants with particular roles. These activities are indicated in the unit-specific notes below.

The **language exercises** at the beginning of each Resource bank unit can be used to revise language from the main Course Book unit, especially if you did the Skills section in another lesson. In any case, point out the connection with the Course Book Skills material. These language exercises are designed to prepare Ss for the role play(s) that follow and in many cases can be done in a few minutes as a way of focussing Ss on the activity that will follow.

A typical two-person **role play** might last 5 or 10 mins, followed by 5 mins praise and correction. An animated group discussion might last longer, and longer than you planned: in this case, drop one of your other planned activities and do it another time, rather than try to cram it in before the end of the lesson. If you then have 5 or 10 minutes left over, you can always go over some language points from the lesson again, or, better still, get students to say what they were. One way of doing this is to ask them what they've written in their notebooks during the lesson.

Revising and revisiting

Feel free to do an activity more than once. After one run-through, praise strong points, then work on three or four things that need correcting or improving. Then you can get learners to change roles and do the activity again, or the parts of the activity where these points come up. Obviously, there will come a time when interest wanes, but the usual tendency in language teaching is not to revisit things enough, rather than the reverse.

Fluency and accuracy

Concentrate on different things in different activities. In some role plays and discussions, you may want to focus on *fluency*, with learners interacting as spontaneously as possible. In others, you will want to concentrate on *accuracy*, with learners working on getting specific forms correct. Rather than expect Ss to get everything correct, you could pick out, say, three or four forms that you want them to get right, and focus on these.

Clear instructions

Be sure to give complete instructions *before* getting students to start. In role plays, be very clear about who has which role, and give learners time to absorb the information they need. Sometimes there are role cards that you hand out. The activities where this happens are indicated below.

Parallel and public performances (PPP)

In pair work or small group situations, get all pairs to do the activity at the same time. Go round the class and listen. When they have finished, praise strong points, and deal with three or four problems that you have heard, especially problems that more than one group has been having. Then get individual pairs to give public performances so that the whole class can listen. The performers should pay particular attention to these two or three points.

1 to 1

The pair activities can be done 1 to 1, with the teacher taking one of the roles. The activity can be done a second time reversing the roles and getting the student to integrate your suggestions for improvement.

Unit 1 Communication

Problem–solving on the phone

- With the whole class, look again at the expressions on page 11 of the Course Book and get Ss to read them with realistic intonation. Then do the same with the expressions here, completing the unfinished ones with possible continuations.

1 d j	**2** a i	**3** e h	**4** c g	**5** b f

(B)

- Point out that 'widget' is used to talk about an imaginary product that a company might produce: it doesn't matter what it is. Divide the class into pairs and hand out the role cards for Phone call 1. Get Ss to sit back to back to simulate the phone calls, or even better, get them to use real phone extensions.

- When the situation is clear, the role play can begin in parallel pairs. (There is quite a big element of information exchange here, as A has to communicate information about the order to B before B can deal with the problem.)

- Circulate and monitor. Note language points for praise and correction, especially in the area of problem-solving.

- Praise good language points from the role play and work on three or four points that need improvement, getting individual Ss to say the correct forms.

- Hand out the role cards for Phone call 2.

- Follow the same procedure for monitoring and correction as above.

- Get one of the pairs to do a public performance of their role play for the whole class.

Unit 2 International marketing

Brainstorming

(A)

- Refresh Ss' memories about the advice for brainstorming on page 19 of the Course Book. Then ask them to correct the expressions here in pairs. Circulate and assist.

- With the whole class, ask Ss for the answers.

---

1 We're trying to come <u>up</u> with some completely fresh <u>thinking</u> on this subject.
2 It doesn't <u>matter</u> what your <u>positioning</u> in the company is. All ideas are (no 'the') welcome.
3 We're going to stop at 5 on the <u>dot</u>, so we have an hour <u>ahead</u> of us to think of something.
4 Don't <u>criticise</u> other people's <u>contributions</u>. At this <u>stage</u>, everything is acceptable.
5 Just say everything that comes <u>into</u> your head. We should <u>consider</u> every idea, <u>however</u> crazy it seems at first!
6 You don't have to <u>stick</u> to the point. We get some good ideas when people <u>digress</u>.
7 Let other people (no 'to') finish when they are <u>talking</u>. Don't butt <u>in</u>.
8 We mustn't get <u>bogged</u> down in <u>details</u> at this stage.

(B)

- Divide the class into groups of three or four, and appoint a leader for each group. Allocate a situation to each group. Point out that money is no problem, at least for the moment!

- When it's clear what Ss have to do, the brainstorming sessions can begin.

- Circulate and monitor, but do not interrupt the flow of the brainstorming. Note language points for praise and correction, especially brainstorming-type language.

- Praise good language points from the discussion and work on three or four points that need improvement, getting individual Ss to say the correct forms.

- Ask representatives (not necessarily the leaders) of the different groups for a brief summary of their brainstorming discussions and conclusions.

Unit 3 Building relationships

Networking

(A)

- Remind Ss about the language of networking on page 27 of the Course Book.

- Divide the class into pairs. Cut up, shuffle and hand out the 'turns' to each pair. Obviously, be careful not to mix the different sets of turns, as this could lead to some surreal conversations!

- Get the pairs to piece together the conversation in parallel.

- You can hand out a complete conversation as printed in this book as a key and get Ss to read it sitting back to back to simulate a phone conversation, paying attention to friendly intonation.

- Ask for a performance of the conversation from one of the pairs for the whole class.

(B)

- In Exercises B and C, students A and B both have access to the same information.

- Point out that the conversation in B takes place in the week *before* the one in A.

- Divide the class into pairs and get them to rehearse the conversation.

- Circulate, monitor and assist with natural expression and intonation of the kind you hear between old friends.

- Praise good language points from the role play and work on three or four points that need improvement, getting individual Ss to say the correct forms.

- Ask for a performance of the conversation from one of the pairs for the whole class.

(C)

- Point out that the conversation in C takes place a few days *after* the one in A.

- Divide the class into pairs and get them to rehearse the conversation.

- Circulate, monitor and assist with natural expression and intonation of the kind you hear between people who have just met.

- Praise good language points from the role play and work on three or four points that need improvement, getting individual Ss to say the correct forms.

- Ask for a performance of the conversation from one of the pairs for the whole class.
- Ask the other pairs what happened when they continued the conversation.

Unit 4 Success

Negotiating

(A)

- Get Ss to look again at the expressions on page 35 of the Course Book, then do this exercise as a quick-fire whole-class activity.

1 d	**2** b, c, f, g	**3** a, e, h

(B)

- Divide the class into groups of four or six, with two or three Ss on each side.
- Cut up and hand out the relevant role cards and give Ss a few minutes to study them.
- Explain the situation to the whole class, and that the points system is meant to represent the priorities of each side. In the final agreement, points will be calculated on a pro rata basis, so, for example, if the local authority makes 45 teachers' assistants redundant, they will get 37.5 points.
- Explain that each side will give reasons for its demands. For example, teaching union representatives might point out that their main priority is avoiding redundancies among teachers because they are the backbone of the system and more important than anything else. They might say that under present circumstances, building the new technical school can wait a few years, etc.
- When everyone is clear, the role play can begin. Circulate and monitor. Note language points for praise and correction, especially negotiation language.
- When the groups have reached a conclusion, bring the class to order and praise good language points from the role play and work on three or four points that need improvement, getting individual Ss to say the correct forms.
- Then ask a representative from each group for an account of what happened, and the final score. Compare and contrast the discussions and scores from each group.

Unit 5 Job satisfaction

Handling difficult situations

(A)

- Get Ss to look at the expressions on page 48 of the Course Book, then do this exercise in pairs.
- Circulate and assist.
- Ask the whole class for the answers.

1	I'm terribly sorry. How clumsy <u>of</u> me!
2	Excuse me, but I really must be <u>off</u>. It was nice talking to you.
3	It's very nice <u>of</u> you to offer, but I'm very busy at the moment.
4	Sorry I'm <u>late</u>, but the traffic was a nightmare.
5	That's really bad news. I'm really sorry to <u>hear</u> that.
6	I don't know how <u>to</u> tell you this, but I've had an accident with your car.
7	I must <u>apologise</u>. I thought the meeting was *next* Tuesday.
8	The same thing happened to me. I know how you <u>must</u> be feeling.
9	You <u>mentioned</u> that you might be able to help me out.
10	<u>Could</u> you possibly help me to finish this report?

(B)

- Divide the class into pairs and hand out the role cards.
- Point out that situations 1–5 are between colleagues, and situations 6–10 between potential supplier and customer. They are just meant to be separate, isolated exchanges, not form a continuous conversation.
- Point out that Ss can give the real reason for saying 'no' in an appropriately polite form, or if more suitable, a pretext.
- When the situation is clear, the parallel exchanges can begin.
- Circulate and monitor. Note language points for praise and correction, concentrating on appropriate and tactful expressions. For example, in situation 1, B could say: 'I'm rather busy at the moment. I've got an important deadline coming up. Sorry I can't help', etc.
- Praise good language points from the expressions and work on three or four points that need improvement, getting individual Ss to say the correct forms.
- With the whole class, ask different pairs for different exchanges.

(C)

- Practise intonation of the expressions with the whole class.
- Do as a quick-fire whole-class activity. Ask different pairs to enact different exchanges, adding other comments according to the context, for example, for situation 10: 'Yes, I'd like that. I haven't been sailing for a long time. It'll be great', etc.

Unit 6 Risk

Reaching agreement

(A)

- Remind Ss about the expressions on page 51 of the Course Book, then ask them to match expressions 1–7 with their equivalent versions.

1 d	**2** a	**3** g	**4** e	**5** b	**6** c	**7** f

- Point out that in the situation that follows, negotiators should be using expressions a–g from A, rather than expressions 1–7!

- Divide the class into groups of four: two buyers and two suppliers in each group.

- Explain the basic situation. The idea here is that Ss concentrate on clarification in a negotiation, rather than the other stages. The activity is an information exchange to clear up misunderstandings about what has been decided. Get the Chief Buyer in each group to start by saying:
  – 'Let's just run over what's been agreed.'
  Point out expressions for correcting, such as
  – I don't think that's what we decided.
  – There's some sort of mistake there, surely.
    etc.

- When the situation is clear, the parallel clarification sessions can begin.

- Circulate and monitor. Note language points for praise and correction, especially in relation to the language of checking and clarification. Also, be strict with Ss saying numbers correctly. Work on the language of clarification and summary, as well as the stress and intonation of exchanges such as:
  – 'So we agree that we'll buy 20,000 dresses at 35 euros each?'
  – 'No, it was 25,000 dresses at 37 euros each.'

- Bring the class to order. Praise good language points from the role play and work on three or four points that need improvement, getting individual Ss to say the correct forms.

Unit 7 e-commerce

Presentations

- Point out the link with the presentations language on page 59 of the Course Book.

- Get Ss silently to read through the example presentation here individually or in pairs, identifying the steps.

> OK, it's two o'clock. Let's make a start (10). Good afternoon everyone (7) and thank you all for coming (1). My name's Steve Suarez and I'm head of the Anglo-Latin American Chamber of Commerce (6). This afternoon, I'm going to talk to you about doing business in Latin America. I'm going to begin by giving an overview of the different markets in Latin America, and then look in more detail at two key markets that I know a lot of you are interested in: Brazil and Mexico. I'll talk for about 45 minutes, and then we'll open up the session for a general discussion (14). But if you have any questions while I'm speaking, please feel free to ask them at any point (2). Can I just ask how many of you have been on business to Latin America? Can we have a show of hands? (13) Thank you.
>
> When I was in Rio last year, I was being shown round the city by an importer of European machine tools. We were having a beer together when he said, 'You know Steve, the problem with exporters who try to break into the Brazilian market is that they approach Brazil as if it was just like the Spanish-speaking countries of South America. But I can tell you, it's a very different kind of market, that's for sure!' (3) ...

- Go through the answers with the whole class.

- Make enough copies so that every student has a series of steps. Hand them out. Ss can talk about subjects in their presentations that they have already used in earlier presentations. The idea here is to concentrate on the opening few seconds of the presentation, as this is key.

- Get Ss to write out the text of their presentation corresponding to the steps you have given them. Circulate, monitor and assist.

- Give Ss time to memorise as far as possible what they have written. Circulate and help with natural delivery.

- With the whole class, get individual Ss to come to the front and give the beginnings of their presentations, corresponding to the steps you have given them. Keep the pace moving.

- If you have a very large class, get some Ss to give the beginnings of their presentations now, and other Ss in later session(s).

Unit 8 Team building

Resolving conflict

- Draw Ss' attention to the link between these expressions and those on page 73 of the Course Book. Ask them to identify the errors in the expressions here in pairs or individually. (All the headings are correct.)

Expressing your feelings I'm really <u>worried</u> about … **Making suggestions** <u>We can always look</u> into other possibilities … **Expressing satisfaction** Yes, that <u>sounds</u> like an ideal solution. **Expressing dissatisfaction** That's <u>just not</u> feasible.	**Agreeing action** Right. Now we've fixed our goals, let's plan a course of action to put them into <u>effect</u>. **Showing sympathy** I'm sorry to <u>hear</u> that. **Stating common goals** <u>Ideally</u>, we should all be working together on this. **Identifying the real problem** What are you really <u>concerned</u> about here? **Resolving the conflict** We must <u>reach</u> some sort of compromise on this. **Reviewing the situation** We should get together next month and check on <u>progress</u> towards our objectives.

B

- Divide the class into groups of three. Student A is the Sales Manager. B is a senior rep and C is a junior rep. All three have copies of the different proposals and the amounts that each would save. A has no role card apart from this information. Explain that A's role is to chair the meeting, explain the proposals, and get reactions from the members of the sales force, who are representing their colleagues, not just putting their own point of view. Emphasise that C also has a conciliatory role between the sales force head and B, the senior sales person.
- Hand out the relevant role cards to Students B and C.
- Give Ss time to absorb the information.
- When the situation is clear, the role play can begin. Circulate and monitor. Note language points for praise and correction, especially in relation to language for resolving conflict.
- Bring the class to order. Praise good language points from the role play and work on three or four points that need improvement, getting individual Ss to say the correct forms.
- Ask different groups to explain briefly what happened in their meetings and which combination of cost savings they chose.

Unit 9 Raising finance

Negotiating: tactics

- Point out the connection with the expressions on page 81 of the Course Book.
- Ask Ss to do the exercise individually or in pairs.
- Check the answers with the whole class, discussing any difficulties.

1 Let's check ~~up~~ the points we've covered so far. *(summarising)*
2 How do you see ~~at~~ the future development of the plant? *(open question)*
3 Have you considered setting up ~~to~~ operations in other European Union countries? *(closed question)*
4 I regret that this is the case, but under European Union ~~the~~ competition laws, there's no way we can offer more government money. *(softening phrase)*
5 I'd like to suggest something. If your government can guarantee the currency here will be relatively stable against the currencies of other countries over ~~when~~ the next five years, there's a much bigger chance of us investing here. *(signalling phrase)*
6 I'm sorry, but if you do not offer us a ~~more~~ bigger incentive, we'll have to look elsewhere. *(softening phrase)*
7 How about ~~for~~ this? If you can guarantee to employ 5,000 people, we can sell you some government-owned land at a very reasonable price. *(signalling phrase)*

B

- Explain the situation and divide the class into groups of four: two senior Kara managers and two UK government officials.
- Give Ss copies of the information for their side of the negotiation. Point out that the idea here is not to have a complete negotiation, but to apply the language seen above in A and in the Skills section of the Course Book, following the stages separated by continuous lines.
- When the situation is clear, the role play can begin.
- Circulate and monitor, especially the language relating to this unit. Note language points for praise and correction.
- With the whole class, praise good language points from the role play and work on three or four points that need improvement, getting individual Ss to say the correct forms.
- If there is time, reverse the roles and do the activity again, getting Ss to integrate corrections and improvements from the first run-through.

Unit 10 Customer service

Active listening

(A)

- Tell Ss they are going to look specifically at active listening in interviews, in this exercise by the interviewee.
- Ask them to discuss the points in pairs or threes.
- Circulate and monitor. Explain any difficulties.

1 The ideal amount of eye contact varies from culture to culture. In an interview situation this could vary from o to almost 100%, depending on the culture.

2 This and other mannerisms are best avoided everywhere. But in some cultures, this particular mannerism is viewed especially badly.

3 This might show you are paying attention, but it's probably better to adopt a more neutral position. Ask Ss to show how they would sit in an interview.

4 Some people might do this to show they are paying attention, but it probably would be seen as disrespectful in most places.

5 Not good. Creates a barrier between you and the interviewer and looks disrespectful.

6 More acceptable in some places than others, but probably best avoided.

7 In some cultures, this gesture is used (consciously or unconsciously) to show that you don't understand. Probably best avoided.

8 Probably the right thing to do in many places, but may be interpreted as being over-passive in some cultures.

9 In the UK, 'sir' is rarely heard outside the army and the schoolroom. More commonly used in the US, for example to ask strangers for directions in the street. May be heard in both places in very conservative institutions. Might be good to say 'Mr Brown', 'Mrs Smith', etc. occasionally.

10 Done in some cultures, but not others.

11 Acceptable in many cultures, but be careful not to ask about something that has already been explained.

12 Probably safer to do this than pretend you have understood and then find you answered a question that was not asked.

(B)

- Divide the class into groups of three. A is Head of Recruitment at Novia and is interviewing B for the job of Head of Research at their Canadian labs. C is an observer, who will note the stages of the interview, and the sort of language used in the questions and answers, especially in relation to techniques for active listening.
- All three members of each group should get copies of Karl Eriksson's CV, and be given time to study it. Explain any difficulties.
- When the situation is clear, the role play can begin in parallel threes.

- Circulate and monitor, but do not pre-empt the role of the observer, who should be noting the stages in the interview and the language being used.
- When the interviews are over, ask the observer from each three to give an account of what happened and the language used.
- Praise good language points from the role play and work on three or four points that need improvement, getting individual Ss to say the correct forms.

Unit 11 Crisis management

Asking and answering difficult questions

(A)

- Relate this to the language for asking and answering difficult questions on page 97 of the Course Book.
- Explain the situation here and get Ss to do the exercise individually or in pairs.
- With the whole class, ask Ss for the answers and explain any difficulties.

1 Could you tell me how many tons of oil have leaked from the tanker?

2 Would you mind answering the question? What is your policy on compensation for those affected?

3 Do you deny that serious environmental damage has been caused?

4 Do you mind if I ask whether the oil tanker had (or has) a good safety record?

5 I am interested in knowing if you consider Natoil to be a safety-conscious company?

6 Isn't it true that you don't care for the environment, only profits?

7 May I ask why you did not react more quickly?

8 Are you saying that you deny responsibility?

9 Could you clarify what efforts are being made to clean the affected beaches?

10 What can you tell us about the long-term effects on seabirds and other animals?

(B)

- Tell Ss that the questions in A anticipated this role play. Read 'The facts so far' with the whole class.
- Divide the class into groups of four or five. In each group, two Ss represent the government side, and there is a journalist from each newspaper. Hand out the relevant role cards.
- Point out that at this press conference, the officials are very defensive, trying to minimise their involvement in the disaster. The journalists are very persistent and do not believe the officials.
- When Ss have absorbed all the necessary information, the role play can begin.
- Circulate and monitor. Note language points for praise and correction, especially in relation to asking and answering difficult questions.

- Praise good language points from the role play and work on three or four points that need improvement, getting individual Ss to say the correct forms.
- If there is time and interest, organise another press conference, where the politicians are more open and forthcoming.

Unit 12 Management styles

Socialising: putting people at ease

Ⓐ

- Relate this exercise to the one on page 105 of the Course Book. Point out the way that questions in informal speech can be shortened like those in 1–4. Work on friendly delivery.
- Get your Ss to do the exercise individually or in pairs.
- With the whole class, ask for the answers.

1 c	**2** d	**3** a	**4** f	**5** b	**6** e

- Then ask Ss to have a continuous conversation in parallel pairs, incorporating the expressions 1–6 and a–f as naturally as possible. Circulate and monitor.
- Ask one of the pairs do a public performance for the whole class.

Ⓑ

- The idea here is that Ss must incorporate their one-liner seamlessly into a small-talk conversation without Student A realising what is on Student B's card.
- Cut out copies of the cue cards. Hand out copies of the first five or six randomly to Ss in a way that prevents Ss from seeing each other's cards: one one-liner for each student. Do the small talk conversations in parallel pairs. To keep things simple, do not monitor for language in this activity.
- Tell Ss that they can start by discussing what they are each going to have for lunch (from an imaginary menu).
- Student A then starts the conversation in a general way, e.g. by saying
  – What have you been up to since we last met?
- Ss must then try to 'steer' the conversation so that they can place their one-liners inconspicuously!
- At the end of the conversation, each student tries to guess the other's expression.
- If Student A guesses correctly, A 'wins'. (A variation on this is to have A, B and C, where C is an observer, guessing what is on the cards of both A and B.)
- Ask Ss about their tactics for placing their one-liners, how easy / difficult it was, etc.
- If there is time and interest, do the activity again, handing out new one-liners, perhaps getting one pair to perform for the whole class.

Unit 13 Takeovers and mergers

Summarising in presentations

Ⓐ

- Make the link with the Skills section on page 113 of the Course Book.
- Ask Ss to do the exercise individually or in pairs.
- Circulate and monitor.
- With the whole class, ask for the answers, explain any difficulties.

1 A zoo is a combination of three things: a visitor attraction, an education centre, and an animal conservation centre. *(making points in threes)* ✓
2 Firstly we'll look at zoos as visitor attractions, then we'll examine them from the educational point of view, and last but by no ~~way~~ means least, we'll turn to the conservation issues. *(ordering)*
3 What are the key issues ~~in~~ relating to animal conservation in zoos? *(rhetorical question)*
4 As I pointed out ~~more~~ earlier, planning a zoo requires great expertise. *(referring back)*
5 Of course, if a dangerous animal escapes from your zoo, this is an absolute disaster. *(emotive language)* ✓
6 These days visitors have higher expectations. They're saying we want more, more, more! *(repetition)* ✓
7 For ~~the~~ example, zoos have a big role to play in the conservation of certain types of monkeys. *(exemplifying)*
8 Have I covered ~~over~~ everything you wanted me to cover? *(asking for feedback)*

Ⓑ

- The idea here is for Ss to put into practice the language for ordering, referring back, etc. The points on theme parks, football stadiums, etc. have been provided as subject matter in which they can use the key language.
- Hand out a subject card to each student. Emphasise to Ss that the points are suggestions, and that they should feel free to mention others.
- Allow time for Ss to prepare their presentation, concentrating on the language for the particular functions in A.
- If short of time, tell Ss that they won't have to make the complete presentation, just be ready to illustrate the key phrases in context.
- Ask individual Ss to come to the front of the class and give their presentations, where necessary 'fast-forwarding' to the next point where they use a key expression, explaining what they would be saying between the key expressions.
- Note language points for praise and correction, especially in relation to presentations language.
- Praise good language points from the presentations and work on three or four points that need improvement, getting individual Ss to say the correct forms.

Unit 14 The future of business

Telephoning: getting the right information

(A)

- Remind Ss about the language for telephoning on page 121 of the Course Book.

- Divide the class into pairs. Cut up, shuffle and hand out the 'turns' to each pair. Obviously, be careful not to mix the different sets of turns, as this could lead to some surreal conversations!

- Get some students to work in threes on Conversation 1 and other Ss to work in pairs on Conversation 2.

- Circulate, monitor and assist.

- Hand out copies of the complete versions and get Ss into threes to read aloud the first conversation together, sitting back to back to simulate a phone conversation: Maria, the switchboard operator and John Reed.

- Get Ss in pairs to read aloud the second conversation in pairs: Maria and Tim Reed, paying attention to friendly intonation.

- Ask for a performance of each conversation from one of the pairs for the whole class.

(B)

- Explain that there will be a series of phone conversations following on from the first one in A.

- Divide the class into pairs. Student A is Maria, Student B, Tim.

- Hand out copies of the role cards progressively for each situation, so as not to pre-empt the final dénouement.

- Get Ss in parallel pairs to role play the first situation. Circulate and monitor.

- Get one pair of Ss to do their version of the role play for the whole class.

- Do the same for the second situation.

- For the third situation (three weeks later), hand out the role cards to just one pair, so that they do a performance for the whole class. Tell Ss that in this situation, they can interpret 'end suitably' as they wish, without going over the top, of course!

Resource bank

UNIT 1   Communication

Problem-solving on the phone

A Look again at the expressions for problem solving on page 11 of the Course Book. For each category 1–5, there are two new expressions in a–j. Match each expression to its category.

1 Stating the problem

2 Offering to help

3 Apologising / showing understanding

4 Making suggestions

5 Requesting action

a) I'll see what I can do.

b) Could you deal with this?

c) Have you thought of checking the database?

d) I'm phoning about a mix-up that there's been with …

e) You must be very upset.

f) I'd be grateful if you could find out …

g) This is just an idea, but …

h) I know how frustrating this must be.

I) I'll get on to this right away.

j) I'm calling to see what's happening with …

B Work in pairs on this situation. Use the expressions on page 11 of the Course Book, plus the expressions a–j above.

Phone call 1

A You work for Rod Engineering. You have received a consignment of widgets and related parts and supplies from Reliable Widget Supplies. (Widgets are essential components in the machines that Rod makes.) However, the consignment you received does not correspond to the order you made by phone last week.

You ordered:
- PBX widgets: 10,000 units
- widget sheets: 4,000 square metres
- widget oil: 500 litres
- Grade D widget powder: 10 tonnes

You received:
- BVX widgets: 10,000 units
- widget sheets: 1,000 square metres
- widget oil: 5,000 litres
- Grade E widget powder: 10 tonnes

B You work for Reliable Widget Supplies (RWS).
- Note down the problems with one of your customers.
- Say you can't check A's order on screen because your computer network is down.
- Ask A to give details of the order for
  - widgets
  - widget sheets
  - widget oil
  - widget powder.
- Say you will phone back later when you've found out what went wrong.

Phone call 2

A
- B phones you back.
- Note down B's explanations.
- Ask how they are going to rectify the situation.
- Say if you are happy with the solutions offered.

B
- You phone A back.
- Explain what went wrong and offer apologies and solutions.
  - PBX 10,000 widgets. The person taking the order on the phone misheard, and noted 'BV' instead of 'PB'. The correct widgets will be sent today.
  - Widget sheets. RWS was low on widget sheets last week and was only able to send 1,000. Now you have more in stock and will send another 1,000 today and 2,000 next week.
  - Widget oil. You don't know what happened. With the next delivery, you will ask the delivery driver to bring back the 4,500 extra litres.
  - Widget powder. Grade E has replaced Grade D, and is even better. It costs the same as Grade D. Tell A that they will be very pleased with the results!

UNIT 2 International marketing

Brainstorming

A Look again at the good and bad advice about brainstorming on page 19 of the Course Book. Then correct these expressions at a brainstorming session related to it.

1 We're trying to come off with some completely fresh thinkings on this subject.

2 It doesn't mind what your positioning in the company is. All ideas are welcome.

3 We're going to stop at 5 on the point, so we have an hour up front of us to think of something.

4 Don't critic other people's contributes. At this stadium, everything is acceptable.

5 Just say everything that comes across your head. We should considerate every idea, whatever crazy it seems at first!

6 You don't have to glue to the point. We get some good ideas when people digression.

7 Let other people to finish when they are talk. Don't butt inside.

8 We mustn't get bogging down in detailings at this stage.

B Hold brainstorming meetings about these situations. (Money is not a problem at this stage!)

1 Behind its main building, your company owns a piece of unoccupied land. The company is doing well and its Chief Executive wants to spend money on facilities for staff. Brainstorm the different ideas for facilities that could later be put to employees in a vote. These ideas have already been suggested:
  • ornamental garden   • go-kart track   • gym ...

2 It's your company's 50th anniversary. You and your colleagues have been asked to brainstorm suitable ways of marking and celebrating this important event.

3 You work in the R&D department of a chemical company. You have developed an invisible, odourless glue that can be applied to paper, textiles, plastics and even metal. The glue is sticky enough to hold something in place, but it comes unstuck if someone pulls on one of the things that it is being used to hold together. Brainstorm the possible applications for this glue.

4 You work for a European airline. There is now a delay of 30 mins or more in the departure of 45 per cent of the flights, and there have been instances of air rage in the departure lounges, with angry passengers abusing staff. Brainstorm all the ideas you can think of for keeping passengers calm while they are in the departure lounges.

5 Your city owns a huge disused power station on a prestigious riverside site. The building is an impressive listed monument from the 1930s, and it cannot be demolished. You and your fellow city councillors brainstorm the different uses to which it could be put.

Networking

A Look again at the useful language for networking on page 27 of the Course Book and rearrange the 'turns' that your teacher will give you into a logical phone conversation.

JM: Jane Montgomery.

LP: Oh, hello. My name's Linda Persson. I'm a friend of Silvana Belmonte. She said I might be able to track you down through your New York office. I hope you don't mind me phoning. Is this a convenient time, or shall I call back later?

JM: No, this is fine. How is Silvana?

LP: Very well. She said to give you her regards.

JM: The last time I saw her was at our office in Rio two or three years ago. What's she up to these days?

LP: She's still working in advertising down there. In fact that's why I'm calling. I work for Smithson, you know, the European food products company.

JM: Ah, Smithson, right.

LP: We're looking for an advertising agency to help us get into the American market. Silvana said you had a lot of contacts in advertising here in New York.

JM: Yes, I know one or two people. Maybe I could help you out there. Do you work in marketing or general management?

LP: Marketing. I'd be very grateful for any ideas you could give us. The US market is unknown.

JM: Why don't you come round to my office later this week, and we could go out to lunch. It's near the Metropolitan on East 86th Street: Montgomery and Associates, 450 East 86th.

LP: How about Wednesday? Shall we say about one?

JM: That would be good. Just ask for me at reception. See you then.

LP: Looking forward to it. Bye for now.

JM: Bye.

B This conversation takes place the week *before* the one above in A. Student A is Linda Persson. Student B is Silvana Belmonte. They are old friends: they did an MBA together at Harvard 10 years ago. Linda is on holiday in Rio, visiting Silvana who lives and works there.

- You reminisce about your time together at Harvard.
- Silvana talks about her job in advertising in Rio.
- Linda talks about her work at Smithson, their plans to get into the US market, and their need for a US-based advertising agency.
- Silvana mentions Jane Montgomery, who might be able to help: she knows a lot of people in advertising in New York.
- Linda asks Silvana if she has Jane's number.
- Silvana says she'll find it if she looks for 'Montgomery and Associates' on the Internet.
- Linda thanks Silvana.

C This conversation takes place a few days *after* the one above in A. Student A is Linda Persson. Student B is Ross Klein, of the advertising agency Daponte Klein Jameson. They were put in touch by Jane Montgomery and they are meeting in the DKJ offices in New Jersey.

- Ross meets Linda at reception and takes her to his office, asking if she found the address OK.
- Linda says it was no problem.
- Ross says that DKJ used to be in Manhattan, but they recently moved to New Jersey (easier to commute and to park): Linda shows interest.
- Ross asks if she would like some coffee, tea or juice and Linda responds.
- They talk about their mutual contact, Jane Montgomery, and Linda explains how she met her.
- Ross says he understands that Linda works for Smithson, and that they are looking for an advertising agency in the US.
- Linda confirms this, and they continue the conversation.

Negotiating

A Look at the expressions for 1) signalling, 2) checking understanding and 3) summarising on page 35 of the Course Book. Then put each of the expressions a–h under the correct heading.

a) Let's just summarise the key points again.

b) If I understand you correctly, you're not willing to make a concession on this.

c) What sort of lead-time do you have in mind?

d) Do you mind if I make a suggestion here? Let's adjourn for lunch.

e) Right. That seems to be it. Just to recap …

f) So, you're offering a 10 per cent discount if we can pay 30 per cent up front, is that right?

g) To put that in non-technical language, you're bankrupt, is that correct?

h) Great! We have a deal! We'll go through the main conditions again now, and then our lawyers can draw up a contract based on them.

B A local government authority in a big city has budget problems. Schools are paid for through local taxes, and the authority must cut spending on schools in order to stay within this year's budget. City officials meet members of the teaching union to discuss the cuts.

Local authority officials

- In order to cut enough from the budget, you must gain at least 180 points by obtaining the agreement of the teaching unions to a combination of these items:
- Making teachers redundant
  100 teachers or more: 100 points
  50 teachers: 50 points
  no change: 0 points.
- Making teachers' assistants redundant
  60 assistants: 50 points
  30 assistants: 25 points
  no change: 0 points.
- Asking teachers to take early retirement
  50 teachers or more: 30 points
  25 teachers: 15 points
  no change: 0 points
- Cutting maintenance of school buildings
  10% cut or more: 50 points
  5% cut: 25 points
  no change: 0 points
- Cutting expenditure on school books
  10% cut or more: 10 points
  5% cut: 5 points
  no change: 0 points
- Cancelling the construction of a new technical school: 10 points
- If the unions agree to your maximum demands, you will score 250 points.

Teaching unions

- In order to protect the interests of your members, you feel you must gain at least 180 points by reaching agreement on a combination of these items:
- Making teachers redundant
  100 teachers or more: 0 points
  50 teachers: 75 points
  no change: 150 points.
- Making teachers' assistants redundant
  60 assistants or more: 0 points
  30 assistants: 15 points
  no change: 30 points.
- Asking teachers to take early retirement
  50 teachers or more: 0 points
  25 teachers: 20 points
  no change: 40 points.
- Cutting maintenance of school buildings
  10% cut or more: 0 points
  5% cut: 10 points
  no change: 20 points.
- Cutting expenditure on school books
  10% cut or more: 0 points
  5% cut: 2.5 points
  no change: 5 points.
- Cancelling the construction of a new technical school: 5 points.
- If the local authority agrees to your maximum demands, you will score 250 points.

UNIT 5   Job satisfaction

Handling difficult situations

A Look again at the expressions for handling difficult situations on page 43 of the Course Book. There is one wrong word in each of the utterances 1–10. Cross it out and put the correct word.

1 I'm terribly sorry. How clumsy with me!

2 Excuse me, but I really must be out. It was nice talking to you.

3 It's very nice from you to offer, but I'm very busy at the moment.

4 Sorry I'm later, but the traffic was a nightmare.

5 That's really bad news. I'm really sorry to listen that.

6 I don't know how for tell you this, but I've had an accident with your car.

7 I must apology. I thought the meeting was *next* Tuesday.

8 The same thing happened to me. I know how you should be feeling.

9 You mentions that you might be able to help me out.

10 Might you possibly help me to finish this report?

B Work in pairs. Student A makes requests or invitations, B politely says 'no', and A replies suitably.

Student A

In situations 1–5, you and Student B are work colleagues with the same seniority. Politely ask Student B to do these things, and reply politely to the reason they give.

1   Help finish a report

2   Answer your phone while you're out

3   Give another colleague, C, a sensitive message that might make C annoyed

4   Go for a drink after a meeting

5   Have a game of tennis at the weekend

In situations 6–10, you have invited a potential supplier, Student B, to your country.

6   See the sights of the city

7   Go to a karaoke bar

8   Go to a nightclub

9   Come and have dinner at my house

10   Go sailing at the weekend

Student B

In situations 1–5, you and Student A are work colleagues with the same seniority. Say 'no' politely, using a different expression each time. You might give the real reason shown below, or not, depending on the situation.

1   Too busy – other important deadlines

2   Can't be bothered

3   Not your job, and you feel used

4   Long day – too tired

5   Not very good at tennis

In situations 6–10, you are a supplier who has been invited by a potential customer, Student A, to their country.

6   Have been there before – ugly city

7   Can't sing

8   Don't drink alcohol and can't dance

9   Potentially embarrassing – not done in your country

10   Prefer to be by yourself

C Now change roles, and practise saying 'yes' in as many different ways as possible to the requests and invitations. Here are some suggestions. Try to think of other ways of saying 'yes'.

- Yes, no problem.
- Yes, that would nice.
- Yes, I'd like that.
- Yes, thanks. That would be great.
- Yes, good idea.
- Yes, I can do that.

UNIT 6   Risk

Reaching agreement

A Look at the useful expressions for reaching agreement on page 51 of the Course Book. Match each expression 1–7 to another version of the same expression a–g.

1 Does anyone have really serious objections if we … ?

2 I totally and absolutely disagree with you.

3 I agree with you a hundred and ten percent on that one.

4 I've said this before and I'll say it again because no one takes any notice …

5 It's blindingly obvious we should …

6 This is bad news, but we're certainly going to be forced to …

7 I'm going to summarise because I don't think you've understood and there are bound to be problems if I don't go over the main points.

a Well hold on. I'm not sure I agree with you on that one.

b I think it's pretty clear we should …

c Well, unfortunately, I think we'll probably have to …

d Does anybody have any strong feelings about … ?

e I keep repeating this, but as I've said several times already …

f Can I just clarify that by looking again at the main points …

g I think I'd agree with you there.

B Buyers for a department store chain are negotiating with clothing suppliers. They have been negotiating all day. The Chief Buyer for the department stores thinks they have reached agreement and summarises what he / she thinks has been agreed. The suppliers disagree and indicate this politely.

Buyers

You think you have agreed the following:

20,000 women's dresses @ 35 euros each

15,000 men's jackets @ 30 euros

12,500 pairs of women's slacks @ 27 euros

10,000 pairs of men's trousers @ 25 euros

Delivery: 1 month from now

Payment: 90 days after delivery

Currency of payment: euros

Suppliers

You think you have agreed the following:

25,000 women's dresses @ 37 euros each

15,000 men's jackets @ 35 euros

10,000 pairs of women's slacks @ 25 euros

8,000 pairs of men's trousers @ 27 euros

Delivery: 3 months from now

Payment: 30 days after delivery

Currency of payment: US dollars

UNIT 7 e-commerce

Presentations

A Look at the beginning of this presentation. Which of the steps a–k does the speaker go through, and in what order? (He does not go through all of the steps mentioned.)

1 thanks the audience for coming
2 tells the audience if / when they can ask questions
3 tells a story
4 states a problem
5 offers an amazing fact
6 introduces himself
7 greets the audience
8 greets latecomers
9 tells latecomers where there are seats available
10 brings the audience to order
11 asks if everyone can see the data projection screen
12 asks if everyone can hear at the back
13 asks a question
14 announces the structure of his talk

OK, it's two o'clock. Let's make a start. Good afternoon everyone and thank you all for coming. My name's Steve Suarez and I'm head of the Anglo-Latin American Chamber of Commerce. This afternoon, I'm going to talk to you about doing business in Latin America. I'm going to begin by giving an overview of the different markets in Latin America, and then look in more detail at two key markets that I know a lot of you are interested in: Brazil and Mexico. I'll talk for about 45 minutes, and then we'll open up the session for a general discussion. But if you have any questions while I'm speaking, please feel free to ask them at any point. Can I just ask how many of you have been on business to Latin America? Can we have a show of hands? Thank you.

When I was in Rio last year, I was being shown round the city by an importer of European machine tools. We were having a beer together when he said, 'You know Steve, the problem with exporters who try to break into the Brazilian market is that they approach Brazil as if it was just like the Spanish-speaking countries of South America. But I can tell you, it's a very different kind of market, that's for sure!' ...

B Prepare the beginning of a presentation on a subject of your choice, going through the steps that your teacher will give you.

Scenario 1	Scenario 2	Scenario 3
1 Greet the audience.	1 Ask if everyone can hear at the back.	1 Bring the audience to order.
2 Thank the audience for coming.	2 Introduce yourself.	2 Ask if everyone can see the screen.
3 Introduce yourself.	3 Offer an amazing fact.	3 Introduce yourself.
4 Start to tell a story.	4 Announce the structure of your talk.	4 State a problem.
5 Greet latecomers.	5 Go into the first point of your talk.	5 Tell latecomers where there are seats available.

Resource bank

UNIT 8 — Team building

Resolving conflict

A Look again at the expressions for resolving conflict on page 73 of the Course Book. Correct the mistakes in these expressions used in talking about problems. (All the headings are correct.)

Expressing your feelings
I'm really worry about …
Making suggestions
Always we can look into other possibilities …
Expressing satisfaction
Yes, that sound like an ideal solution.
Expressing dissatisfaction
That's not just feasible.

Agreeing action
Right. Now we've fixed our goals, let's plan a course of action to put them into effectiveness.
Showing sympathy
I'm sorry to heard that.
Stating common goals
Idealistically, we should all be working together on this.
Identifying the real problem
What are you really concerning about here?
Resolving the conflict
We must gain some sort of compromise on this.
Reviewing the situation
We should get together next month and check on progression towards our objectives.

B After a year of very bad sales at Repro Photocopiers, the Sales Manager (responsible for three senior reps and nine junior reps) has been told to cut expenses by $300,000. Repro believes in its managers consulting staff about changes. The Sales Manager meets members of the sales force to discuss ways of doing this.

Proposal	Savings $
• Reduce the number of reps by 10 per cent and increase sales target of each rep	80,000 per senior rep, 50,000 per junior rep
• Replace all sales reps' cars with smaller models	130,000
• Reduce the maximum amount to be spent on each lunch with clients from $100 to $50	30,000
• Annual sales conference to be held locally in the US rather than in Cancun, Mexico, the usual venue	35,000
• Move the sales team to a smaller office within the company HQ	30,000
• Abolish the perk of a yearly clothing allowance	25,000
• Economise on stationery	5,000

Student B   Senior sales force member
You are a senior member of the sales force, representing the three senior reps. You could imagine firing junior reps, but not senior ones. You cannot accept the loss of status that would go with a smaller car and a reduced expense account. You can just about accept the idea of giving way on some of the other issues, but you are not in a conciliatory mood.

Student C   Junior sales force member
You are a junior member of the sales force, representing all your junior colleagues. You try to conciliate between the senior rep and the head of the sales force. You would prefer one or two senior reps to be fired rather than junior ones, because their results last year were particularly bad, but you can't say so openly, of course. You are less status-conscious than your senior colleagues and willing to consider the other budget reduction proposals.

Resource bank

UNIT 9　Raising finance

Negotiating: tactics

A Look again at the negotiations language on page 81 of the Course Book. There is one word too many in each of the expressions 1–7. Cross out the extra word in each expression.

1　Let's check up the points we've covered so far. *(summarising)*

2　How do you see at the future development of the plant? *(open question)*

3　Have you considered setting up to operations in other European Union countries? *(closed question)*

4　I regret that this is the case, but under European Union the competition laws, there's no way we can offer more government money. *(softening phrase)*

5　I'd like to suggest something. If your government can guarantee the currency here will be relatively stable against the currencies of other countries over when the next five years, there's a much bigger chance of us investing here. *(signalling phrase)*

6　I'm sorry, but if you do not offer us a more bigger incentive, we'll have to look elsewhere. *(softening phrase)*

7　How about for this? If you can guarantee to employ 5,000 people, we can sell you some government-owned land at a very reasonable price. *(signalling phrase)*

B The above expressions come from a negotiation between Kara, an Asian car company that wants to build a plant in the UK, and British government officials. Role play part of these negotiations, following the instructions for each side. (You don't have to use the expressions in A above.)

Kara company representatives	British government officials
• Summarise the situation so far: • British government will provide £100 million in state aid and sell government land cheaply for building the plant. • Kara will guarantee 5,000 jobs. • Key issues remaining: price for land, and UK currency stability.	• Agree that summary is correct. • Price for the land not an obstacle; can be discussed later. • Say that British government is aiming for currency stability, but can give no guarantees.
• Agree to come back to land price later. • You need guarantees on British currency stability so costs of components from outside the UK will be stable.	• Again say you can offer guarantees. • Ask about Kara's future plans in the UK if this investment is successful.
• Say that you envisage long-term commitment.	• Ask if Kara have considered other countries for their plant.
• Avoid answering question directly, but say all options are open. • Suggest that you discuss the price of the land.	• Agree to the suggestion.

Resource bank

UNIT 10 Customer service

Active listening

A This Resource unit looks specifically at active listening in interviews. Discuss these ways of behaving at a job interview to show that you are listening actively, and group them into a list of dos and list of don'ts, giving your reasons.

1 Face the interviewer, but keep direct eye contact only about half of the time. Do not stare continuously at the interviewer.

2 Run your fingers through your hair.

3 Hold your chin between your thumb and your forefinger.

4 Hold your hands together vertically, with only the fingertips touching.

5 Cross your arms in front of you.

6 Cross your legs.

7 Scratch your forehead.

8 Speak only when spoken too.

9 Use a polite form of address to the interviewer when answering questions, e.g. 'Sir', 'Mrs Smith', etc.

10 When the interviewer asks about your qualifications, show the certificates relating to them.

11 Ask the interviewer a question about the job if there's something you want to know.

12 Ask the interviewer to repeat a question if you have not understood.

B Student A is interviewing candidates to head the North American research centre of Novia, a large pharmaceuticals company in Montreal, Canada. Student B is a candidate for the job. Student C is an observer. Role play the interview, showing that you are listening actively to the other person.

Karl Eriksson's CV

- 1999–present **Deputy head of research, Novia Pharmaceuticals Research Labs, Reading, England** Assisted head of research in all types of drug trials. Supervised staff (250 researchers) in the absence of the head of research

- 1990–1999 **Researcher, Novia Pharmaceuticals Research Labs, Hamburg, Germany** Worked under research team leader on anti-cancer drugs. Specialised in computer simulations of drug effectiveness.

- 1986–90 **PhD in Pharmacology, Stanford University, California**

- 1983–86 **Degree in Pharmacology, Stockholm University**

- 1982–83 **Gap year** Backpacked round Asia

- 1975–82 **Secondary school, Kalmar, Sweden** Science specialisation

- Good interpersonal skills

- Computer skills: advanced programming skills in drug testing software

- Languages: Swedish (mother tongue), fluent German and English, intermediate Italian (have been taking evening classes in the UK)

- Interests: Ice hockey, sailing, travel, languages

Student A   Head of recruitment, Novia Pharmaceuticals

You consider yourself a sympathetic interviewer. Try to use the language for active listening on page 89 of the Course Book, as well as the extra expressions you found.

You have a copy of Karl Eriksson's CV. Base the interview on it. In particular, you want to know

- why he wants to leave England for Canada
- if he speaks French (the working language of the research labs is English, but he will need French outside)
- how he looks back at his time in Hamburg and the US
- why he didn't go straight to university from secondary school
- how he feels about having lived outside Sweden for so long
- what his interpersonal skills are like. (Ask him how he would deal with particular situations like disputes between colleagues.)
- how he keeps his knowledge of computer applications in pharmaceuticals up-to-date

Student B   Karl Eriksson

- You're looking for new challenges in a new job. You think of yourself as a permanent expat (=someone who works abroad), and like the idea of moving on regularly. (So do your family: wife and two teenage children.)
- Professionally, you're happy with your time in Reading, but you're fed up with the weather (and you want more opportunities to play ice hockey, which is not popular in England).
- Hamburg was also a good experience. Apart from specialising in cancer drugs, you learnt that you're good at managing people.
- You keep up with computing in pharmaceuticals by reading a lot and going to professional conferences about it.
- You have pleasant memories of your studies. You like the world of commercial pharmaceuticals. You could never have become a university teacher.
- Your gap year was an enriching experience, and you hope your children will do the same thing.
- You feel you have a gift for languages (but be modest about this!) and could learn French quite quickly.

Student C   Observer

- Be ready to provide a (tactful) report on what happened during the interview.
- Note the stages in the interview and the language being used.
- Also note the body language and the way it relates to the language being used, either to reinforce it or contradict it.

Resource bank

UNIT 11 Crisis management

Asking and answering difficult questions

A Complete these questions from journalists to officials at a press conference about an oil spill from an oil tanker that has sunk off the coast. Each slash represents one missing word. Put the words in brackets into their correct form.

1 Could / tell me / many tons / oil / (leak) / the tanker?
2 Would / mind (answer) the question? What / your policy / compensation / those affected?
3 Do / deny / serious environmental damage has (be) (cause)?
4 Do / mind if / ask whether / oil tanker (have) /good safety record?
5 I / interested / knowing if / consider Natoil / be / safety-conscious company?
6 Isn't / true that / don't care for / environment, only profits?
7 May / ask why / did / react more quickly?
8 Are / (say) / you deny responsibility?
9 Could / clarify / efforts are (be) made to clean the affected beaches?
10 What can / tell us about / long-term effects / seabirds / other animals?

B Role play the press conference where the above questions were asked. Students in Group A are government officials and senior managers at Natoil, the state oil company. Students in Group B are journalists from national, local and professional newspapers.

The facts so far. The accident happened last night when a tanker sank in stormy weather. The coastline has been polluted. 10,000 seabirds have been killed and many more are likely to die because of the oil. Cultivation of shellfish may also be affected.

Minister for the Environment. You maintain the line that damage will be limited. The wind direction is about to change, and this should blow the oil away from the coast. You think that the estimate of 10,000 seabirds killed is exaggerated. You do not think there is any danger to shellfish, as they are 200 km away from the site of the spill.

These are the facts as you see them, and you are sticking to them. If the journalists ask any questions not covered by the information above, you use a 'blocking' answer, or ask the Chief Executive of Natoil to answer it.

Chief Executive, Natoil. The shipwrecked tanker did not belong to Natoil: it was subcontracted. You do not see the accident as Natoil's responsibility, but that of the shipping company whose tanker it was. In any case, you think the long-term damage will be minimal.

These are the facts as you see them, and you are sticking to them. If the journalists ask any questions not covered by the information above, you use a 'blocking' answer, or ask the Minister for the Environment to answer it.

Journalist from 'Petroleum Inquirer'. You ask questions about the general situation, but also particularly about the rumour that the captain of the tanker was drunk at the time of the accident. You want to know what action is being taken to ascertain the complete facts surrounding the accident, and what action the government will take against Natoil and the shipping company.

Journalist from 'Environment Concern'. You ask questions about the general situation, but also particularly about the effect of pollution on the coastline.

Journalist from 'Shellfish Trade Weekly'. You ask questions about the general situation, but also particularly about compensation for fishermen if their fishing grounds are destroyed by oil.

Resource bank

UNIT 12   Management styles

Socialising: putting people at ease

(A) Two business contacts who know each other quite well are talking. Match the questions 1–6 to their answers a–f. Then have a natural conversation containing them.

1 Good flight?	a) It's been a hell of a year. Let's hope things calm down a bit.
2 Family alright?	b) I've been trying to work on my technique, but you know how difficult it is to find the time.
3 Been busy recently?	c) Fine, but my luggage didn't turn up. I think it's probably still in Brussels.
4 Hotel OK?	d) My son has been feeling a bit off: you know, a bug that's been going around. But he's OK now.
5 How's the golf?	e) It's been a very wet autumn, and now they're forecasting snow.
6 What's the weather been like with you?	f) Very comfortable, but the traffic noise is a bit of a problem.

(B) This is a role play where two business contacts are making small talk over lunch. They know each other quite well. One of the business people must include a particular expression in what he / she says. The other must guess which one it is.

Jobs
The labour market is getting really tight here. We're having trouble finding specialists in our field.

Hobbies
I try and go sailing every weekend. But you know how difficult it is to get away!

Families
My son's into the latest rock music. I just can't keep up with the trends these days!

Weather
It's more and more unpredictable. First we had the flooding. Then it felt like summer in the middle of February!

Holidays
We're going walking in the Pyrenees for a week. Less crowded than the Alps from what I hear.

Food and restaurants
You must try the latest Japanese place while you're here. It's difficult to get a table, but I've booked for this evening.

The market
Business is booming. But we're worried that the recession in the US will eventually affect us here.

IT topics
Our company intranet is finally working just like we want it to.

The building you are in
I love modern architecture. So much light and space! It gives you this feeling of freedom!

Cars
Have you tried the latest Jaguars? They're really amazing. I'm thinking of getting one.

How you travelled here
Everything went very smoothly. No hold-ups. No lost luggage. Magic!

Resource bank

UNIT 13 Takeovers and mergers

Summarising in presentations

A A specialist in zoo management is giving a presentation about her subject. In most of these extracts from her talk there is one extra word that does not fit. Cross out this word. Some of the extracts, however, are correct. If an extract is correct, put a tick (✓) against it. (The labels in brackets are all correct.)

1 A zoo is a combination of three things: a visitor attraction, an education centre, and an animal conservation centre. *(making points in threes)*

2 Firstly we'll look at zoos as visitor attractions, then we'll examine them from the educational point of view, and last but by no way means least, we'll turn to the conservation issues. *(ordering)*

3 What are the key issues in relating to animal conservation in zoos? *(rhetorical question)*

4 As I pointed out more earlier, planning a zoo requires great expertise. *(referring back)*

5 Of course, if a dangerous animal escapes from your zoo, this is an absolute disaster. *(emotive language)*

6 These days visitors have higher expectations. They're saying we want more, more, more! *(repetition)*

7 For the example, zoos have a big role to play in the conservation of certain types of monkeys. *(exemplifying)*

8 Have I covered over everything you wanted me to cover? *(asking for feedback)*

B You are an expert talking about running a particular type of visitor attraction. Use your own expressions for the functions in brackets in A above in giving your presentation. Some key issues are given to help you, but you can mention others, of course.

Theme park
- Interesting attractions for an increasingly sophisticated public
- Transport and access to the park
- Crowd and queue management for popular attractions
- Value for money: parades, etc.
- Safety
- Cleanliness
- Restaurants

Football stadium
- Architecture and atmosphere
- Sitting versus standing. Safety of terraces: should terraces for standing be allowed?
- Facilities for spectators
- Facilities for players
- Facilities for broadcasters, photographers, etc.
- Policing
- Ticketing
- Transport and access

National park
- Traffic and crowd control
- Damage by people to paths, fences, etc.
- Litter
- Relations with local people, including farmers
- Possible charging for entry
- Building of tourist facilities versus need to keep the place 'untouched'
- Manage restaurants and shops directly, or franchise them? Control?
- Allow other activities, e.g. mining?

Open-air rock concert
- Choice of venue
- Choice of bands
- Ticketing
- Keeping out gatecrashers (=people who haven't paid)
- Facilities for musicians
- Facilities for fans
- Crowd control
- Transport and access

UNIT 14 The future of business

Telephoning: getting the right information

A Look again at the useful language for telephoning on page 121 of the Course Book and rearrange the 'turns' that your teacher will give you into a logical phone conversation.

Conversation 1

Switchboard: Iberia Wine Importers, good morning.

Maria: Hello. Can I speak to Tim Reed in Accounts?

Switchboard: Do you know the extension?

Maria: No, I'm afraid I don't.

Switchboard: Sorry to keep you waiting. ... I'm putting you through.

John Reed: Reed.

Maria: Is that Tim Reed?

John Reed: No, this is John Reed. You seem to have got the wrong extension. I'll try and transfer you back to the switchboard.

Switchboard: Switchboard.

Maria: I phoned just now but I got put through to the wrong extension.

Switchboard: Which extension did you want?

Maria: Tim Reed in Accounts.

Switchboard: Sorry, I don't follow you. There's no one in Accounts by that name.

Maria: But I've been dealing with him for years!

Switchboard: Let me just check. Reed ... Reed ... Reed. Ah, here he is. Timothy Reed. Putting you through.

Conversation 2

Maria: Hello, Tim. Got through to you at last! This is Maria Soares at Vinhos Portugueses in Porto.

Tim: Hi Maria. Has the switchboard been playing you up? There's a new receptionist every week. It's a nightmare. Anyway, what can I do for you?

Maria: I'm phoning about an invoice we sent some time ago. As far as we can see, it still hasn't been paid.

Tim: Have you got the invoice number and the date?

Maria: 193 987A. It was dated 1st March, and it was for 120,534 euros.

Tim: 193 987A. 1st March. Sorry, I didn't get the amount.

Maria: 120,534 euros. It was for 5,000 cases of Vinho Verde we shipped in late February.

Tim: Right, I've got that. Vinho Verde. Nice wine, but I can't see any trace of it on our system.

Maria: Are you saying you've lost the invoice?

Tim: Maybe we never received it here in Accounts. The mail distribution in this place is hopeless. I'll check it out and get back to you as soon as I can.

Maria: Thanks Tim. Be hearing from you soon, I hope.

Tim: You can count on me, Maria. Bye for now.

Maria: Bye.

B Maria and Tim have a series of conversations over the following weeks. Role play these conversations, using the key information for each one.

Maria   **One week later**

- You have heard nothing from Tim.
- You call him again and get through first time. Make small talk.
- Say politely that you've heard nothing from him, despite sending two e-mails.
- Listen sympathetically to his explanations and say that you're looking forward to receiving payment.
- End the conversation appropriately.

Tim   **One week later**

- Maria phones you again. She gets through first time.
- Apologise for not having contacted her. (Find an excuse.)
- The invoice has just turned up: someone found it behind a cupboard in the post room.
- Promise that it will be paid soon by bank transfer.
- End the conversation appropriately.

Maria   **Two weeks later**

- You still haven't received payment. Phone Tim again.
- No small talk this time: get straight to the point. Your company is in serious financial difficulty because of non-payment of this invoice.
- Say that you are really concerned about the situation. Ask Tim what he means when he says the invoice will be paid 'soon'.
- End politely but coldly.

Tim   **Two weeks later**

- Maria phones you again.
- Apologise for the fact that the invoice still hasn't been paid.
- You understand the financial difficulty caused. Say that the invoice will be paid soon.
- End politely.

Maria   **Three weeks later**

- Phone again.
- You are desperate for payment. Your boss has threatened to make colleagues redundant if payment is not received.
- When you hear that Iberia Wines is in receivership, ask why Tim didn't tell you before. You feel really let down.
- End suitably.

Tim   **Three weeks later**

- Maria phones you again.
- Explain that Iberia Wine Importers is bankrupt and unable to pay its bills.
- Apologise and say that you had no idea this was going to happen. You only found out yesterday.
- Sympathise with Maria.
- End suitably.

IntLang Corporate Training (S) Pte Ltd
55A Cantonment Road
Singapore 089754
Phone (65) 324 3868 Fax: (65) 324 8331

Pearson Education Limited
Edimburgh Gate,
Harlow,
Essex CM20 2JE
England
and Associated Companies throughout the world.
© Pearson Education Limited 2001

First published 2001
Third impression 2002
ISBN 0 582 434637

Set in 9/12pt MetaPlus

Printed in Spain by Mateu Cromo, S.A. Pinto (Madrid)

www.market-leader.net

Acknowledgements

We are grateful to the following for permission to reproduce copyright material:

The Economist Newspaper Limited for an extract from "Risky returns", published in *The
Economist* 19th May 2000 © The Economist Newspaper Limited, London 2000; Financial
Times Limited for extracts from "Learn to listen and let go" by Vanessa Houlder, published in
Financial Times 22nd January 1997, "The first and second information revolutions" by Tony
Jackson, published in *Financial Times* 10th March 1997, "Managing separation after that perfect relationship", published in *Financial Times* 5th May 1997, "Four styles of chairman",
published in *Financial Times* 24th September 1997, "Making brands work around the world",
published in *Financial Times* 30th January 1998, "Stay tuned to consumer taste", published
in *Financial Times* 31st March 1998, "Tying in an asset", published in *Financial Times* 28th
September 1998, "Beyond the suggestion box" by Nikki Tait, published in *Financial Times*
7th April 1999, "Caught in media crossfire: business education crisis management" by Kathy
Harvey, published in *Financial Times* 22nd November 1999, "Pioneering venture takes fledg-
lings a step further", published in *Financial Times* 25th November 1999, "A low regard for
high-tech", published in *Financial Times* 23rd December 1999, "Europeans must get a foot in
the virtual shop door" by Patrick Forth and Neil Monnery, published in *Financial Times* 15th
February 2000, "Volvo digs deep in Korea", published in *Financial Times* 13th June 2000,
"Can't get no satisfaction", published in *Financial Times* 19th June 2000, "Avoid merger most
horrid", published in *Financial Times* 19th September 2000, "Wal-Mart finds German failures
hard to swallow", published in *Financial Times* 12th October 2000, "US cybercops face challenge", published in *Financial Times* 25th October 2000, and "Flexible employment: job
shares can work for everyone" by Dido Sandler, published in *Financial Times* 8th November
2000; Guardian Newspapers Ltd for extracts from "Building new skills in Brazil" by Roger
Cowe and Colin Walkey, published in *The Guardian* 27th February 1999, and "What price a
job change?", published in *The Guardian* 13th November 2000; Independent Newspapers
(UK) Ltd for extracts from "After the crisis at work, enter the counsellors" by Kate Hilpern,
published in *The Independent* 2nd May 1999, and "Steering an uncertain course to a future
of services, not goods" by Hamish McRae, published in *The Independent* 6th October 2000;
Tim Jackson for an extract from his article "IT retailers face 'last mile'", published in
Financial Times 5th June 2000; Michael Porter for an extract from his article "Successful
Japanese companies are the ones with strategy", published in *Financial Times* 5th July 2000;
and Beth Taylor, a Senior Consultant with Meridian Consulting, for an extract from her article
"A well-appointed position: Employees moving to new positions could benefit from a com-
pany culture checklist", published in *Financial Times* 10th October 2000.

In some instances we have been unable to trace the owners of copyright material, and
would appreciate any information that would enable us to do so.

Layouts by Jennifer Coles

Photocopying